THE
MAKING
OF A
MIRACLE

THE
MAKING
OF A
MIRACLE

The Untold Story of the
Captain of the 1980 Gold Medal–Winning
US Olympic Hockey Team

MIKE ERUZIONE

with Neal E. Boudette

HARPER

An Imprint of HarperCollinsPublishers

HarperCollins books may be purchased for educational, business, or sales promotional use. For information, please email the Special Markets Department at SPsales@harpercollins.com.

FIRST EDITION

Unless otherwise noted, all photographs are courtesy of the author.
Title page photograph by Seth Wenig/AP/Shutterstock, Inc.

Library of Congress Cataloging-in-Publication Data has been applied for.

ISBN 978-0-06-296095-5

20 21 22 23 24   LSC   10 9 8 7 6 5 4 3 2 1

To my parents, Helen and Eugene "Jeep" Eruzione,
who instilled in me the values of hard work, dedication, and family

CONTENTS

FOREWORD

BY AL MICHAELS

Forty years later, it's still brought up to me almost daily: An early Friday evening in upstate New York. A team that believed in itself when few others did. A game that will be remembered forever.

I was in my fourth year at ABC Sports and very happy to have the hockey assignment at the Olympics, calling the games alongside the recently retired Ken Dryden, one of the greatest goalies in NHL history. We were witness to this improbable, maybe even impossible, run by the United States team. They were a collection of mainly college kids, primarily from Minnesota and New England, led by a taskmaster coach, Herb Brooks, who convinced them they could take on the world. And at the center of it all was Team USA's burly captain, a twenty-five-year-old former Boston University star, one Mike Eruzione.

Mike and company had reached the medal round of the tournament at Lake Placid and were now set to face off against Goliath—the Soviet Union, inarguably the best team in the world. Just thirteen days earlier, that Soviet team had pummeled the US team, 10–3, in an exhibition game at Madison Square Garden.

Astonishingly, the American team had hung right in and were tied 3–3 with the Soviets with ten minutes left, when in the high slot, thirty feet in front of the net—*ERUZIONE SCORES!!! MIKE ERUZIONE!!! USA 4, SOVIETS 3!!!*

The next ten minutes felt like ten hours—the clock was in quicksand. I simply focused on the mechanics of the telecast, just calling each pass, each save, nothing but rudimentary play-by-play. The crowd was going crazy; our broadcast platform was shaking from the noise. This was when you could *feel* the sound. Finally, there were twenty seconds left. Then ten, with the crowd counting down in unison. And then with about six seconds left, the puck gets cleared out to center ice, all but sealing the win.

I'm like almost everyone in America at this point. *Can you believe this?!*

A word pops into my head: *miraculous.*

A split second later, it gets morphed into a question and answer:

Do you believe in miracles? Yes!!!

Six words that in my heart punctuated the moment.

There was nothing I had prepared, nothing written down. In my mind, the US had no chance to win the game—the Soviets wound up outshooting them 39–16—but Herb Brooks, Mike Eruzione, and the rest of team knew otherwise and provided the greatest American sports moment of the twentieth century.

Two days later—and forgotten by many—the Americans still had to beat Finland to clinch the gold medal. And of course they did, which led to the medal ceremony a few hours later, when Captain Eruzione summoned the entire team to join him on the platform in the greatest celebration scene I've ever witnessed. In a way, that celebration has never stopped.

Mike also came up with my favorite line about the Soviet game. A few years ago, he told me, "You know, if I sometimes get a little down, I just pop that tape in. And the best thing about it? Every time I shoot, the puck goes in!"

Enjoy Mike's book. Relish the story of everything that happened before, during, and since that puck went in.

THE
MAKING
OF A
MIRACLE

CHAPTER 1

FEBRUARY 22, 1980

I wasn't on the ice when it ended. As the final minute wound down, I was on the bench, standing, not sitting. Who could sit? Mark Pavelich was on my left, Jack O'Callahan on my right. They were on their feet, too. The whole team was up, leaning over the boards, shouting, exhorting the six guys on the ice. Herb Brooks, the man who had engineered this absolutely incredible, unimaginable scene, was standing behind me, arms folded, with that same blank expression, even at the moment of the greatest achievement of his life, probably the greatest achievement of any hockey coach, anytime, anywhere, ever.

As the seconds ticked off, all I could think was "Get it out. Get it out. Get the puck out." If we could just chip the puck out of our zone, that would be it. The game would be over. Get it out, and not even the greatest hockey team in the world would have enough time to score, to tie the game, before the final horn. Get it out, and we've pulled off the most shocking upset in Olympic history.

To me, and to my nineteen teammates, it was just a game. We didn't see it as a piece of the Cold War, a showdown between the world's two superpowers, East versus West, communism versus freedom. I understand why people saw it that way and why, even all these years later, millions of people all across the United States remember where they were and who they were with when it happened. But to the twenty of us players, as it was happening, it was one Olympic hockey game—and not even the final one of those in Lake Placid in 1980. It was just a game between two teams. One was made up of amateurs, college players, and a couple teenagers. The other team were professionals, men, veterans. It was a game played in a little village in upstate New York before only about nine thousand people, while the rest of the country sat down for dinner or turned on the evening news or went about their business with no idea, no clue, what was about to happen.

From the bench, I saw the puck skid over the blue line by the far boards. Out. There were still two seconds left on the clock, but nothing was going to hold us back. Pav, OC, and I hopped the boards. Neal, Buzzy, Bah, Janny, Bobby Suter, Wellsy, and the rest did the same. We charged out, running, jumping, galloping across the ice, skipping like kids on Christmas, all headed for Jim Craig, our goaltender. The only person missing was Herb. When the game ended, when the arena erupted, he disappeared.

I hugged one teammate after another. I found one guy, embraced, then turned to look for the next, embraced him, looked for another, and another, and another. At the far end of the ice, in the stands, my mother and father, my cousin, my high school football coach hugged and cried. I glanced up at the scoreboard: 4–3. It finally hit me: the goal I'd scored twenty minutes earlier had been the difference, the winning goal. I hadn't realized that until then. Then another thought took over my mind: all along I had believed. Once we had learned we were going to play them, I'd thought it was possible. It was a long shot for sure, but I'd thought if we played well, if we did certain things, we'd have a chance. I'd thought we could win. I had believed from the beginning. I had believed back when I was eighteen, when I had been all set to become a gym teacher. When a chance meeting had changed the course of my life, I had believed I could play big-time college hockey. When it had come to the Olympic tryouts, I hadn't been the fastest skater, I hadn't been the biggest player, and I hadn't been the most talented, but I had believed. I had believed I could play and contribute. That's just how I was brought up. That's how it was in my family. You worked. You worked and worked and you waited, and if an opportunity came up, you kept working. And if you believed in yourself and tried as hard as you could, well, at some point something good would happen.

And now something good, something really good and wonderful and incredible and amazing, had happened, and at that moment, that's when I stopped believing. The thought just kept going through my head as I moved from one teammate to the next.

I can't believe it.

I can't believe it.

I can't believe it, I said to myself, over and over.

I can't believe it.

I can't believe we beat the Russians.

CHAPTER 2

THREE FLOORS, NO DOORS

It all started on the tennis courts across the street from the high school. The town I grew up in, Winthrop, Massachusetts, didn't have an ice rink when I was a kid. In winter, someone flooded the tennis courts, and before long there was a sheet of ice for kids to skate on. Sometimes I'd go to the golf course and find a sand trap where water was frozen and skate by myself on my own personal rink. Other times kids would skate at the swamp next to the golf course and play pond hockey for hours. When you got thirsty, you chipped a hole in the ice with the toe of your skate blade and drank the swamp water. At the time, the only skates we had in my house were my sister Connie's white figure skates. They were too big for me, but I laced them up as tight as I could and joined other boys playing hockey. Hockey's a pretty macho sport, so you can imagine what that was like, wearing my sister's white figure skates. It didn't help that the skates had blue pom-poms on the toes, either. When Connie got out of school, she'd come to the tennis courts and take her skates back. I'd go home with frozen toes. To warm them, my grandmother would turn on the oven and open the door. I'd sit on a chair with my feet inside.

Winthrop is right next to Boston, but in some ways it's like a different world. It sits on a peninsula that juts out into Boston Harbor, just northeast of the city. Logan Airport is right across the water, so planes come and go over Winthrop all the time. There are only two roads that lead to the town. You can get to Winthrop from East Boston by crossing the bridge over the Belle Isle Inlet, or you can come in on Winthrop Street, which runs along a narrow neck of land that connects to Revere. Since there are only two ways into Winthrop, it's an isolated place. No one passes through the town to somewhere else. If you come to Winthrop, it's because you either live there or you got lost.

The town has about 18,000 people jammed into less than two square miles of land. Most roads are residential streets. There's hardly a place where you can drive even thirty miles per hour. Most homes are two-story shingled houses on postage stamp–sized lots. Just about everyone can cut their lawn in ten minutes. Almost all the shops are owned by people who live here. We don't have any of the big-box stores and chain restaurants so familiar in just about every other town in the country. We have no Starbucks, no Target, no McDonald's, no Wendy's, no Walmart, no Panera Bread, no malls, no major supermarkets, no car dealerships, no strip malls, no highways. Winthrop is a sheltered place. It's like an enclave, a fortress.

That close-knit community existed outside our front door as well as in our home. My father was Eugene Eruzione. In Italian, our last name means "eruption." I don't know any other people with that name. My grandparents came from small towns in Italy near Naples and ended up in East Boston. My father grew up in a triple-decker, three-family house, and my mother, Eleanor Fucillo, lived in the three-family house next door. My mother and father knew each other as kids and went to grade school and high school together. He was a man about town and went out with some other girls. But my mom never dated anyone else. After graduating from high school, my father served in the marines in World War II on a navy ship. When he came home, he married the girl next door.

I grew up surrounded by a big extended family. When I was little, Uncle Tony bought a three-family house in Winthrop and three parts of my family moved in together. My father had twin sisters, Annette and Ann. Annette—we called her Auntie AT—married my mother's brother, Tony. My other aunt, Auntie Ann, married Jerry Jaworski, who was from Poland. My family lived in the middle apartment. It was me, my mother, my father, my four sisters—Connie, Nanci, Jeannie, and Annette—and my younger brother, Vinny. Eight people in five rooms—a kitchen, dining room, two bedrooms, and a bathroom. The girls were in one room, Vinny and I in the other. My parents set up their bed in the living room.

Upstairs, Uncle Tony and Auntie AT had five kids: Tony, Gail, Linda, Laurie, and Richard. Uncle Jerry and Auntie Ann had three kids: Karen, Geraldine, and Bobby, or Bubba, as we call him. Three mothers, three fathers, and fourteen kids, all living like one giant family. You could go anywhere you wanted. We called it "Three floors, no doors." If I didn't like what my mother was cooking, I could go upstairs or downstairs and see what was on the table there.

When I was a kid, I thought all this was normal. I thought everybody had a family like mine. I always assumed we had a typical home, a typical house—a little loud and lively, but no different from anybody else. Kids coming and going, running around, playing in the yard constantly. You were never on your own. In summer we had all-night barbecues with the whole family and lots of friends. The biggest was always on the Fourth of July, my father's birthday. The horseshoe games would go on until one or two in the morning. I'd go to bed and fall asleep listening to my father playing his guitar and the aunts and uncles singing. A few of the neighbors thought we were a little crazy and called the cops on us plenty of times because of the noise. The house was painted a dark green color. Some people referred to it as the Green Monster.

My cousin Tony is five years older than me, and we did everything together. We went around Winthrop on a bike, Tony pedaling, me on the handlebars. We played one-on-one football against each other. In the backyard, Tony would pay me a dime to stand in our hockey goal while he and his friends took shots. I'd get hit with so many pucks, I'd run into the house crying. One time we made a rink out of boards and old windows. I checked Tony, and the glass broke and sliced his arm open. Some days we were so tired we ended up falling asleep next to each other, the two of us in his bed. Next to the house was a small side yard, and that was "Three Cousins Stadium," our ball field. An old broomstick was our bat. Tony and Richard and Bubba and I would pitch metal bottle tops and hit them with the broomstick. We called that "stoppers." We'd cut a rubber sponge ball in half. That made it harder to hit. That was called "half ball." One day Tony took some little wooden baby blocks that were sitting around the house, and we started hitting those. That was "block ball." Every day we played sports. Every day we competed.

In our house, everyone worked. My father was a maintenance mechanic at the Watertown Arsenal and Charlestown Navy Yard, and eventually at the Deer Island Sewage Treatment Plant in Winthrop. He worked nights as a waiter at Santarpio's Pizza, a restaurant in East Boston. He had a weekend job as a welder. On Saturdays, Connie cleaned the bathroom. Nettie— that's what we call my sister Annette—swept the front stairs. Nanci changed the sheets on the beds. Vinny and I took out the trash and shoveled the walkway in winter. My mom did the laundry. You did your job, whether you liked it or not.

We didn't have a stereo or a television until I was about twelve. Our car was an old red-and-white taxicab. One time my dad was driving and the steering wheel came off as we were going down the road. I looked over at him, and he was holding the steering wheel in his hands and it wasn't connected to anything. He hit the brakes and got the wheel back on before anything happened. My father didn't have the money to take us on vacation or to restaurants. I usually didn't have money to go to the movies or get an ice cream with other kids. My father used to say, "You want money? Go to work." I did. I caddied at the nine-hole golf club in Winthrop and earned a dollar or two for a round. I'd go home and give the money to my mother, and she'd put it in a tin that she kept in the kitchen. In winter, I shoveled snow. I'd go out in the morning and knock on doors and shovel for hours. Then I'd give that money to my mother, too.

My father went by the name "Jeep." When he was a kid, there was a comic strip character named Jeep who was always getting into trouble. That was my father. He enjoyed his beer and liked to bet on the horses at Suffolk Downs. You could always tell when he won because he'd come home and start handing out five- and ten-dollar bills. To anyone, whoever happened to be in the house, cousins, friends, even kids from the neighborhood. "Here ya go, my horse won!" One night he was out playing poker and came home late with his winnings—a little black dog. He tried to sneak into the house with the dog under his coat but fell on the stairs and gashed his forehead. He had the dog hidden in the bathtub by the time my mom found him, blood dripping down his face. "I brought you a surprise!" he said. My mother was so thrilled to see the dog that she forgot about being mad at him. Another time he came home from work and parked the car in front of the house. My brother, Vinny, looked out from the porch on the second floor and saw him frantically trying to douse flames under the hood. Vinny ran downstairs. "Dad! Dad! Let it go!" he shouted. "The insurance will pay for it!"

My dad turned to him, panic on his face. "No, it won't! I just canceled it this morning!"

That was Jeep.

My father wasn't a learned man, and he wasn't a wealthy man, but he had a gift, a talent: he made people around him feel good. If you were with my father, you were having a good time. If he wasn't telling jokes or singing songs or playing his guitar, he was doing something else to entertain everyone in the house. When Jeep was around, you felt happy. Sometimes he'd take me with him to Santarpio's when he was waiting tables. After closing time, he'd sit and have a few beers with his buddies, and I'd collect the salt and pepper shakers from the tables. There was sawdust on the floor, and I'd look around with a flashlight for dimes and quarters. If my mother called, one of the guys would say, "Jeep just left." My father would sit back and have a few more beers. I was at Santarpio's once when some of the bookies who hung out there got tipped off that there was going to be a raid. So they had me stuff all their betting slips into my pockets. The police came in and found nothing, and I just sat in the corner. I had free pizza and Coke for about a year.

My mother's name was Eleanor, but everyone called her Helen. She never did anything for herself. She never had a night out, never had a day off. But she was the boss in the house. My father got paid once a week, and on Fridays, he had to hand over his paycheck—all except twenty dollars. That was his spending money for the week. For my mom, the six kids were everything. At Christmas, she would scrimp and save to get us presents. There was never a pile of stuff, but I always seemed to get what I really wanted, a baseball glove or maybe a hockey stick. We're Italians, so my mother had a pot with sausage and gravy on the stove every day. She and my father made their own wine. My mother used the recipes her mother had brought from Italy and cooked chicken cacciatore, veal parmigiana, eggplant parm, ravioli. Her meatballs were famous. She'd get up early in the morning and make two massive pans of lasagna. It was a simple recipe for lasagna, no meat; it had a special ingredient—ricotta cheese—and it was like heaven. Neither of my aunts could drive, so my mother took them shopping every week in the red-and-white taxicab. Auntie AT and Auntie Ann would sit in the back. They didn't want to be in the front with my mother driving. They'd buy all the food for the three families for the week and pull up to the house with the car jammed with bags and bags of pasta and fruit and flour and vegetables. We kids would scatter because we knew my mom was going to make everyone carry groceries. No one wanted to get stuck hauling groceries up all those stairs. My mother would order me and my cousins, "Grab some bundles!" We heard that so much that it became her nickname: Auntie Bundles.

My mother was the discipline in our house. You did not talk back to her or use bad language. You respected your parents, your teachers, your sisters, your cousins. If you were fresh, she'd give you a whack. Sometimes she'd get mad at me and I'd hide under the bed. She'd take my hockey stick and jab at me to get me to get out of there. Whenever I was in really big trouble, I got dragged to Jesus. She'd haul me over to the wall where there was a cross and say, "You tell Jesus what you did. Are you going to lie to Jesus?" If I admitted to something, I was in for a spanking, but I knew Jesus wasn't going to hit me. So I fibbed. No, I didn't do it. My mom would give me a look, and she probably knew I was lying, but she'd let me go. I'd smirk, and my sisters would just roll their eyes that I had gotten away with it. We still laugh about it to this day—lying to Jesus.

In school, I was an antsy kid. I had a lot of energy. One time when I just couldn't sit still, a teacher used a whole roll of tape to strap me into my chair. When we had art in school, I would draw nothing but pictures of sports, especially hockey players. All the time. My second-grade teacher, Mrs. Franklin, used to say, "Michael, there's going to be a time when you're going to realize that there are other things in the world besides ice rinks and hockey players."

My parents always supported me and my sisters and brother in whatever we wanted to do, but they had a rule: you couldn't quit. They didn't have the money to buy me hockey skates if two months later I was going to decide I didn't like hockey. So I kept using my sister's white skates with the blue pom-poms.

But my mom could find ways. Back then, there were these things called S&H green stamps. If you shopped at certain supermarkets or gas stations or department stores, you'd get green stamps—they looked like postage stamps. Today you get frequent-flier miles or reward points from your credit card. In those days, you collected green stamps. The more you spent, the more stamps you got. You'd go home and lick the backs and paste them into a book. After a while, you could cash in your book of stamps for all kinds of things: a toaster, an iron, furniture. One cold day I came home from school and there was a pair of black Hyde hockey skates on the kitchen table. My mother had taken all the stamps she'd collected for a year and cashed them in. She was tough, but she had a heart of gold.

Once I got those skates, I spent hours at the frozen tennis courts. I just loved to skate. When I was in high school, I'd get up early and skate before school, and go out and skate more when I had study hall.

A lot of the time, I didn't see much of my father. He was always working. But there were other fathers in the house. I used to sit and watch Red Sox games downstairs with my Uncle Jerry. Uncle Tony would take me and cousin Tony down to the ball field and hit grounders. First Tony would field them and throw to me at first base. Then we'd switch. One winter I heard there was going to be a hockey camp nearby run by one of the players from the Bruins. But it cost seventy-five dollars, and where was I going to get that kind of money? Uncle Tony said he'd loan it to me. After the camp, I could work and save and pay him back.

I loved the hockey school. Right after it ended, we had a snowstorm, and I grabbed a shovel and started knocking on doors. A week later, we had another storm, and then another.

In the month after the camp, it probably snowed five times. Before long, I had seventy-five dollars and went upstairs. "Uncle Tony, here's the money," I said. He took it and paused a moment. "You've learned a good lesson about paying your debts, Mike," he said. Then he handed the money back to me. It's something I've never forgotten.

That's just how it was in our house. Nobody ever said it. It wasn't written down anywhere. But you were there for each other. You looked out for each other. We were twenty people, all on the same team. When one family had a baby, it was as if all three were getting a new baby. If one family was short on money, the others pitched in. We had our share of disagreements, and you didn't always get along with everybody, but you still took care of each other. "You only have your family" was what my mother said. Sometimes she'd dream and say that if she ever hit the lottery, she wanted to buy a big piece of land and build houses where everyone could live together forever. I didn't know how that could ever happen, but to this day, I do know that wherever I go, whatever I do, I always have a little bit of 274 Bowdoin Street with me.

CHAPTER 3

"THERE'S NO SPOT FOR YOU"

Today kids start specializing in one sport at ridiculously young ages. Six, seven, eight years old, and they start playing one sport year-round. When I was a kid, Winthrop had a police officer who had played for the Boston Braves in the minor leagues. People thought he was a god. And that's what I wanted to be: a baseball player. When I was nine, I tried out for the top level in Little League. One coach pulled me aside and told me to hold back, not try that hard. He wanted to make sure that no other coaches picked me. I didn't. I did my best, and as it turned out, that coach still got to pick me. Our team ended up winning the league championship, and I was hooked. I loved baseball.

At the time, there wasn't much opportunity to play hockey in Winthrop. The town didn't have a rink and didn't start a high school hockey team until right before I got to high school. I got started in organized hockey in Revere, the next town over. Winthrop had a learn-to-play program over at the rink in Revere. We had some coaches who ran drills and taught us the game. Every week you had to pay to skate: twenty-five cents. As you stepped onto the ice, you gave the coach a quarter. If you didn't have the money, they marked it down in a ledger and you paid the next week. They still have that ledger in Winthrop, and I still owe a couple dollars. When I was eleven, a few players from Winthrop and I joined a team in Revere. One of them was a buddy of mine, Eddie Rossi. My mother would get up at 5:00 a.m. to wake me up and give me breakfast. She cut up oranges for me to take to the team. She drove me and Eddie to games all over: Revere, Chelsea, Lynn, Saugus. I got better and better, and my father saved his tip money from Santarpio's to buy me new skates, first a pair that cost seven dollars, then eleven dollars, then fourteen dollars. But hockey was just something I played in winter. Baseball was my favorite sport.

In high school, I had a baseball coach who had played some minor-league ball and had come back to teach at his high school. Jim Evans was a stickler for fundamentals, a real student of the game. He'd drill us over and over on different game situations: what to do if a ball is hit to the outfield with a man on second, where to throw the ball with bases loaded. He'd hit ball after ball, and he wouldn't end practice until we got it right ten times in a row. It would be getting dark, but he wouldn't end practice until we did it. He wanted us to be ready for any situation, so that no matter the score, no matter the inning, we knew exactly what to do. My hockey coach, Paul O'Brien, was my science teacher. He wasn't a screamer coach. He made practices fun. But he was still demanding. In one game my freshman year, I got into a fight with a kid from Beverly, Bill Gilligan. In high school hockey, fighting automatically brought a one-game suspension. But for Coach O'Brien, that wasn't enough. He suspended me for the entire season. I practiced with the team, but I did not play in a single game, not one. No surprise, that was the last fight I ever got into in high school.

Near the end of my sophomore year, my sporting life took an unexpected turn. I was in phys ed one day when my teacher came up, grabbed the front of my shirt, and pinned me against the wall. That was Bob DeFelice. The following fall he was going to become the head football coach, too. With my shirt in his fist and a finger in my face, he announced, "You're going to play football."

The Winthrop football team was coming off a tough season, and Coach DeFelice wanted to get athletes from other sports to play football to improve the team. Pinning me against the wall was his way of recruiting me. How was I supposed to say no to that? Coach DeFelice had grown up in Winthrop himself. He had been a baseball and football star in high school and had even spent three years in the Red Sox farm system. When I joined the football team, he was twenty-eight years old and looked like a marine, with a buzz cut, a barrel chest, and a wad of tobacco in his cheek. He barked out orders like a drill sergeant, too. He was in better shape than any of us players. After practice, we'd see him running laps around the track. After that he'd go back to his office and watch game films. Most of the time we called him Deefa. Sometimes we called him Vince because he reminded us of Vince Lombardi. Deefa used to tell us all the time, "Ability and a dime will get you a cup of coffee." What he meant was that talent alone isn't going to take you very far. You have to be willing to work hard to be successful.

Practices were grueling, and there was only one way of doing things, and it was his way. You didn't show up late, and you didn't forget your equipment. You wore your socks the right way. Your shirt was tucked in. You paid attention when he was talking. If you didn't, he'd grab you by the face mask and twist until you were on the ground looking up at him screaming in your face. If you missed a block or ran the wrong play, if he didn't like your effort, he'd smack your helmet or kick you in the butt, literally. I was afraid of him. I practiced and played as hard as I could because I didn't want him in my face if I screwed up. Coaches can't do that today, but that's how it was back then, and Deefa wasn't doing it to be mean. He was an intense competitor, and he was trying to light a competitive fire in us and turn us into something. As tough as Deefa was, I found I loved football. I was five feet six and weighed about 140 pounds, and I played safety and wide receiver and ran back punts and kicks. I loved the hitting, the tackling, the intensity. I loved baseball, but football became my passion.

My first season in football, we won just one game. In the big Thanksgiving Day game against our rival Revere, we trailed 28–0, made a big comeback, but lost 28–26. A couple days after the game, Coach DeFelice called me into his office and shut the door. This time he grabbed me by the shirt collar. Again he put a finger into my face. He said I wasn't working hard enough and not doing the extra things, the little things, to become a really good player. I think he thought that if we'd played a little harder, we could have beaten Revere. Maybe we would have stopped one of their touchdowns or scored one more of our own. That day, he challenged me to be tougher, more focused, to come back as a senior and become a leader on the team.

One thing that was on Bob's mind back then was the turmoil that was going on around us. It was the late 1960s, the Vietnam War era, a time when a lot of kids were getting involved with drugs, and there was a lot of rebellion against authority. Deefa was trying to scare me into keeping out of trouble. If a coach did that today, you'd probably have parents running to the principal and calling their lawyer. But it was different back then, and it worked. His talk that day affected me. I have nothing but respect for Coach DeFelice and love the guy to this day. That time he confronted me and made me a better football player. He made me a better athlete and a better person. It was one of the greatest things any coach ever did for me.

Playing three sports was probably one of the best things that happened to me in high school. In baseball, you develop hand-eye coordination that is directly related to handling a puck. You can take the toughness of football and transfer it right to the rink. I also learned lessons not from one coach but from three, each with a different style. If I hadn't played baseball and football, I don't know where I would have gone in hockey.

Whatever season it was, I always had the biggest and loudest cheering section in the crowd. My mother and father, my sisters and brother and cousins and uncles and aunts would come to watch. No one was louder than Jeep. He was nonstop. "Go, Mikey! Shoot, Mikey! Pass it to Mikey!" If I scored or made a good play, he would put two fingers into his mouth and make an ear-splitting whistle. Everyone in the crowd always knew who Mike Eruzione's father was. One time in Little League baseball, Jeep was watching from center field when I slid into home plate. The catcher dropped the ball, but the umpire called me out anyway. Jeep climbed over the center-field fence and ran to the infield. Jeep argued and argued and argued and wouldn't let up. Finally, the umpire said, "If you know so much, you call the game!" And Jeep did. He took the mask and chest protector and yelled, "Play ball!" He stayed behind the plate the rest of the game—and the rest of the season. That was Jeep.

In a football game my senior year, I was playing safety and the other team had scored on a couple of pass plays. We were still ahead but needed another score to ice the win. We got the ball back, and Jeep came down out of the stands and called to Deefa on the sidelines. "Bobby! Bobby!" he yelled. "Throw the ball to Mikey! Hey, Bobby, you gotta throw the ball to Mikey!"

Deefa turned, and he was steamed. Here was Jeep Eruzione telling him how to run his team. Deefa pointed to the bleachers. "We have to get your kid to cover people! Now get the hell back in the stands!" Jeep started to say something more, and Coach DeFelice snapped, "Get back in the stands!" Jeep just turned and climbed the steps back to his seat.

At hockey games, my mother wouldn't even sit with him. She sat with Mrs. Rossi, my friend Eddie's mom. There was one game when the puck was just jumping into the net for me. I had a hat trick, and Jeep was going crazy. Helen and Mrs. Rossi just watched him. Then I got a fourth goal, and Jeep was beside himself. Late in the game, I got a fifth goal, and Jeep leaped up out of his seat—and fell down on the bleachers. He got up and looked around, hoping no one had noticed. My mom and Mrs. Rossi acted like they didn't see anything, but they were laughing hysterically.

High school sports were a big deal in Winthrop and still are. In a town that small, most everybody is related to someone on the football team or has friends who are. Saturday games would get big crowds, and there was nothing bigger than the Thanksgiving Day football game against our bigger neighbor Revere. For that matchup, there would be four or five thousand people in the stands. We beat Revere about as often as they beat us, and when we won, we got a hero's welcome. Winthrop loves to celebrate its own.

When I was a senior, Winthrop had plenty to cheer about. It was Coach DeFelice's second season as football coach, and we won one game after another. I played safety and made a bunch of interceptions. I returned punts and kickoffs, a few for touchdowns. Every once in a while, Deefa put me in at wide receiver, too. That talk he had given me had had an impact. When the big Thanksgiving Day game came around, we had a record of 7–1, and the whole town of Winthrop was hoping we would end the season with a win against Revere. Deefa was an old-school coach. We ran the ball on almost every play, almost never passed. But for Revere, Deefa had us practice a trick pass play—a halfback option. The quarterback would hand off to the running back, who would make it look like a run but then stop and heave a pass downfield to a receiver going long. He picked me to be the halfback for that play. We worked on it day after day, and parents and fans saw us running it in practice. Everyone in Winthrop knew we were going to spring it on Revere. It was the worst-kept secret in town. On Thanksgiving Day it rained, and the game was postponed until Saturday. That Friday, Deefa had us back on the soggy field, practicing the trick play. We tried it probably twenty times and completed the pass maybe only twice.

But in the game, I couldn't wait for Deefa to call for it. On our first possession, our quarterback handed off to me, I started running to the right, and the whole Revere team bought it. Downfield, our receiver was wide open. I remember thinking, Don't overthrow him, don't screw it up. I lofted the ball, and it hung in the air. The receiver, a kid named Mike Welch, actually had to wait for it to come down, and Mike was tackled right after he caught it at the five-yard line. If I'd thrown a better pass, it would have been a touchdown, but we scored a few plays later, anyway. That set the tone for the game. Little Winthrop had big, bad Revere on its heels. With a few minutes to go, it was a nail-biter. We led 14–8 but had the ball and scored a touchdown on the final play to win 20–8. Our locker room was insane. We passed out cigars and jumped around like we won the Super Bowl. We dumped water buckets on Deefa and pushed him into the showers. He was completely soaked, but he wasn't mad. He was laughing and yelling with the rest of us.

Bob DeFelice was one tough SOB, but he made me a competitor. He turned us into winners. What I took away from playing for him was that you don't have to like your coach. He doesn't have to be your friend. And sometimes you may think a coach is being too hard on you or unfair, but if you just keep working, it may all work out in the end.

My senior hockey season started a few days after the Thanksgiving Day game, and Winthrop kept right on winning. I played center on a line with two friends, Steve Christopher and Chris Costonis. We scored two, three, or four goals every game. My father had always demanded that I hustle. In baseball, if you get a walk, you run to first base. If you pop up, you run it out anyway. I tried to play hockey the same way: full speed every shift. Late in the season, I was second in the league in scoring with sixty-one points, one point behind a kid from Beverly, Bill Gilligan—the kid I'd had the fight with freshman year. We played Beverly in the last game and lost 8–0. Bill Gilligan got a bunch of goals and assists and won the scoring title. That wasn't the last I'd see of Billy Gilligan, though.

Baseball was still my best and favorite sport. If I was going to play in college, baseball seemed like the best bet. One year in high school, I was selected to play in some all-star baseball games at Fenway Park for the top players in New England. The Hearst All-Stars, it was called. My mom and dad and family got to see me play two games on the same field as the Red Sox. I figured for sure I'd get to play the following year, too. But the newspaper that had sponsored the tournament merged with another paper, and the tournament ended. There was a lesson there. You never know what life is going to throw at you. You have to take advantage of opportunities when you can, because nothing is guaranteed and nothing lasts forever.

When I was a senior, Winthrop had a great baseball team. Once when we had several rainouts in a row, Coach Jim Evans had me pitch. I walked several batters and made some wild pitches, but I threw a no-hitter. I gave up a run because I balked once when runners were on first and third, but we won 2–1. We finished the season as conference champions, and by then I was sure that athletics was my ticket to college. Two kids who had played baseball in Winthrop were playing at the University of New Hampshire. Eddie Rossi, my hockey friend, was skating for Harvard. Bill Gilligan, the kid who had beaten me for the league scoring title in hockey, was headed for Brown University. Other hockey players I'd played against were going to Boston College, Boston University, UNH, and Northeastern. Surely someone would offer me a scholarship, too.

Maybe it was my size. The Winthrop newspaper used to refer to me as "Mike Eruzione, the mighty mite," not exactly the most awe-inspiring nickname. Whatever it was, none of the Boston-area schools recruited me. Not one. The only recruiting letter I got came from the hockey coach at Merrimack College, a Division II school. I decided to do a postgraduate year at a prep school, Berwick Academy in Maine. The school offered some financial aid, and I thought it would be a good place because Berwick played hockey against the UNH junior varsity. That would give me a chance to play in front of the UNH coaches. I thought I could play a year at Berwick, get bigger and stronger, and a scholarship to UNH would be a slam dunk. I played football, hockey, and baseball at Berwick and became more serious about academics. The hockey team took a trip to Sweden and Norway, my first time on an airplane and my first time out of the country. When we played the UNH junior varsity team, I fell in love with the campus in Durham. By the end of the year, I'd grown three inches and added thirty pounds. I talked to the UNH football and baseball coaches. They seemed to like me, although no scholarship offer came. Then word got back to me that the UNH hockey coach, Charlie Holt, wasn't interested. Sorry, there's no spot for you, I was told. Coach Holt doesn't think you're good enough for Division I hockey.

Surprise, disappointment, frustration: I felt all of those. I couldn't understand what it was about me, why none of the coaches at the big schools wanted me. I had put all my eggs into one basket, too. I'd been so sure that I'd get an offer from UNH that I didn't have a backup school. Swallowing my pride, I took up the offer to play hockey at Merrimack and dropped the idea of playing three sports. I was eighteen years old at that point. I wasn't thinking I could have a career in hockey. The Olympics—it wasn't even a consideration. I didn't have that in mind as a goal or a possibility. Playing hockey in the Olympics seemed about as likely as becoming president.

Eventually, I felt good about going to Merrimack. I sent in my $200 deposit. I was going to be only the second person in my immediate family, after my sister Nanci, to go to college.

My mother and father were proud of me. I figured I'd have four good years in Division II hockey, major in education, and then go back home to Winthrop, get a job teaching and coaching at my high school—just like Coach Evans and Coach DeFelice. My cousin Tony had actually done just that: after playing football at Xavier University in Cincinnati, he had moved back home and gotten a job at Winthrop High. He was going to be one of Deefa's assistants on the football team that fall.

That's what I was going to do, too—until I met Jack Parker.

CHAPTER 4

A CHANCE ENCOUNTER

I spent the summer of 1973 playing baseball in a senior league, my hockey gear stowed in the garage until fall. A few high school friends were playing in a summer hockey league, and one day in August one of them stopped by the house on Bowdoin Street. Their team was short a few players. Could I fill in?

The game was at a rink a couple towns away, in Billerica, and I played the way I always played. I skated hard and hustled. I scored a few goals and set up a couple others. After the game, the referee came up to me and asked where I was going to play in college.

"Merrimack," I said.

"Why aren't you going to a Division I school?" he asked.

"Because no Division I schools are talking to me."

"Well, I'm talking to you."

Jack Parker was from Somerville, a tough working-class section of Boston. He had played hockey at Boston University in the 1960s and now was an assistant coach, responsible for recruiting new players and coaching the JV team. BU was a powerhouse. The Terriers had won back-to-back national championships in 1971 and '72. The school had top players from not only the Boston area but also kids from Ontario and Quebec. In high school, I had hoped to play at UNH or maybe Northeastern. I'd never thought I'd have a shot at playing at BU.

I didn't know it at the time, but Coach Parker was actually scrambling to find a few players. He had been recruiting a kid from Montreal: Pat Hughes, a highly regarded forward. Jack had gone up to Montreal to visit Hughes and his parents and told them about BU and its brand-new rink, Walter Brown Arena. When he left, Coach Parker had thought for sure he had Hughes all lined up to become a Terrier.

But about a week before I played in that game in Billerica, Hughes had called Coach Parker to say he'd decided to go to the University of Michigan instead. Coach Parker had also thought he had a commitment from a player from Toronto, and that kid had backed out at the last minute, too. It was August. The start of school was about a month away. Coach Parker had two open scholarships to fill. When he suited up to ref that summer-league game, he was in a bind.

It boggles my mind whenever I think about that moment in time. If those two players hadn't backed out, Coach Parker never would have struck up a conversation with me that day. He never would have asked where I was going to play college hockey. I never would have gone to BU. I would have played at Merrimack, and no one outside Winthrop would have ever heard of Mike Eruzione. What if I had decided not to play hockey that day? My life would have taken a completely different course. I wouldn't have played four years at BU. I wouldn't have been invited to try out for the 1980 Olympic team or any team representing the United States. The Olympics, Lake Placid, the game against the Soviets, the winning goal, the gold medal, all the things that people associate with my name today—I wouldn't have been part of any of that. Maybe it wouldn't have happened at all. Everything that has happened for me since then—meeting presidents, having a career in television, being asked to give speeches, the movie *Miracle*, lighting the torch at the 2002 Winter Games in Salt Lake City, playing golf with guys such as Charles Barkley, John Elway, Joe Pesci, Dan Marino, and Mario Lemieux at celebrity golf tournaments, having opportunities to speak to a US Ryder Cup team, the Miami Dolphins, the St. Louis Cardinals, and plenty of other teams over the years—none of that would have been possible without Jack Parker. None of it. I still just shake my head when I think about it now, almost forty years later.

The next day, I sat down in Coach Parker's office off Commonwealth Avenue, and he spelled out the offer: $3,200—a full scholarship and a lot of money for a kid from Winthrop. My father had been right: if you work hard, at some point you'll get a break. Here was mine. I told Coach Parker I was in. I was going to be a Terrier.

When we started preseason practices at BU, I noticed that most of the twenty-three players were Canadians. I was intimidated. I wasn't the big recruit here. I was the kid from Winthrop who hadn't been recruited at all. Some of those guys had had lots of schools chasing them and multiple scholarship offers to choose from. A lot of them were established big-time college players, and a few were national champions, having won the title with the BU team of 1972. I knew I didn't have the skill and speed of a lot of them, so I tried to make up for it with hustle and hard work.

I also noticed that a lot of them had new skates. If you were on the varsity, BU gave you a new pair of skates. Since the season was just getting under way, the coaches hadn't named freshmen to the varsity. Until I made the varsity, I would have to use the same old skates I'd had in high school. After one of the first practices, I sat in the locker room looking at my skates, the leather cracked and torn, the blades spotted with rust. "These things suck," I said, and tossed them into the trash. The kid sitting next to me looked at me like I was some kind of a nut, and we got to talking. His name was Rick Meagher, from Belleville, Ontario.

One of the upperclassmen, Vic Stanfield, helped me out. His brother, Fred, played for the Bruins and had a hockey shop in Danvers. He gave me a deal on a new pair of skates called Hyde Jelineks. I paid fifty bucks for them, which was all the money I could scrape together. They weren't black like most hockey skates. They were red. The next day I was the only player on the ice at Walter Brown Arena in red skates.

Rick Meagher was a freshman, too. He and I actually had something in common: he was the other player Coach Parker had recruited at the last minute to fill those two open scholarships. Rick's brother Terry was a sophomore and a rising star at BU, but Ricky had planned to go to Clarkson University, one of the other top eastern hockey schools at the time. After Jack had signed me to fill one of his open scholarships, he called the Meagher home in Belleville to fill the other. He asked if Ricky wanted to come to Boston University and play with his brother. Right before school started, Ricky switched from Clarkson to BU.

It wasn't long before I was palling around with Ricky all

the time, taking him home to Winthrop on weekends for my mom's Italian cooking. On the ice, he was something to watch. He was a little shorter than me, but he was lightning quick, he could stop and change direction on a dime, and he just had a sense of where other players were. If you kept your stick on the ice and went to the net, Ricky would find you.

Jack Parker had recruited me, but the head coach, Leon Abbott, had never seen me play. He didn't know anything about me, and he wasn't going to play me. He was going to play the guys he knew and had recruited himself. One day I showed up for practice, and a list posted in the locker room showed who was practicing with the varsity and who would practice with the JV team. I wasn't on the varsity list. The JV dressed in a different room. They skated at a different time. It almost felt like you weren't really on the team. And I had never been cut or put onto any JV team. I had been on the varsity in every sport in high school. When I saw my name on the JV list, I couldn't believe it. I was practically in tears. My only response, though, was to work. That's what Jeep would have told me: quit whining and start skating.

After a couple hard skates with the JV, I was moved to the varsity, and when we played our first game, I was on the fourth line. I didn't get a lot of ice time, but at least I was in the lineup. In the third game of the season, a home loss to Vermont on December 1, 1973, I scored my first goal for BU. A few days later, I scored against Princeton and then again against Harvard. The guy who was getting me the puck was Rick Meagher. By then, anytime one of the guys on the team asked, "Where's Ricky?" the answer was always, "He's with Mike." It turned out that Ricky came from a big family a lot like mine. They were Irish instead of Italian, but they were regular people like everyone at Bowdoin Street. His father worked for the railroad and had been born on the Fourth of July, just like Jeep. His mother and mine both knew what it was like to have to stretch the grocery money to feed everybody. Almost every weekend, Ricky went home with me to Winthrop. My mother would put him to work in the kitchen, peeling eggplant and chopping vegetables. My mom would do Ricky's laundry as well as mine. There were still so many cousins in the house that one more person didn't matter.

The big turning point for me, though, turned out to be a bad break for Leon Abbott. He was in his second season at BU and was in hot water with the administration. There was a controversy over the eligibility of two Canadian players on the team, Bill Buckton and Peter Marzo. Apparently, they had been given small amounts of money to cover room and board expenses while they were living away from home and playing junior hockey in Canada before they had come to BU. The question was whether those room and board stipends violated NCAA rules. It was not a lot of money, maybe a few hundred dollars, and it was stupid because one kid could get a prep school scholarship worth thousands of dollars and full room and board, and that was fine. And there were plenty of other players in college hockey who had gotten room and board money, but the BU situation became a big deal because it ended up in court. In the end, Buckton and Marzo were ruled eligible and stayed on the team. But the administration thought Leon should have known about the payments and should have informed the university that they could be an issue. In late December, we were preparing to play in a tournament. On the Saturday before

Christmas, I was in the locker room with the other players getting dressed when the athletic director and Coach Parker walked in.

The AD said, "Gentlemen, we just fired Leon Abbott for violating NCAA rules. Jack Parker is now head coach. Good luck." He turned and walked out without saying another word. Coach Parker was left standing there. His head must have been spinning. He'd found out just fifteen minutes before that he was suddenly head coach. He said, "Practice starts at ten. Be on time," and then he left, too. The players were stunned. A lot of them had been recruited by Leon and had played for him the previous season. He was a good coach, and they liked him. But I was the happiest guy in the room. The coach who had barely known I was on the team was now gone. I saw an opening for something else, too. I got up, walked across the hall to the coach's office, and knocked on the door. Coach Parker called me in. He was at the desk with his head in his hands. The last thing he needed at that moment was freshman Mike Eruzione coming in to complain about ice time or to ask about playing on a different line. He was wondering, What now? What does this kid want?

"Coach," I said, "can I get a new pair of skates?"

He stared at me for a moment. "Didn't you get a pair at the beginning of the year?"

"No, Coach Abbott told me he wasn't sure if I was going to make the varsity."

"Mike, I think you'll make the varsity," he said, relief spreading across his face. "Go see the equipment manager."

Jack Parker would eventually coach for forty years at Boston University. He'd win three national titles and 897 games. He'd become a legend in college hockey. But his very first act as head coach was getting me a new pair of skates.

Every underdog story involves a bit of luck, and my life has been defined by three incredible lucky breaks, three points where something fortunate happened and changed the course of my life. Without those three moments, everything would have been different. One was being on the ice, in the right place at the right time, on February 22, 1980, in Lake Placid, New York, in the Olympics against the Soviet Union. Another was my chance encounter with Jack Parker in August 1973. The third happened in the summer before I went off to BU, and that was the night Donna Alioto let me walk her home.

The Alioto family lived down the street and around the corner from my house. They had thirteen kids, six of them girls. The girls used to line up their lounge chairs on the sidewalk and lie in the sun in their bathing suits. The third oldest in the family was Donna, and she had beautiful green eyes. She was two years younger than me and was friends with my sister Nettie. Anytime I was going to the beach or the ball field in the summer, I made sure to walk past the Alioto house, hoping maybe I'd see Donna. As I was preparing to go off to BU, I got Nettie to ask Donna if she'd go out with me. Each time Donna said no, she already had a boyfriend. But I kept bugging Nettie, and Nettie kept bugging Donna, and finally the answer was yes. One night that summer a bunch of kids were hanging out at a park in Winthrop. Donna was there and I was there, and I walked her home.

A few days later, I went over to her house. Donna's sister was getting married, and her parents were having the wedding and reception at their home. I showed up and said hello and talked for a little while. On my way out, I grabbed a case of beer to take with me. I was playing hockey that day, and it was the only place I could get beer on a Sunday. It was something Jeep would have done. Donna didn't think it was funny at the time, but we laugh about it now. A couple days later, I took her out for our first date: pizza at Santarpio's, the restaurant where my father worked. It wasn't the fanciest place, but it was within my budget—Jeep picked up the tab.

I dated Donna on and off when I was at BU. She would come to games at Walter Brown Arena with my family, but afterward I would hang out with the guys at a bar on Commonwealth Avenue called the Dugout. It was located down some steps below street level and was the hangout of the BU hockey team. A lot of the players worked there as bartenders or bouncers. We drank beer there after games, and it was always mobbed with students and fans. Boston sportswriters would show up to talk to players for their stories. On the jukebox, they had "O Canada" for the Canadian guys on the team. I didn't take Donna to the Dugout. She was still in high school. I was a college man. My father had Santarpio's, and I had the Dugout. That was where I hung out with teammates.

I sent Donna some funny cards and notes to keep in touch, but I'd go weeks without seeing her. Sometimes I wouldn't hear back from her for a while and I'd call and ask what was wrong. She'd say, "You're being a jerk." In hindsight, I probably was. But I usually could find a way to make her laugh, and then everything would be okay again, or so it seemed. One weekend, Ricky and I were in Winthrop and Donna was babysitting for a family in town. He and I dropped by the house to see her. Another guy was already there—her old boyfriend. I stormed out. "You can have her!" I shouted over my shoulder. A couple days later, we were back together, though.

The firing of Leon Abbott paid off for me in other ways besides a new pair of skates. When Coach Parker took over, he decided to give everybody equal ice time for the first couple games, so he could get a fresh look at each player's abilities. He also moved me from the fourth line to the second line. We lost three of the first six games under Coach Parker, and at that point the season was on edge. One coach had been fired. The new coach had no head-coaching experience. And we weren't playing up to our potential.

In one game, two of our players were sent to the penalty box at the same time. They happened to be the two best penalty killers on the team. Coach Parker looked down the bench to find someone else to put onto the ice. I think most of the other guys were looking straight ahead, but I was looking back at him, nodding to tell him, "I'll go, Coach. I'll go."

"You know how to kill penalties, Mike?" he asked.

"Yup," I said and hopped over the boards. Killing penalties is all about beating the other team to the puck and winning battles along the boards and in the corners. It doesn't require great skill. It takes heart, intensity, energy—the things that made up my game. We killed the two-man advantage that night, and after Jack gave me a regular turn on the penalty kill. A little over a month before, I had been practicing with the JV. Now I was skating regularly and killing penalties. That's what happens when you have a coach who believes in you.

Coach Parker was only twenty-eight, but he understood hockey better than most coaches twice his age. His philosophy was that you create offense by playing good defense. It may sound backward, but it's simple logic: you can score only if you have the puck. So your first job is to stop the other team and take the puck away. If you have the puck, you can score and the other team can't. The more you have the puck, the more shots and scoring chances you get, the better the chances you'll win the game. It's not that complicated, but you have to play tough defense for it to work.

It wasn't easy playing for Jack. Under his approach, you had assignments and responsibilities even if you weren't near the puck. Forwards—the center and wings—score most of the goals in hockey, but on Jack's team the forwards were a big part of the defense, too. You couldn't just hang out at the red line and wait for the defensemen to get you the puck. Forwards had to come back, backcheck, cover their man. He pounded that into us. He wasn't happy if you made a mistake in the offensive end, but defensive mistakes pissed him off. If you took your time getting back into the defensive zone, he'd chew you out, in practice or in games. If you didn't hustle or play with intensity, you heard from him. You had to be thinking and working every second you were on the ice.

Yet it wasn't hard to pump yourself up to go all out. Coach Parker had a fire in him. He's one of the most competitive people I've ever met, and he was thinking about hockey all the time. Sometimes he'd get an idea, and if we didn't have time for an actual practice, he'd have us go out onto the ice in shoes and street clothes. He would position guys on the ice to explain some play he had in his head, for the power play or penalty kill, and then he'd move us around like chess pieces. "Mike, you pass to Ricky and then go to the corner. Ricky, pass to the D." In those days, Coach Parker was so wound up he smoked three packs of cigarettes a day. He'd grab a smoke before a game, come into the locker room, and the smoke would still be coming out of his mouth. He talked in a rapid-fire way, words coming at you in quick bursts, and his intensity radiated out into the locker room. There was an element of fear, too. If he didn't like a call on the ice, he'd go off on the referee, yelling, screaming, face red, veins bulging on his neck. I'd see that and think, Oh boy, I better not screw up.

On game days, Coach Parker was in a zone. I remember a couple of us went into his office once, and he was lying on the couch he had in there, smoking a cigarette, staring at the ceiling. "BC tonight, boys," he whispered. "BC." He took great pride in being a Terrier. To him, there was no greater honor than to wear the BU jersey. And he just hated to lose, especially to Boston College. The two schools don't just share a city and a name; they share the same street. BU is located at one end of Commonwealth Avenue, BC at the other end, three miles to the west in Newton, just beyond the Boston city limits. The rivalry goes beyond the ice. The two schools recruit the same players. They compete for media attention. When Jack was a Terrier center in the 1960s, he never lost a game to BC, and as head coach he preferred to keep his record as close to perfect as possible. It was more than just a rivalry for me, too. BC hadn't recruited me. They hadn't wanted me, hadn't even given me a look. You bet I wanted to beat them.

We had some great players on the 1973–74 team. Vic Stanfield was one of the best defensemen in college hockey. Our goalie, Ed Walsh, one of the few Americans on the team, was one of the best in the East. And we had a load of terrific players. We had nine guys who averaged more than a point per game—almost half the team! Before long, Coach Parker's way started to click. We won eight games in a row, often by lopsided scores. Ricky and I ended up on the third line together, and it was a blast playing with him. One night we beat Boston College 11–2. Ricky scored two goals, I got one. We scored nine goals against Clarkson, one of the top teams in the East, and then nine more against RPI.

When we got to the Beanpot, the annual tournament among the four big hockey schools—BU, BC, Harvard, and Northeastern—we lost in the finals to Harvard. The winning team had a defenseman from Winthrop: Eddie Rossi, my buddy from youth hockey. But we got back on a roll and found ourselves playing for the championship of our league, the Eastern Collegiate Athletic Conference, and we faced Harvard again.

For that game, Boston Garden was packed. Harvard scored forty-six seconds into the game. A bit later, I tipped in a shot to tie the score. Ricky scored to give us the lead. Late in the game, Harvard had a power play, but Ed Walsh was superb in goal. When the horn sounded, we piled off the BU bench to mob Ed. It was 4–2. We were ECAC champions.

Winning the title meant that Boston University was the top team in the East and would play in the national championship tournament, which was also being held at Boston Garden that year. It wasn't the big media event that the Frozen Four is today. It was just a four-team tournament: the top two eastern teams and the two best from the West. But for the players and coaches, it was a big deal. Eastern and western schools hardly ever played each other back then. Most years, western schools won the national title, and they thought their more physical brand of hockey was better. They thought they had better players. Eastern schools tended to have smaller, faster players and played more of a finesse game, a skill game. That was better hockey, in our view. You also found more Canadian players on the rosters of the eastern schools. At BU, we had heated rivalries with BC and Harvard, Cornell and Clarkson. But when it came to the final four, I wanted to knock those western schools down a peg or two.

The East-West rivalry tended to heat up every four years when the Olympics rolled around. If the Olympic coach was a western guy, he seemed to pick a team made up mainly of western players. If it was a coach from back East, he might favor eastern players. When the final four came to Boston Garden in March 1974, the rivalry was as hot as ever. Eastern schools had won three of the previous four national championships: Cornell in 1970 and then BU in '71 and '72. Wisconsin had won it back for the West in '73.

In the first game, we faced the University of Minnesota. I knew little about Minnesota and even less about its coach, a guy named Herb Brooks, then in his second season. The game didn't go well for us. They jumped out to a 3–0 lead; we battled back. In the third period, Ricky picked up the puck at center ice and flew up the left wing. He crossed the blue line and deked the Minnesota defenseman out of his skates. Then he made a move on the goalie and somehow picked the top corner. It was as amazing as any goal I've ever seen, and it tied the game 4–4. Then, with under a minute left, Minnesota was called for a penalty. It was a big opportunity for us. We would play the last forty-four seconds of the game with five skaters while Minnesota had four, giving us a great chance to win the game, especially with all the guys we had who could put the puck into the net.

We were in their zone when Minnesota knocked the puck out to center ice. Our defensemen had trouble gathering the puck, and a Minnesota forward tipped it away and skated in alone and scored. Our hopes for a national championship ended right there, on a shorthanded goal with thirteen seconds left. Two days later Minnesota beat Michigan Tech to win the title. Talking to reporters after the game, Herb Brooks hit on the East-West rivalry. He pointed out that every player on the Minnesota roster was an American. In fact, every one of them was from Minnesota. That was a big deal to him, having a team of all-American players, all-Minnesota players. "We respect Canadians, but we respect the people of the United States, too," he said after the game, a comment that seemed aimed at Boston University with all the Canadian guys we had. It wouldn't be the last time he'd bring up the topic of Canadian players.

The loss was disappointing, but it had been a great season for me. My father had always told me, "If you work hard, some day you will have success." I felt like my effort was finally paying off at BU. I had a fiery coach who believed in me. Jack Parker had given me an opportunity, and I had worked to make the most out of it. I had scored twenty-one goals, the most on the team. I wasn't the fastest skater or the best stick handler, but I hustled, and I had an ability to make plays. That's what they talk about today: guys who make plays. The Patriots beat the Seahawks in Super Bowl XLIX because Malcolm Butler made a play. He wasn't the best player on the field, but when the Patriots needed a big play, he intercepted a pass on the goal line. I seemed to make plays. If Ricky got me the puck in front of the net and I had an opportunity to score, I could pick the corner. If Ricky was open, I could get him the puck. People were noticing, too. A *Boston Globe* story called me "Pete Rose on skates."

I also had a new best friend. Ricky and I both ended up with forty points. I was named best defensive forward in New England, which was a nice award. In the draft for the World Hockey Association, a new league that had sprung up to rival the NHL, I was chosen in the second round by the New England Whalers.

It was hard to believe. Just nine months before, I had been headed to Merrimack College to become a gym teacher. Now I was one of the top scorers on one of the best college teams in the country, and even a pro hockey career no longer seemed like a crazy idea.

CHAPTER 5

THE BRAWL IN DENVER

When I played college hockey, I never lifted weights. I never went to the gym. I don't know if any of the guys did. We didn't have the kind of strength and conditioning programs they have today. But I worked out—by lugging hundred-pound bags of sand in the hot sun.

My summer job was painting bridges—small bridges like the overpasses on the Massachusetts Turnpike. To start with, a couple other guys and I had to scrape the stinking, reeking bird crap off the steel girders, inches of it. Then we sandblasted the old paint off. An older guy worked the sandblaster. My job was to make sure he didn't run out of sand. So I hauled bags of sand from the truck up to the bridge, sometimes two at a time. Up and back, up and back. I had to wear coveralls, and in the summer sun, it was like I was in a furnace. Sometimes I'd come home ten or fifteen pounds lighter than I had been at breakfast. I had to drink a lot of water, so I went to the bathroom a lot. Almost every day my underwear would be sticky with the lead paint we used. My mother was buying a new package of underwear almost every week.

Eddie Rossi worked there, too, and he also lined up a lot of painting jobs at Harvard, which was a nice break from doing bridges. Other times we had jobs at the sewage treatment plant where my father worked. I'd start painting a single water pipe, moving the ladder every couple of feet. One pipe might run three or four miles inside the plant, and I would follow that pipe all day, painting it blue. I'd come back the next day and follow a different kind of pipe, painting it red or green. Talk about a pain in the neck. I spent the entire day looking up with my neck, reaching up with my arms.

It's funny to think of that today. Now college players work out all summer, on ice and off ice. Some go to prospect camps run by NHL clubs. The best under-twenty players skate in a tournament against Canada and other countries to get ready for the Ice Hockey World Junior Championships. The college season may be over, but the hockey never stops. I can't imagine any of the better players having summer jobs, and if they do, they're definitely not painting bridges.

In my sophomore season at BU, almost all the players from the year before returned. We won every game we played at home, all eleven of them. We had twelve guys—half the team—who scored twenty points or more on the season. Vic Stanfield was an All-American and led the team with seventy points, an incredible total for a defenseman. In thirty-two games, we scored 221 goals, an average of almost seven a game. Coach Parker again had Ricky playing center and me on his left wing, and we terrorized the other teams. I led the team in goals with twenty-seven, Terry Meagher had twenty-six, and Ricky had twenty-five. A lot of writers picked us to win the national title.

For home games, Jeep would lead a caravan of family and

friends to watch us play. It seemed like half the people in Walter Brown Arena were from Winthrop. As usual, the Eruzione section was loud. My sister Jeannie would come home with bruises on the backs of her legs from hitting the bench seats every time she jumped up to cheer. Jeep whistled at every goal by me or Ricky. And of course, Jeep, who knew absolutely nothing about hockey, always had an opinion. One night I scored two goals and had a chance for a hat trick on a breakaway. I shot it wide. After the game Jeep said, "You should have deked the goalie."

"I should have deked?" I asked him. "What do you know about deke? What does deke mean?"

He shrugged. "I don't know. That's what the guy behind me said." That was Jeep for you.

That 1974–75 BU team piled up one win after another. We beat Harvard and Eddie Rossi in the Beanpot. When we played Harvard again for the ECAC title, Ricky and Terry scored two goals each and I got one in a 7–3 victory. By then Jack Parker was being called a coaching prodigy. He was just twenty-nine years old, and in less than two seasons as a head coach, he had led us to two league championships and we were headed to the NCAA tournament for the second year in a row. Ricky was named an All-American, meaning he was one of the top five players in the country. I was named best defensive forward in New England again, which was nice, I suppose.

That year's final four was played in St. Louis, and again we were slotted as the top eastern team. In the semifinal game, we faced Michigan Tech, the number two team from the West. We'd been a fast team all year, playing the go-go hockey Coach

Parker demanded, but for some reason, we were awful, off our game. It was probably our worst game in my four years at BU. The score was 9–5. For a second time, we had a chance for a national championship and went home disappointed.

At the end of that season, Coach Parker called me into his office and told me I had been selected to play for the United States in the 1975 World Ice Hockey Championship. I'd had no idea I was even in the running. Jeep, Uncle Tony, and Uncle Jerry had all served our country in World War II. This was my first chance to represent our country. To me, it was an honor to wear the USA jersey, and my mother and father couldn't have been prouder.

The tournament took place in West Germany, and it was the first chance I had to see the Soviet hockey team. By then, everyone knew they were the best in the world. They had come to North America and embarrassed NHL teams—the Canadiens, the Bruins, the Rangers. In international hockey, no one could touch them. By 1975, they had taken the gold at three Olympics in a row and nine of the last ten World Championships. They hardly ever lost a game.

I didn't know much about the Russians. I knew just a few of their names—there was one guy, Valeri Kharlamov, who was a great skater, and the captain, Boris Mikhailov. When they played the NHL teams, they seemed every bit as good as the top NHL guys such as Phil Esposito and Guy Lafleur.

They were considered amateurs by the Olympics organizers, but the only thing they did was play hockey. In Russia, their teams were sponsored by the Red Army or labor unions or factories, so they didn't have jobs, they just trained year-round. They'd get up, run three miles, lift weights, do gymnastics and calisthenics, and *then* hit the ice for practice. That was one reason they always won—they were always in better shape than the other team.

They had also played hockey a different way, a better way. In North American hockey, you got the puck, rushed up the ice, and fired the puck the first time you had a chance. Maybe you made a pass or two, but the idea was to get lots of shots. If you took thirty shots, a few were bound to go in. And if you didn't have a play or a shot, you threw the puck into the corner and chased after it, hoping you could bang and check your way into getting possession again. It was a straight-ahead, physical game.

The Soviet style was based on passing and keeping possession of the puck. The Soviet coaches didn't worry about how many shots the players took, but they actually counted how many passes they made. The idea was to keep the puck, swirl, and weave until they found an opening. Their style was suited to the rinks used in Europe and for the Olympics, which are two hundred feet long and one hundred feet wide, fifteen feet wider than NHL rinks. The extra space leaves lots of room for skating and passing, less for checking and hitting.

When the Russians got the puck into their opponent's zone, they wouldn't shoot at their first opportunity. They might pass ten times before taking a shot. The puck would bounce around like it was in a pinball machine. When they played exhibition games over here, NHL teams would be running in circles trying to figure out what was going on. And then suddenly a Soviet player would have the puck and a wide-open net to shoot at. Soviet teams would play NHL clubs and be outshot 35–15, and it would look like the North American players were all over them most of the game. But the Soviets would win 5–2 or 6–3, and most of their goals were of the highlight-reel variety.

And at the other end of the ice, they had one of the best goalies in the world, Vladislav Tretiak.

When the US team got together before the 1975 World Ice Hockey Championship, I knew it was going to be hard for us. Everyone did. We were college guys, mostly twenty or twenty-one years old, thrown together for the tournament. We had some good players. One of my teammates was a kid from Babbitt, Minnesota, Buzz Schneider. Everyone called him Buzz. Hardly anyone knew his real name, William. Buzzy could skate like the wind. The Babbitt Rabbit, they called him. But we weren't really a team. We had about a week of practice together and flew to Germany. The coach was "Badger Bob" Johnson, the head coach at the University of Wisconsin. He had a son, Mark, who was a hockey player, a good one, but he was too young to play that year. Badger Bob's motto was "It's a great day for hockey," and I don't know if I ever played under a coach who had more energy and love of the game than he did.

Badger Bob had traveled to the Soviet Union and studied their game. In the short time we practiced together, he made us try some of their training methods. He had us get up early and go for walks in the morning air, and we took saunas. He tried to teach us some of the Russian game, the passing and possession. But you can't learn that in a few days, and there weren't many Olympic-sized rinks for us to practice it on.

When we got to Germany and played Czechoslovakia, the second-best team after the Soviet Union, we lost 8–3. More astounding were the shots on goal. In a normal hockey game, thirty shots would be a lot. The Czechs had ninety-three.

When the game ended, the crowd gave a standing ovation—not for the Czechs but for our goalie, Jim Warden. We were going to meet the Soviets in a preliminary game, and I just stayed positive. "We can beat these guys," I kept saying. "We can beat these guys." Badger Bob laughed every time he heard it.

When we faced them, they beat us easily, 10–5. The one bit of good news was that Buzz Schneider had a hat trick, scoring three of our five goals. In the second round, we played them again, and they were bored. They knew they could beat us and just wanted to get the game over with. Since they weren't giving it much effort, the game was actually close. Halfway through the third period, it was only 3–0. Then I intercepted a pass and went in alone on Tretiak. I fired the puck between his legs, five-hole. That made the score 3–1, with 10:15 left in the game. Suddenly the Soviets woke up. In the final ten minutes of the game, they scored ten goals. *Ten.* The final was 13–1.

"You shouldn't have scored, Mike," Badger Bob told me after the game. "That just pissed them off."

At that tournament, we played ten games and lost every one. The United States was a long way from being a serious contender in international hockey.

That summer the US Olympic organizers had tryouts for the team that would play the following February at the 1976 Winter Olympics in Innsbruck, Austria. Badger Bob was again going to coach. If I made the team, I'd have to sit out a year at BU, and we had a lot of upperclassmen returning, all guys I knew and liked playing with, including nine seniors. We had missed out on a national championship twice, but this was going to be the best team yet. The Terriers were going to have a shot at a national championship, and I wanted to get one before I left BU. Forget the Olympics, I decided.

The 1975–76 season would be the most momentous of my college career, and it would stick with me for years to come—and not in the best way. In that season, I'd get a sense of the mind and methods of Herb Brooks, the man who, four years later, would be my coach in the Olympics. The season would end in a bizarre and violent spectacle, and the full meaning of what had taken place wouldn't be clear to me until I made it to Lake Placid, where I'd experience firsthand how Herb could get into the heads of his players. In 1980, I was on the winning end of a big upset Herb orchestrated. In 1976, unfortunately, I wasn't.

In the fall of 1975, Ricky and I were back for our junior year. He had been named an All-American the previous season and was one of the best players in college hockey. We had a terrific goalie in sophomore Brian Durocher and a raft of other outstanding players: Mike Fidler, a great goal scorer, Bill Buckton, Peter Marzo, Bill Robbins, and on and on.

The players we chose to be our captains were Peter Brown, an offensive defenseman, and Terry Meagher, now a senior. Peter was an intense guy. He'd get into your face if he didn't think you were working hard enough or focused enough. Terry was a very different player from both Peter and Ricky. Ricky was a shifty, dynamic skater who scored highlight-reel goals, often making it look easy. Terry was a hard worker, always hustling. He scored goals by digging and battling for the puck. Our power play, when the other team had a man in the penalty box, was almost unstoppable. Terry would stand in front of the net and pick up rebounds, tip shots in.

Off the ice, you couldn't meet a nicer guy. He was only a year older than me but was always looking after other guys. "How ya doing, Mike? How's school? How's the family? You doing okay?" He was almost like a father on the team. Everybody respected him.

We also had a tough freshman defenseman, a wiseass from Charlestown named Jack O'Callahan. When we started practicing, I could see he had an intense competitive drive. He had been accepted by Harvard but had chosen to play at BU— because he wanted to play for Jack Parker. He was willing to pass up a Harvard degree to do that.

That season we won our first four games, lost one to Michigan Tech in a tournament, and then won ten in a row. We were the number one team in the nation. It was fun practicing with that team and even more fun when we played games.

Even when we fell behind, I could see it in the eyes of the other team. At any time, we could erupt and take over. We knew it. And whoever we were playing knew it. The game was never over. That was one of the things I loved about playing for BU and playing for Coach Parker: the confidence, the pride we had, the feeling that we could win every time we stepped onto the ice. I wasn't just playing college hockey; when I pulled on the scarlet-and-white jersey with the terrier on the front, it meant I was among the elite.

I was having a blast playing with Ricky. We had chemistry, and it led to a lot of goals. I had a knack for being in the right position to score. Sometimes Ricky would put the puck onto my stick. Sometimes the puck just seemed to find its way to me. It would just come to me in the right place at the right time. Every home game, Walter Brown Arena was rocking, loud, with its low ceiling, the stands packed, the BU band firing up the students. For the second year in a row, we never lost a game at home. People started joking that going into Walter Brown Arena was like going to Death Valley because nobody came out of there alive.

We reached the Beanpot final and bombarded BC's freshman goalie, Paul Skidmore. He stopped forty-three shots. BC had last beaten BU in the Beanpot in 1965, but they did again that night. It was only the third game we lost that season. Five days later, half a world away in Innsbruck, the US Olympic team—the one I hadn't wanted to be a part of—suited up for a crucial game against West Germany, which was not a particularly good team. Win, and the United States had a silver medal. But the US team was outplayed and lost 4–1. I guess I made the right decision.

In March, we got our revenge on BC in the first round of the ECAC tournament. The lead kept changing hands throughout the game, until it was tied 5–5 with three minutes to go. With fifty-three seconds left, Ricky put in a rebound off my shot. Coach Parker was pretty happy after that game.

In the ECAC championship game, we faced Brown University. One of its top players was from Beverly—Bill Gilligan, the same kid I had fought when I was a freshman in high school, the kid who had beat me for the league scoring title. That game went my way, though; we won 9–5. Terry Meagher had scored thirty goals on the season. He was named most valuable player of the ECAC tournament.

As Ricky and I skated off the ice, Coach Parker was following behind us with his assistant coach, Don "Toot" Cahoon.

"How about that?" Jack said to Toot. "Three ECAC championships in a row!"

I turned around and said, "Yeah, and when we win a fourth next year, no one will believe it."

We headed to the NCAA tournament in Denver as the top-ranked team in the nation, with an incredible 25–3 record. Brown, the other eastern school in the final four, was almost as good at 22–6. Michigan Tech, at 33–8, was the top team from the West. The team with the weakest record in the final four was the University of Minnesota, the same school we had lost to when I was a freshman. They were 26–14–2 and were almost not selected for the final four. They would be our semifinal opponent.

My mother and sister Nanci flew out to Denver for the tournament. Nanci worked for Eastern Air Lines and got free plane tickets. Jeep stayed home. You couldn't cattle prod him onto a plane. He was terrified of flying. Like everybody else, my mother and Nanci thought this would finally be our year and looked forward to seeing me win a national championship. Some writers called us "the best team ever to come out of the East" and predicted it would be a "dream final" of BU against the best from the West, Michigan Tech.

I felt confident. I knew what kind of a team we had. I thought we were going to win. At that time, I don't think I even remembered who the Minnesota coach was, but it was the same guy who'd beaten us two years before: Herb Brooks. To start the game, Coach Parker sent out my line, our third line. Right after the puck dropped, I checked a big Minnesota defenseman, Russ Anderson. I might have gotten my stick up a little, but it was nothing dirty. Anderson didn't like it at all. He chased after me and rammed me into the boards. He was sent off for cross-checking. As I skated to the bench, I was pumped: not even a minute into the game, and we get to use our great power play unit. It was a great opportunity to grab an early lead and set the tone of the game.

Just 1:08 into the game, there was a face-off on their end. Terry and a Minnesota forward, Joe Micheletti, began jostling as they lined up. Micheletti jabbed Terry in the ribs. Terry whacked him across the skates. The ref saw the retaliation and sent Terry off. BU's thirty-goal scorer was off the ice. The guy in the Minnesota box, Russ Anderson? He'd scored two goals that season and had 111 penalty minutes.

But that was only the start of it.

The penalty box was next to the Minnesota bench, and there was no divider between where Russ Anderson was sitting and where Terry would sit. As Terry skated over, taunts, insults, and F-bombs came from the Minnesota players. "Hey, MVP, where are ya now?" "Preppie import!" "Go home, ya frog!" Terry's not French Canadian, but the Minnesota guys didn't know that. Even more worked up than the players was the Minnesota trainer, Gary Smith. As Terry skated by, he leaned over the boards and yelled, "I'm going to get you!"

The whole Minnesota team was going wild. Somehow they had come into this game whipped up into a frenzy, like they were out of their minds, pumped up and almost crazed with aggression and energy. They had gotten into a fevered mind-set somehow, some way.

Once Terry was in the box, someone spat on him. He jabbed his stick at the bench and spat back. The spit hit Smith, the trainer, and he went nuts. He grabbed Terry's stick, yelled, "I'm going to knock your head off!" and took a swing at Terry.

Then Russ Anderson jumped on Terry. As they wrestled in the penalty box, Mike Fidler, one of our top scorers and as tough as anyone, skated to the Minnesota bench and challenged them to fight. A Minnesota forward, Tom Younghans, sucker punched Mike, and all hell broke loose. Players on the ice dropped their gloves, paired off, and started swinging. Jack O'Callahan, the kid from Charlestown, went after Younghans and began throwing uppercuts.

I was on the bench, wondering, What the hell is happening? One or two guys tried to hop over the boards to join the brawl, but Bob Murray, an assistant coach, and our seventy-year-old trainer, Tony Dougal, grabbed them by the jersey to hold them back. They didn't have enough hands, though. More and more guys hopped over, and they gave up trying to keep us on the bench.

It was mayhem. It was like the movie *Slap Shot*, except it wasn't a movie. All the players were on the ice brawling, gloves and sticks scattered everywhere. O'Callahan had his helmet in his hand and was using it to bash Younghans over the head. Bob Sunderland, one of our defensemen, tried to pull the jersey over a Minnesota player's head and fell to his knees. Tony Dougal was yelling from our bench, and a Minnesota player came over and dared him to step onto the ice—the guy wanted to fight a seventy-year-old man. The officials would pull two players apart, move to another pair, and the first two guys would start again. Pairs of players pulled and clawed at each other's jerseys, trying to get a hand free to land a punch.

It went on for almost twenty minutes. Finally, the lights were turned out, and in the darkened arena the fighting stopped. The teams were sent to their locker rooms while the NCAA officials tried to figure out what to do. In the NCAA, any player who fights is ejected and sits out the next game. Were they going to eject both teams? Disqualify both teams? Would they just give the championship to the winner of the Brown–Michigan Tech game?

Sitting in the locker room, I just kept thinking, This is crazy. This is crazy.

After an hour, they had a decision: The game would resume, and only the two first combatants—Terry Meagher and Russ Anderson—would be ejected. Our top scorer and the Minnesota guy who had scored two goals. Jack Parker was steaming. I'm sure Herb Brooks was smiling inside.

I tried to put all the insanity aside and focus on the game. Things happen in hockey, and you just have to keep playing, keep competing. And we did. After two periods, we led 2–1, but the brawl and losing Terry had taken the wind out of our sails. In the third, Minnesota scored three goals for a 4–2 final.

I slumped onto the bench in our locker room, frustrated and pissed off. How could they have made that decision, to kick Terry out of the game? How could the officials have let that happen? It never should have gotten so out of hand. It was just total frustration. It's the national championship, it's everything you work for, we have a great team, and then this happens, and we lose in the national tournament for the third year in a row in the most bizarre, ridiculous way—all that was running through my mind. How did it happen?

I felt terrible for Terry. The guy had had just eight minutes in penalties the whole season, and he was such an important part of our team. Because he had been ejected, he was ineligible for the consolation game. So that embarrassment of a game had been his last in a Terriers jersey. It wasn't right, and it wasn't fair. For four years, Terry had been a great example of what college hockey should be. It wasn't the way he should have ended his college career.

When Jack Parker talked to the media, he didn't pull punches. The fight had been premeditated, he said; it had been Minnesota's game plan. "Herb Brooks is known as Herb Bush in the WCHA, and now I know why. It is obviously the way he thinks the game should be played. It's the way he wants it. I don't happen to agree with him. No question they came out with the intent of running us."

"Hogwash" was how Herb replied when he got his turn to speak. "What sense would it make to intentionally take penalties and let that power play work for you all night? If he says we came out deliberately trying to run at them, it shows an immature coach and it's sour grapes."

Back then, I thought Jack was probably right. The Minnesota coach probably wanted his guys to beat us physically. We had a very talented team, and it seemed they had planned to stop our speed and skill with aggression. I had no idea where it could have come from. How had they gotten whipped up into such a frenzy? The day of the game, a newspaper had quoted one of the Minnesota players: "All that stuff in the papers about how Boston's the best team, shit, we're going to shove that down their throats. We'll win it. People say we're pushovers, but we'll show 'em. Especially those preppies from out east." That was the mind-set they had taken into the game.

They had come out with a chip on their shoulder, apparently because they thought we were preppies and Canadians, and had used that attitude to get fired up. They had had the right mind-set to beat a more talented team. For me it was a bitter defeat. For years, I could barely talk about the game. Jack Parker couldn't, either. To this day, if you ask Jack O'Callahan about it, he'll go into an F-bomb rant about how we got screwed by the western refs and the western officials.

That season, Ricky was named an All-American for the second year in a row. Very few college hockey players have ever made the All-American team twice, and now Ricky had done it. I had actually had more goals than Ricky that season, but I didn't make the All-American team. For the third time in a row, I was named best defensive forward in New England. This time, it felt like a consolation prize.

CHAPTER 6

EAST VERSUS WEST

A couple weeks after the debacle in Denver, I pulled on the USA jersey again. I had been selected to play at the 1976 World Ice Hockey Championship in Poland. It was a very different team from the one I'd played on the year before. The 1975 team had been all college guys. This time, the United States went with older, more experienced players. Four of the guys on the roster had played for the Minnesota North Stars that season. Two had been in the WHA. Three guys played for the University of Minnesota—the guys my BU team had just brawled with. One of the players on the team who was my age was Buzz Schneider, my teammate at the '75 World Championship. We were both twenty-one at the time.

All of those players had one thing in common: every single one of them was from Minnesota. The coach was a Minnesota guy, too, John Mariucci, who'd coached the University of Minnesota years before. In fact, there was only one eastern guy, one non-Minnesota guy, on the team—and that was me. There wasn't one other eastern guy who was good enough for the team? To me, that was just further confirmation of western bias.

When we played our first game in Poland, I was in the stands in street clothes. Mariucci didn't play me in the next game either, or the one after that. In '75, even though we had lost every game, I'd had fun. I didn't have a good time in Poland. Why'd they bring me over here if they weren't going to play me? I eventually got into the lineup, and with that older team we won three of the ten games we played, beating Poland, West Germany, and Sweden, all pretty good teams, and we tied Finland, another good team. But what I took away from that experience was the East-West rivalry in US hockey. The bitterness had spilled over in the brawl in Denver. But playing here in Poland, I felt it in a whole different way. With a Minnesota coach, an all-Minnesota team, and one eastern guy who didn't get to play that much, I felt the rivalry personally. The message was: if you have a western coach, he's going to play his guys; if you're from the East, it doesn't matter how good you are. It was East versus West.

The most notable game at that World Championship didn't involve the US team. In an early game, the host Poles played the Soviets. Poland wasn't very good in hockey, but they were playing on their home soil, in front of their own fans, and they were playing a country they didn't like. Poland was then a member of the Eastern Bloc, but the Polish people hated the Soviet Union. To them, the Russians were the enemy.

The Soviets knew they were the far better team and could beat the Poles any day of the week. But after two periods, the Poles, playing with energy and emotion, had a 5–2 lead. That great Soviet goalie, the best goalie in the world, Vladislav Tretiak, was pulled from the game. It didn't change the course of the game. Even with the Soviets pulling out all the stops in the third period, the Poles hung on and won 6–4. It was a monumental upset, the greatest upset ever in international hockey at that time. After the game, the Polish fans streamed out of the arena and sang and cheered and hugged in the streets. Drivers honked their horns. It was a wild celebration. They were going crazy. In Poland, they called it a miracle.

Czechoslovakia won the championship that year. In international hockey, the Czechs were the only team that could play at the Soviets' level. But Poland showed that if the Soviets were a little off their game, maybe a little complacent and over-confident, and you played with emotion and energy, they could be beaten.

In my senior year at BU, Ricky and I were named cocaptains. We had lost ten players to graduation but got some talented freshmen. One was Ricky's younger brother, Tony, the third Meagher to play for Jack Parker. Another was a right wing named Dave Silk from Scituate, Massachusetts. Since I was a senior and spent a lot of time in Winthrop, I didn't get to know him well. But I could see he could shoot the puck. We also got a goalie named Jim Craig, from North Easton. Again, because he was a freshman and I was a senior, our paths didn't cross much—or at all, actually. He seemed to be a quiet guy and kept to himself. I probably didn't spend a minute talking to him. That really didn't matter. What mattered was that he was pretty good at keeping the puck out of the net.

We got off to a bad start, losing our first five games. One loss came at home at the hands of Dartmouth on December 1, 1976. It's a game worth noting. We had gone exactly three years to the day since our last loss at Walter Brown Arena. The last home loss had come in my freshman year, against Vermont, when I had scored my first goal. We had won twenty-nine home games in a row. We had gone 1,096 days without a loss at Walter Brown. They're interesting statistics. But I didn't care about winning streaks. What I wanted was a national championship.

To get the team moving, Coach Parker shook up our lines. The biggest move was splitting up me and Ricky. He put Ricky together with the kid from Scituate, Dave Silk. I was on the left wing with two sophomores I'd never played with. I'd been playing with Ricky for three years, we had great chemistry, we could almost read each other's mind on the ice. It was frustrating. I took my frustrations to Jack, and he explained what he was doing. He needed more balance in our scoring. He needed two lines that could score consistently, not just one line loaded up with me and Ricky. It made sense. He was trying to win.

One person who didn't like it at all was Jeep. "Why did he split up my Michael and my Ricky?" he asked my mother again and again as they watched us play.

In our sixth game of the year, against Harvard, we went into overtime, and Tony Meagher scored the winner for us. Soon Coach Parker started playing Jim Craig in most games. Jimmy's story was a little bit like mine. He came from a big family of eight kids. He hadn't been recruited heavily by the top hockey schools when he was in high school. He had gone to Norwich University, a Division II school, but had stayed only four days before leaving. The whole time he was there, he had been sick and had never even attended a single class. He had then gone to Massasoit Community College and joined its hockey team, hoping he'd get noticed by a bigger school. Like me, he had become a solution to a recruiting problem of Jack Parker's. Jack had thought he had a goalie lined up to come to BU, but the kid had chosen Brown instead. So Coach Parker had offered Jimmy a spot with the Terriers. With Jimmy in goal most games, and with our new lines, we started playing better.

Ricky and I were no longer together on the ice, but we were hardly ever apart away from the rink. We were just cut from the same cloth. One night a friend gave me two tickets to a Bruins game and the keys to his Rolls-Royce. Ricky and I felt like kings when we took off for the Garden. Neither of us had ever been in a car like that. But when we got to the toll booth at the tunnel into Boston, we just looked at each other. I didn't have a nickel in my pocket, and neither did he. We had to scrounge in the ashtray and under the seats to come up with twenty-five cents for the toll so we wouldn't miss the game.

At New Year's, we played a tournament at Madison Square Garden. I had two good games and was named MVP. Which was lucky. In the stands for one of the games was John Ferguson. He had played for the Montreal Canadiens and was an enforcer on the ice. Anyone who messed with the Canadiens' stars was probably going to get a pummeling from John Ferguson. True story: he got into his first NHL fight just twelve seconds into his first game. When he came to the Madison Square Garden tournament in 1977, he was general manager of the New York Rangers, and afterward the Rangers claimed me as an undrafted player. That meant they had the right to sign me after college.

On January 19, 1977, we beat Vermont 4–3 in overtime at

Walter Brown Arena. I set up a goal. I made a play. It was a significant assist, too. That gave me 172 points for my career at BU, making me the school's all-time leading scorer. It seemed hard to believe that a guy who hadn't been recruited until the summer before freshman year had now scored more points than anyone else in the long history of Boston University hockey. Even more than Ricky. He was a magician on the ice. He'd been named an All-American in our sophomore season and again in our junior season, and he was no doubt a better hockey player than me. But at that point, he was about a dozen points behind me in total career points. I was proud of my record. I was lucky to have played with a lot of great players who had made it possible for me to score. After that game, I told the *Boston Globe*, "I know it won't last forever. I wouldn't mind seeing someone pass me because that would mean we were doing well." And I meant every word of it.

It was nice to have a scoring record, but what I cared about were team accomplishments. I wanted to win another Beanpot. I wanted to win another ECAC title. I wanted a national championship. Yes, it's nice to score goals and put up big numbers, but I'd rather be part of a great team than be a great player. If Jack Parker needed me to play defensively to win, I was willing to do that. If he needed me to score goals, I'd try my hardest. If he needed me to move the puck and make the guys around me better, well, then, that's what I was going to do. I just wanted us to win.

In February, after we lost to Harvard in the Beanpot final, we had a mediocre record, 13–9–1. Nobody thought BU was going anywhere. The papers were saying that the Terriers' run was finally over. But we had learned a lot about playing as a team, and we won the next five games. Ricky caught fire, too.

In a stretch of three games, he scored nine goals and got five assists. The new kid, Dave Silk, was filling the net, too. He was on his way to scoring thirty-five goals on the season, with Ricky setting him up most of the time.

In the first round of the ECAC tournament, we faced BC at home. Earlier in the season we had tied them and beat them once. Whoever won this game would have bragging rights in Boston. For the loser, the season would be over. Coach Parker did not—*did not*—want to lose. In the third period, we had the game under control. It was 6–3, and Walter Brown Arena was rocking. BC clawed back and tied it. Then Ricky scored his second goal of the game to put us ahead. A minute later BC tied it. And then, off the center ice face-off, Ricky got the puck, blew past the BC defense, and deked the goalie. Just six seconds after BC's goal, Ricky got us the lead back. The guy was amazing. After the game, Coach Parker ripped us apart. "This never should have happened! You thought you had the game won, and you let up! You let them back in!" And he was right. When we had the lead, we let up, made mistakes, and were sloppy in our defense. You have to play all sixty minutes, to the final whistle. Whether you're ahead or behind, you have to keep playing to the last second.

In the semifinals, we faced Clarkson, the top team in the East with a record of 26–6. They had the best player in the country, Dave Taylor. The guy was good, really good. Going into the game, he had 100 points—the first NCAA player to hit the century mark. Years later he'd star for the Los Angeles Kings and be inducted into the Hockey Hall of Fame. But this was a game he'd probably like to forget. The game didn't start until nearly 10:00 p.m. because the earlier semifinal had gone into double overtime. Clarkson jumped out to a 3–0 lead. In the third period, we were still behind 6–4. On the ice, I was playing as hard as I could. On the bench, I just kept saying to myself, "Keep battling, keep playing." Because you never know, strange things can happen. And they did.

Late in the second period of the game, one of our best defensemen, Dick Lamby, slipped, crashed into the boards, and got up with a sprained ankle—and a broken skate. The boot was separating from the sole. Coach Parker told our equipment manager, Carl James, to see if he could fix it. Carl and his assistant decided they could tape Lamby's skate together for just the last part of the game. Carl wound athletic tape around and around the skate as quickly and tightly as he could, while his assistant held the boot and sole together. Finally, Lamby turned to jump back onto the ice, but his foot was stuck. Carl had taped the assistant's hand to the skate. Lamby was kicking his foot, trying to get the hand free. Coach Parker saw what was going on and yelled, "I don't care if you have to cut his hand off with a hacksaw! Get Lamby back on the ice!" I couldn't believe it was happening.

Clarkson was still leading 6–4 with about four minutes to go when they chipped the puck into our end and Dave Taylor, the leading scorer in the country, raced after it, all alone. Jim Craig charged out of his crease to try to beat Taylor to the puck. Taylor got there first. He cut around Jimmy and was fifteen feet away with nothing between him and the goal. I saw it from the bench: Dave Taylor with a wide-open net. "Okay, now the game's over." That was the thought in my head. But as Taylor went to shoot, the puck must have rolled off his blade. Instead of going into the wide-open net, the puck went straight to the corner where the Zamboni comes out—thirty feet wide of the net.

We picked up the puck and raced back the other way. I jumped onto the ice, Lamby hit me with a pass, and I fired it in the net. If Taylor had scored when he had the open net, it would have been 7–4 and game over. Instead, after he missed, my goal made it 6–5 with 3:05 left in the game. It had looked like we were going to lose, but now everybody was really fired up. We were alive. We had a chance. With one more goal, we could go into overtime and have a chance to win this thing. Off the center ice face-off, we got the puck, skated it into the Clarkson zone, and scored again. In less than twenty seconds, we had tied the game. Now there was only a minute left in regulation time. For the last shift of the game, Coach Parker sent me onto the ice. Right after the face-off, Lamby got control of the puck and hit Ricky flying up the left wing. Coach Parker saw the play developing and shouted, "You got Silky on the other side!" As Ricky crossed the blue line, he left the puck behind him on purpose, a drop pass. Right behind him was Dave Silk, the freshman, and he hammered it from fifty-five feet away from the goal, but it was a rocket. The goalie never saw it. Overtime? We didn't need overtime. We scored three goals in the final three minutes to take the lead over the top team in the East. In the final second of the game, a Clarkson player fired a desperation slap shot, but I slid in front of it and blocked it with my shins. A second later, the horn sounded. I was still prone on the ice when Ricky jumped on top of me.

BU, the team everybody had counted out, was now going to play for the ECAC championship for the fourth year in a row. And win or lose, we were going to play for the national championship once again. I run into Dave Taylor from time to time. He's a great guy and a great hockey player. And I always remind him of that game.

The next night, in the championship game, our opponent was New Hampshire, coached by Charlie Holt—the coach who hadn't wanted me. They had a good team and a great player, Ralph Cox, a kid from Braintree who had scored forty goals that season, an incredible total. That night, it was another riveting game. UNH went up 4–2. Then we took a 5–4 lead. They went ahead 6–5, but we got two goals in the third period.

In my first three years as a Terrier, we had overwhelmed teams with talent. In my senior year, we had been a young team, and it had taken us a while to learn to play together. We'd had a lot of talent, but to go as far as we had, we had needed more than talent. This team had grit. Jack O'Callahan played most of the season with a broken wrist and played his heart out. We had commitment, determination, pride, respect for one another. Those qualities exist only if you have the right people with the right values—guys who are willing to work hard, guys who will play for each other more than they play for themselves. That 1976–77 team had great pride in being Terriers, in wearing the BU jersey, in the tradition we had at BU. When it came down to the last twenty minutes, I felt like it was the last ten years of BU hockey versus the last ten years of UNH hockey. I wasn't just playing for the guys who were in the locker room; I was playing for everyone else who had played at BU before me. And that was the difference in the last ten minutes against Clarkson and in battling back against UNH. If you have some talent and a lot of character and heart, you can do some incredible things.

For me personally, I was also playing for Coach Parker. I couldn't have put into words how I felt about him at that point.

He meant more to me as a coach and a person than I can describe. He gave me a chance. He's honest, he's tough, he's intense, he's competitive. He wins, and he wins the right way. He epitomizes what BU hockey is all about. I believed in him then, and I still do.

Shortly after midnight, the ECAC trophy was presented to the BU cocaptains. I had watched other Terrier captains skate with that trophy when I was a freshman, sophomore, and junior. I always wanted to do it. And now I was doing it, with the guy I'd lived with, played with, laughed with for the last four years. Ricky and I held the trophy aloft, over our heads, skating, shouting, smiling as wide as anyone can smile.

I didn't think that winning a hockey game could ever feel any better than this.

From there we headed to the NCAA tournament for the fourth time. We would face the University of Michigan in Detroit. Going into that game, I had 204 career points at BU. Ricky, thanks to his hot streak late in the season, had 203. But I didn't care about that. It was my last chance to win a national championship. I wanted it bad.

I thought we had a team that was good enough to win it all. Against Michigan, Ricky scored a goal in the first period, but Michigan came back to take a 5–2 lead. In the third period, we kicked into gear. Dave Silk, again showing his scoring touch, scored twice, and with just over a minute to play, we trailed 5–4. We were buzzing. We were all over them. I was sure we were going to complete the comeback. I was sure this was going to be the year.

With a few minutes to play, Michigan was called for a penalty.

What a break for us; we could pull Jim Craig and play the last minute with six skaters. Because of the penalty, Michigan would have only four. When we got control of the puck, Jimmy raced toward our bench. Our extra skater was ready to jump onto the ice. Assistant coach Bob Murray had the guy by the back of the jersey, to make sure he didn't jump out too soon.

Jimmy was about three feet from the bench when Bob let our extra skater go. Silky was carrying the puck into the Michigan zone. He was probably the hottest goal scorer in the country at the time. It was a golden opportunity. But Dave never got a chance to shoot. The referee—a western ref—blew the whistle and called us for too many men on the ice. He said our extra skater had jumped onto the ice too soon, before Jimmy had gotten to the bench. It was a ridiculous call. Bob Murray had made sure the extra skater didn't leave too soon. But here it was again: West screwing East. The year before, a western ref and western officials had kicked Terry Meagher out of the brawl game against Minnesota. Now a western ref was calling a BS penalty for too many men. It was the same old crap.

There was still a minute left in the game, and I jumped onto the ice. I remember it like yesterday. I can see it in slow motion. The puck came to me, and I skated over the blue line and took a slap shot. I saw the whole top corner of the net, open. I was about to throw my arms into the air. But the puck sailed just over the crossbar, and a second later the game ended. I remember that shot as well as I remember the goal I scored in Lake Placid in 1980. It's the shot that meant I'd never win a national championship. More than forty years later, it's still clear as day in my mind.

Losing that game to Michigan was the most bitter loss I'd ever had, even worse than the brawl game against Minnesota.

It was my senior year. It was our final shot. And for it to end that way—it's not a memory I like to think about.

In that game with Michigan, Ricky had a goal and two assists. I had an assist. In the all-time BU scoring race, he was now ahead by a point, 206 to 205, with one game left, the consolation game against UNH. For that final game, the final chance for me and Ricky to add to our scoring totals, Coach Parker wanted each of us to have a fair shot at scoring. So he put us back together on the same line, one last time. On the right wing was Dave Silk. The three of us clicked. I got a goal. Then Ricky scored. Then I got an assist. Then he got one.

With forty-nine seconds left in the game, the score was tied and we lined up for a face-off in the New Hampshire zone. On the draw, Ricky tapped the puck between the UNH centerman's feet, scooted past him, and fired it between the goalie's legs. It was crafty play by a great player.

That goal gave Ricky 210 career points on 90 goals and 120 assists. I had 92 goals and 116 assists for 208 points. We were number one and number two in all-time scoring at Boston University. Not bad for two guys Jack Parker had practically grabbed off the street back in August 1973. I was happy for Ricky. I'd had the record for a couple months, but he was a great hockey player and he deserved everything he got. Ricky's a quiet, humble guy. He never talked about himself or grabbed the spotlight. He just went out and played. People sometimes ask me if I'm jealous because I had the record and he took it away. No. Not at all. If you set a record and it's broken by your brother, how could you feel bad?

For the third year in a row, Ricky was named to the All-American East team, an incredible feat. He was a rare hockey player, one of the best ever to play college hockey in the opinion of a lot of people, not just me. I had scored just two fewer points, but again I wasn't named an All-American. I would have been thrilled if I had been, but you can't have two or three guys from the same team named All-Americans year after year. I did win an award, though: best defensive forward in New England. Big surprise. I guess they had to give me something.

In my four years as a Terrier, we had won four consecutive ECAC championships, won one Beanpot, and played in the final four all four years. I had gotten my first taste of international experience playing in the 1975 and 1976 World Championships and had faced the Soviets for the first time. I had even scored on Vladislav Tretiak. But there was one thing missing.

I had never won a national championship.

It's a blot on my career, and it haunts me. It eats at me. To this very day.

Jack Parker always said that to be a truly great team, you have to win a national championship. The following year, Jack would have the Terriers back in the NCAA tournament for the fifth year in a row, and this time he'd win it. Dave Silk scored a goal. Jim Craig was in net. Jack O'Callahan, the captain of that Terriers team, was named MVP. As soon as I left, the Terriers were national champs.

Every once in a while, Coach Parker likes to remind me of this, just to yank my chain. "Well, Mike," he says, "I guess you just weren't good enough."

It's a joke—or at least I hope it is.

CHAPTER 7

"MR. BROOKS IS MY FATHER"

For once there was no mob of Eruziones and Fucillos and Jaworskis filling Walter Brown Arena. Only my mother, father, and Donna attended my graduation from the School of Education. But there was a surprise. My name was called, I went up, and I was given a tube, which I expected to contain my diploma. Instead, there was a note saying I owed $500 for some damage to my dorm. I didn't know anything about damage or who had caused it. What I did know was that I didn't have $500, and Jeep didn't, either. I knew I had graduated, and I didn't need a piece of paper to prove it. I'd get my degree someday, though.

Donna and I were still dating and getting more serious, but I could tell she was unsettled. She wanted to know if this was going anywhere. She didn't want to get married right there and then, but she wanted to know if it was going to happen at some point. A few times she was on the verge of breaking up with me. Nettie and my other sisters even told her to go ahead, do it. Fortunately, I had an ally: her father, Victor Alioto. Whenever Donna started talking about ending it, Mr. A would tell her to hang in there. "Give him a chance," he'd say. "He's a good guy." By the time I graduated, the New York Rangers had invited me to try out for the team the following fall. I loved Donna, but the main focus in my mind at that point was hockey—and how far I could go with it.

In my dorm, after the ceremony, Donna gave me a graduation present, a gold ring inset with a tiger's eye.

"I'm not ready for this," I told her. "Maybe you should take it back."

"No," Donna said, "keep it." And I did.

Four months later, I reported to the Rangers' training camp in Long Beach, New York. Five years after running into Jack Parker, I had a shot at the NHL. The Rangers had a lot of veterans and stars. Phil Esposito, who'd led the Bruins to two Stanley Cups, was the captain. On the ice with the team, I skated hard and hustled, the way I always had, hoping to get noticed. And I did get noticed, but not in the way I'd hoped. At one workout, Espo stopped me. "Hey, kid," he said, "slow down. Our roster is pretty well set. You're not going to make the team."

After two weeks, I was told to see one of the assistant general managers. "We're going to sign you to New Haven," he said. The New Haven Nighthawks, the Rangers' top minor-league team, was going to sign me. To a pro contract? No, the AGM said. I had misunderstood. He said they were going to *assign* me to New Haven. There was no contract, just a train ticket. When I got to New Haven, I needed hockey sticks. The Rangers provided them, New Haven didn't. I called the one person I could count on.

"Donna," I said, "could you go to my house and grab a bunch of my sticks? And then jump on a train to New Haven?"

After another two weeks, New Haven sent me down one more level, to the Toledo Goaldiggers of the International Hockey League. The Rangers and John Ferguson were still interested in me, and to keep my rights they gave me $1,000. That was a ton of money to me, but it was all gone by the time I paid my expenses to get to Toledo and get settled there. I knew it was going to be an uphill battle to get to the NHL. At the time, all the general managers in the league were Canadians, and there was a bias against American players. College hockey was considered a level below Canadian junior leagues. Scoring ninety-two goals in four years at BU wasn't enough to convince people I could play. I would have to work my way up, but it wouldn't be the first time—or the last.

In terms of hockey, Toledo was a totally different world from Boston University. The night I arrived, I watched the first game of the season from the stands, and there was a bench-clearing brawl, twenty-five or thirty guys on the ice, throwing punches, pounding on each other. I was watching that thinking, What the hell did I get myself into?

In the second game I played in, I got tangled up with a defenseman, Tony Horvath. He got his stick up around my neck, my stick was up around his. Before I knew it, his gloves were off and he was punching me in the head. For a minute I stood there like a fool, letting him hit me. Finally I started throwing punches and got a few good shots in. I didn't win the fight, but I didn't lose, either. After the game, the Goaldiggers' coach, Ted Garvin, gave me some advice: "If it seems like it might be a fight, it's a fight."

Every game had three or four fights. One time a guy got thrown out for hair pulling. In a game in Milwaukee, the puck was dropped and the benches emptied instantly. It took the officials fifteen minutes to get control. They called sixty minutes in penalties and not even ten seconds of hockey had been played. One Milwaukee player was ejected for fighting with his knuckles taped, like a boxer. Another time we played the Milwaukee Admirals, so many guys got tossed out for fighting that we had only six or seven skaters on the bench. To make it look like we had more guys, we took our helmets off and put them on top of our sticks. It made it look like we had a full bench. When my shift came up, I put my helmet back on and hopped the boards.

Fortunately, the Goaldiggers didn't need me to fight. We had plenty of guys who would drop the gloves and go toe-to-toe with anyone in the league—including our captain, Ian MacPhee, and another tough guy named Paul Tantardini. We called him Tanner. I always knew we were playing a rough team when I saw those guys taping their hands in the locker room. One practice we had, Tanner and Ian got into a fight. With each other. For the entire practice. The rest of us players just sat on the boards, watching them go back and forth on the ice, throwing punches at each other. Then it continued in the parking lot. Again I asked myself, "What did I get myself into?"

I got to be friends with Tanner. He had skill and put up some good scoring numbers along with a couple hundred penalty minutes. I felt I could always count on him. He never hesitated to jump in to protect one of our players on the ice, and he was a great friend off the ice. Tanner was one of the best teammates I ever played with.

My role on the Goaldiggers was to score goals, and for that the team paid me $3,500—for the entire season. That came to $52.50 a game. To make ends meet, I roomed with two other guys and never had much food in the fridge. I didn't have a car because one of my roommates, Randy Mohns, had one and I got rides from him. I got a check every two weeks, but the Goaldiggers could cut me at any time. It was score goals, or I was out of a job. We played teams in places like Kalamazoo, Fort Wayne, and Muskegon. There were bus rides somewhere every few days. Sometimes we'd play three games in three nights—Friday, Saturday, Sunday. Play, bus home late at night, get up, and play again. On the road we got a food allowance of three dollars a day, which didn't buy much. On the way home, we liked to eat at Arby's and then find a liquor store. And that was the bus ride home: a roast beef sandwich and a six-pack.

Still, I was having fun. The Toledo Sports Arena was a tiny place, about 3,500 seats, and it always smelled of the circus. The ice surface wasn't even regulation size; it was twenty feet shorter than an NHL rink. But it was packed every night, and the Diggers fans were just rabid. They dressed in the team's colors—green and gold—and wore big buttons on their jackets with pictures of their favorite players. When we scored or there was a fight, the cheers were like a jet plane taking off. One time a ref overruled a goal we had scored, and the fans were so incensed they started throwing chairs onto the ice. When it was over, the police had to escort the officials out of the arena. Mobs of fans would wait by our dressing room to meet players and get autographs. There was a group of women and girls you'd see game after game, even on the road. We called them the "Diggerettes."

Ted Garvin was unlike any other coach I had. He had played

fourteen years of pro hockey, all in the minor leagues. Then he'd become a coach in the IHL and won two championships in five years. That had gotten him a shot at the big time. The Detroit Red Wings were the worst team in the league at the time—the "Dead Wings," their fans called them—and they hired Ted Garvin. But those NHL players didn't like having a coach from a minor league, especially one that was two levels below the NHL. The team was awful, and after just twelve games, Teddy was fired. The Goaldiggers were a brand-new IHL franchise and hired Teddy. He won the championship in his first year, and that made him a local hero.

Ted was both coach and general manager, so he was responsible for keeping the Sports Arena filled. He didn't always do it by winning games. One time a reporter called him paranoid. The next night he showed up in shorts, a bathrobe, boxing gloves, and a T-shirt that said, "The Paranoia Kid." He drove around Toledo in a car with his name and the Goaldiggers' logo on the side. Sometimes when he didn't like a call, he'd toss a water bucket onto the ice. The Digger fans never knew what was going to happen, and they loved it.

On the bench, he was a wild card, too. We were losing one game 7–0 when our goalie, Tony Peroski, was having a horrible game. Ted said he was going to fine everyone $100 if we gave up another goal. A minute later it was 8–0. "You guys want to play like that, you don't deserve a goalie!" he huffed. He wasn't kidding. Teddy pulled our goalie, and for the last seventeen minutes, we played with six skaters and an empty net. Tony sat on the bench grinning, because he knew he hadn't played well and Ted was blaming us, not him. The other team was shooting the puck from everywhere on the ice, and they scored eight more goals. It was hilarious. And then there was a thing Teddy used to do with his false teeth.

Almost all the guys on the team were Canadian, and Teddy was skeptical about having some American college player the Rangers had sent him. He told a writer for the Toledo paper that he didn't think I was going to last with the team. In my first few weeks in Toledo, Teddy would snap at me, "Quit playing that Boston College crap."

"I went to Boston University, Ted."

"Yeah, same thing."

But soon I started scoring some goals, and the Toledo *Blade* wrote a story about the new guy from Boston. Teddy said he liked my hustle and enthusiasm. He also said this: "Another reason I decided to keep him was Mike promised to get his mother to make me spaghetti."

I hadn't been on the team for long when we got a new player: Bill "Goldie" Goldthorpe. He had a gigantic blond afro and big, bushy sideburns down to his chin, and everybody had heard of him. He was notorious. He had played in the North American Hockey League, which was even rougher than the IHL, lots of fighting. In one season, he had racked up 285 penalty minutes in just 55 games. He started brawls all the time. I heard he'd once ripped his jersey and shoulder pads off and, bare chested, challenged not just everyone on the other team to fight but everyone in the arena. Players on his own team were afraid of him. Once he had gone into the stands with his skates on to fight some opposing fans. He had gotten one suspension for pulling a linesman's hair, another one for punching one linesman and shoving another. In 1975, while playing for the Syracuse Blazers, he had been suspended and was sitting in the stands in street clothes but jumped onto the ice to join a donnybrook. He had grabbed a stick and swung it at other guys. He had fought one player and then punched the general manager of the team, practically knocking him out. He had been removed from the arena by ten policemen and arrested for assault. Eventually the NAHL kicked him out of the league, banned him for life. That was my new teammate in Toledo.

The day Goldie joined the Goaldiggers, he walked into our locker room and everyone looked up and went silent. He stood there with an equipment bag on his shoulder but had no sticks. Then he looked at the sticks lined up against the wall and took one of mine and one that belonged to my roommate Randy Mohns. I leaned over to Randy and whispered, "Do we say something?" A day or two later, Randy and I thought we ought to be friends with Goldie. We were outside the rink, and Randy and I started kidding around with Goldie about fighting. I didn't like it that he grabbed each of us by the collar and shoved us into a snowbank.

In his first game as a Goaldigger, Goldie was still in the locker room when warm-ups started. Paul Tantardini skated over to the Muskegon players, grinning with glee, to let them know what they were in for. "He's here! He's here!" He didn't have to say who. Ten minutes into the game, Goldie started a bench-clearing brawl. After he got into another fight in his second game, the commissioner of the IHL wanted no more of it—he kicked Goldie out of the league. A couple of days later, Goldie got picked up—by New Haven, the place I was trying to work my way up to. "What the hell am I doing wrong?" I wondered. At that point, I had twelve goals, second on the team, but the player New Haven had picked up was a guy who specialized in punching people in the head.

Anyone who's seen the movie *Slap Shot* knows the climactic scene. The Charlestown Chiefs are in the championship game. The other team has loaded up with the biggest goons around. The most feared puncher is a guy with a giant afro named Ogie Ogilthorpe. Goldie Goldthorpe was the inspiration for that character. So yes, when I was in Toledo, I played two games with the real Ogie Ogilthorpe.

As the season wore on, the puck kept going into the net for me. Some people created a Mike Eruzione Fan Club. On the street and at the mall, people would shake my hand; some would hug me. It was unreal. To them, I was a star, a hero. I missed Winthrop, but being in Toledo felt good. Besides, how could you not have fun when you had a goalie who owned his own bar? Tony Peroski had a place called Tony P's Breakaway Lounge, and he hung out there all the time. They had disco dancing and guys got out there like they were John Travolta. One night we were there, and Ted Garvin walked in and saw six of us drinking, out late. The next day we played horribly and lost. The Toledo *Blade* had a headline: "Six Pack Causes Goaldiggers to Lose Game." Teddy had ratted us out and told the press we had been out drinking the night before.

About halfway through the season, Ted traded for a hard-nosed defenseman: Tony Horvath, the guy I'd had my first fight with. Then the Rangers sent us a goalie, Lindsay Middlebrook. He was two inches shorter than me, but we called him "the Great Wall of China" because nothing got past him. With those two guys, the Goaldiggers got hot and zipped through the playoffs. That happens sometimes in hockey: a team gets just the right mix of players, wins some games, starts feeling confident, and suddenly it seems nothing can stop them. In the finals, it came down to a seventh game against the Port Huron Flags in the Sports Arena on a warm day in May. The place was packed, and between so many bodies in the building and the warm weather, the ice was melting beneath our skates. Thick fog formed on the ice, and you could barely see the puck. The refs had to stop the game every four or five minutes and have players skate around and around to clear the mist. It was surreal. During the stoppages, I laughed to myself. "How is this happening in a professional league?" It took forever to finish the game, but the Great Wall of China was off the charts that day. We beat Port Huron and won the IHL's Turner Cup.

I headed back to Winthrop with a title, but that wasn't going to get me a cup of coffee. It sure didn't get me a pro contract. In June, the Rangers fired John Ferguson. The new GM didn't want any of Ferguson's players, and the team released me. I would have to find a new path to playing hockey. In hindsight, it worked out. If John Ferguson hadn't been fired, I'd probably have signed with the Rangers, and I'd never have tried out for the Olympics the following year.

That summer, in 1978, the US Olympic Committee organized the first-ever National Sports Festival, a mini Olympics for amateur athletes in all sorts of winter and summer sports. In the three previous Olympics, the Soviet Union and East Germany had dominated the medals race in both the Winter and Summer Games. The festival was intended to give US athletes an opportunity to compete and train in non-Olympic years and to draw attention to amateur athletics. Even though the festival took place in the summer, hockey was included. The 1980 Winter Games were going to be played in Lake Placid, and the Olympic Committee didn't want the US hockey team to be embarrassed on home soil.

I wasn't invited to the '78 festival. I had played for the Goaldiggers. I was a pro. My chance to play in the Olympics had come and gone in 1976, when I had decided to stay at BU. I knew some of the players who were there in Colorado Springs for the '78 festival: Jack O'Callahan, Jim Craig, Dave Silk, all BU guys I'd played with. Buzz Schneider, my friend from the 1975 and '76 World Championships, was also there, along with a whole lot of western guys. When the Minnesota team played the New England team, a fight broke out, and suddenly everybody on the ice was throwing punches. And of course, Jack O'Callahan was in the middle of it, fighting a Minnesota player named Steve Christoff. The East-West rivalry was as bitter as ever.

The Lake Placid games were still a year and a half away, but Herb Brooks was there to get an early look at players for the 1980 team. Eight or nine other college coaches were there to help Herb evaluate the talent. Jack Parker was one. That says a lot about both men. Jack and Herb hadn't spoken since the BU-Minnesota brawl in Denver in 1976. But Herb knew that although he had full control of the Olympic team and the selection process, he needed help from the best hockey minds in the country to ensure that the best team was selected, and he knew Jack had a keen eye for talent and knew the eastern players' abilities and qualities well. Bill Cleary, the Harvard coach, was also on the advisory committee Herb had set up. Coach Cleary had played on the 1960 Olympic team that had won the gold medal in Squaw Valley, California. Herb Brooks had also been on that team, but he hadn't made it to Squaw Valley—he had been cut right before those Games, the last man to be dropped from the team.

The '78 festival wasn't meant to be a tryout for the 1980 Olympics, but Herb already knew the kind of players he wanted. "The plan that I'm hoping to implement consists mainly in getting away from the 'I, me, myself' type of thinking that exists in American hockey today," he told the media covering the festival. "People look at the Russians and Czechs and Swedes and say we don't have a chance to win the gold medal in 1980. I don't think that's necessarily the case."

It amazes me when I think back on that today. Eighteen months before Lake Placid, Herb Brooks believed the United States could beat the Russians.

In September, I got a tryout with the Colorado Rockies, the worst team in the NHL. I went out to Denver, skated hard, played in one exhibition game, and got sent down to their minor-league team, the Philadelphia Firebirds. I played six games for them, but it was a confusing situation. Players were bouncing all around, sent to Denver, called back, then sent to other minor leagues, called back again. I never knew where I stood with them or what they wanted. That was when Bob Murray, the former BU assistant coach who was now my agent, got a call from Herb Brooks. Herb told Bob that I was actually eligible for the Olympics, that that contract I had signed with Toledo wasn't considered a professional contract under Olympic rules. The Olympics? I hadn't been thinking about that at all. Until that phone call to Bob Murray, I'd thought I was a professional.

Suddenly, a tryout for the Olympic team, at the 1979 National Sports Festival the following summer, was a possibility. There was one other issue regarding my amateur status that turned out to be a lucky break, too. I'd still be considered an amateur as long as I had played less than ten games with pro teams. I had played six for the Firebirds, three more between Colorado and New Haven.

One more game, and I'd never have gone to Lake Placid.

I returned to Toledo for a second season with the Goaldiggers. I'd play there until the Olympic tryouts, and if I made the Olympic team and played well, maybe an NHL team would give me another shot. It seemed like a good plan. For that season, the Goaldiggers paid me $7,200—a raise. The team also bought me a used Dodge van—no more bumming rides from my teammates. Lindsay Middlebrook was gone and playing in the NHL, but the other guys I was friends with were back: Jim McCabe, Tony Peroski, Randy Mohns, Paul Tantardini. One new player was Greg Neeld. It was incredible to see him play. Years before, he'd lost an eye to a high stick.

By then Toledo was like my second home. Donna came to visit, so we weren't apart all the time. Once, to get time off work, she told her boss she had the flu. Her father called in for her every day for a whole week. "Donna's still sick, can't get out of bed." Her visits weren't exactly romantic getaways. An apartment occupied by three hockey players is not exactly the place you want to hang out with your girlfriend, and a lot of times I couldn't be with her. I had road trips and practices and games. Still, she stuck with me.

There was a lot less fighting in the IHL that year, and hockey was fun. The Goaldiggers were winning games, and I was scoring goals. I was twenty-three, I was playing hockey, I was making $7,200, *and* I had a van. I couldn't believe the life I was living. Some days I'd smile and think to myself, You are killing it, Mike. Just killing it.

For a couple days in that season, anyone who cared about hockey turned their attention to Madison Square Garden in New York. In February 1979, a team of the biggest stars in the NHL played a three-game series against the Soviet Union's national team. It was called the Challenge Cup—the best players from Canada against the best from the Soviet Union. The NHL team was loaded with future Hall of Famers—Ken Dryden, Bryan Trottier, Mike Bossy, Phil Esposito, Martin LaPointe, Guy Lafleur, Gilbert Perreault, Marcel Dionne. It was a dream team before there was such a thing as a dream team. The Soviets had that goalie, Vladislav Tretiak, and some of the players I'd played against in 1975 and '76. Boris Mikhailov was the captain. He was like the Gordie Howe of Russia. Valeri Kharlamov, a slick playmaker, was definitely one of the best in the world. Vladimir Petrov played center between the other two. Those three guys had been playing together for eight years, not just on the same team but on the same line. They knew one another's moves so well that they were almost unstoppable in the Olympics. There were other guys, but I couldn't remember or pronounce their names. In the Challenge Cup, the NHL won the first game, the Soviets the second. In the deciding third game, Tretiak sat on the bench and the Russians played their backup goalie, a blond kid named Vladimir Myshkin. It didn't matter. The Russians won 6–0. They had blown out a team of the very best guys in the NHL, an embarrassment for the league and for Canada.

That was the Soviet team that would be playing in the Olympics in Lake Placid a year later.

The Goaldiggers rolled through the season, but in one game we were playing poorly and losing. Between periods Teddy Garvin was mad because he thought we weren't playing tough enough. Not enough guys were getting into fights. Not enough guys were getting stitches. Then suddenly it happened: Teddy took out his false teeth and threw them onto the floor. "I lost my teeth playing junior hockey!" he fumed. Next to me, Greg Neeld put a hand to his face. "Oh, yeah?" he said. "This is what *I* lost in junior hockey." In his palm was his glass eye.

By March, Herb Brooks and the coaches helping him had a rough list of the guys who had a real chance of making the 1980 Olympic team. When some of them got together for a meeting, my name came up. Someone said, "You can't take Eruzione, he's a troublemaker, bad attitude, a 'bad liver.'" Bill Cleary, the Harvard coach, spoke up and said that that wasn't his impression at all from seeing me play for four years at BU. Afterward, he called Jack Parker, and then Jack called me. I think it had to do with the 1975 World Championships. We hadn't won a game in Germany, and I had joked around a lot with the guys, and I guess someone had decided I was a problem or not serious enough. Whatever the case, I didn't want to go to the National Sports Festival in Colorado that summer with a cloud over my name. I didn't want to lose my chance at the Olympics because of something somebody had said about me that was totally untrue.

It happened that the University of Minnesota, coached by Herb Brooks, was playing in the NCAA final four in Detroit at the time. I hopped into my rickety van and headed for Olympic Stadium. I got there in time to see some of a game between Minnesota and New Hampshire. Minnesota had a kid with long blond hair named Eric Strobel. He had a hat trick. Another Minnesota kid was a freshman, just nineteen, but he was electric with the puck. His name was Neal Broten. New Hampshire had the leading scorer in the country, Ralph Cox. Standing there watching those guys play, I mumbled to myself, "Man, those guys are good."

After the game, I went to the Minnesota locker room. "Mr. Brooks?" I started to say, "I'm Mike Eruzione," but he cut me off.

"I'm Herb. Mr. Brooks is my father. And I know who you are."

"I don't know who said this. I've never been a troublemaker. I've always been a good player, and I've always tried to be a good teammate and a good leader," I said. "I'm not a bad liver."

"Don't worry about it," he told me. "I look forward to seeing you in Colorado." I hopped back into my van relieved—for now at least.

When the Goaldiggers reached the playoffs, I couldn't play. I'd hurt my knee. Everybody knew I was trying out for the Olympics, and one teammate didn't like it. Before a game, I was standing outside the locker room on crutches. Ian MacPhee, the captain, came up and grabbed me by the throat. "I don't give a shit about that Olympic crap," he growled. "You're ruining my career." He apparently thought I was well enough to play and was only sitting out to make sure I was healthy for the Olympic tryouts. I guess he also thought he might get noticed by pro scouts if the Goaldiggers won another Turner Cup. I've had very few negative moments in hockey, but that was one of them. It was one of the few times I was disappointed in a teammate. I thought Ian would've respected me enough to know that I would have played if I could. It didn't matter. The Goaldiggers got knocked out in the first round. My career in Toledo was over.

The 1979 National Sports Festival was like nothing I'd ever seen: 2,300 athletes competing in thirty-one sports, from hockey and figure skating to basketball and track. It was a mini Olympics, with an opening ceremony and medals for the winners. Sixty-eight players were in the hockey competition, and they were divided into four teams. Jack O'Callahan, Dave Silk, Jim Craig, and a few other guys who had played at BU were on the New England team. The Midwest team was made up of Minnesota players. The Great Lakes team was mostly Michigan guys; I was on that team because I had been playing in Toledo. The Central team was an at-large group with players from different states.

Herb Brooks and the coaches on his advisory board watched us closely. NHL scouts were in the stands, too, because a lot of the players had been drafted by NHL teams. One was Ken Morrow, a big, bearded defenseman from Michigan who'd played at Bowling Green. He was on the Great Lakes team with me, and I had no doubt he was going to make the Olympic team. The New York Islanders had drafted Kenny and were eager to sign him. The question was whether he would take the time to play in the Olympics or sign with the Islanders and start making NHL money right away.

There were other guys who seemed to have a really good shot at making the team. There was the kid I had seen in Detroit, Neal Broten. Jim Craig, my BU teammate back in 1977, had done a great job in goal at the '79 World Championships, which had taken place a few months before in Moscow, with Herb Brooks as coach. There was a defenseman from Minnesota, Bill Baker, a tall, smooth skater. There was another defenseman, Mike Ramsey, just eighteen. The talk was that he was going to be taken in the first round in the upcoming NHL draft. No American-born player had ever been taken in the first round. A few weeks after the festival, he became the first.

One guy who seemed a complete lock to make the team was Mark Johnson, a quick center from Wisconsin. Mark's father, Badger Bob Johnson, was the coach at Wisconsin, and he had a bitter feud with Herb. The two coaches could barely be in the same room with each other. A lot of hockey people thought Herb wasn't even going to take Mark because of the hostility between Herb and Badger Bob. But in the college hockey season that had just ended, Mark had had forty-one goals and forty-nine assists in just forty games—an average of more than two points a game, which was unheard of. Any coach who didn't take Mark Johnson, whatever the circumstances, had to be insane.

After a couple of days of off-ice training and practices, I called home. "Ma, there's sixty-eight guys here, and they can all fly," I said. "I'll probably be home in a week."

Still, I was going to work as hard as I could.

If I didn't make it, I could go back to Winthrop and get into coaching. Jack Parker had told me he'd be glad to have me as an assistant. The four teams played each other once and then went to a final round to determine the medal winners. The opening game was Midwest against New England. Both had players who had squared off in that BU-Minnesota brawl in Denver in 1976 and the other brawl in the 1978 Festival, and they picked up where they had left off. There was no brawl, but the game was filled with hard checks and cheap shots from both sides. When it ended, the hostility was as intense as ever. The Minnesota team showed up New England, winning easily 10–5.

I didn't experience much of the East-West rivalry on the Great Lakes team. We had guys from a lot of different places. I became friendly with Ken Morrow and a teammate of his from Bowling Green State University, Mark Wells, a good center. Our game against the Minnesota players was competive but not heated. I hung out with Buzz Schneider a lot. It was funny. He came from Babbitt, Minnesota, a tiny town of 1,400 people, up in the Iron Range, and I came from Winthrop, two totally different places, yet he and I had a lot in common. He had never painted bridges but he had worked in iron mines and construction. He had spent a few years in the IHL, battling and riding buses. We were among the oldest guys at the tryout. And we both played left wing. On days we had no games, he and I would leave our dorm and walk over to Cecil's, a motorcycle bar nearby. One night we were having a few beers and going down the list of all the left wings at the festival. "He's not going to make it . . . he's not going to make it," we said, crossing out names. Finally, five names were left; Herb was going to take only four. Buzzy and I looked at each other and realized what that meant. Practically at the same time, we said, "One of us isn't going to make it."

When it came down to the gold medal game at the festival, it was Great Lakes against Minnesota, and we beat them 4–2. After the medal ceremony, all the hockey players were called into a banquet room to hear who had been chosen for the Olympic roster. I felt confident. I had had five goals and was tied with Ken Morrow for the most points on our team. But

I wasn't completely sure. We waited and waited, and finally, around 11:00 p.m., Herb Brooks appeared. "If you hear your name, please stay. If you don't, thank you for participating," he said.

The first name he read off was Ken Morrow. I held my breath a second and thought, "Gee, I hope this isn't in alphabetical order." Herb read more names: Mark Johnson, Buzz Schneider, Rob McClanahan, all western players. Then a few eastern guys were mixed in: Jim Craig, Jack O'Callahan, Dave Silk. Eventually he said the words I was hoping to hear: "Mike Eruzione."

CHAPTER 8

"WE'RE A FAMILY NOW"

After Herb read off the last name, we had our first meeting as a team right there, late at night, in Colorado Springs. The first thing Herb said was, "I'll be your coach, but I won't be your friend." I heard that and thought, Man, this is going to be a long year. The next thing Herb said was, "If you don't want to be here, then leave, because there are hundreds of people who would like to be in your shoes." That was his first message to the team. He wasn't going to be nice or friendly with anyone, and if you wanted to be part of the team, you'd better check your ego at the door and be ready to give 100 percent—come to the rink with a lunch pail and a hard hat, Herb would say. Twenty-six players were selected for the initial roster. Only twenty would go to Lake Placid. I'd made the team, but the Olympics were still not guaranteed, for me or anyone else. Six more players would eventually be cut.

We were allowed to go home for two weeks, and then near the end of August we reported to Lake Placid, where we learned what the next six months were going to be like. We got up each morning and skated at the new arena built for the 1980 Games, the Olympic Fieldhouse. It was one skating drill after another. We were constantly moving, constantly skating for two hours. Herb kept saying the Russians were the best-conditioned athletes in the world, and if we were going to have any chance to keep up with them, we would have to work harder than any of us had imagined. The last drill of each practice was the one everybody hated. We started at one end, skated to the blue line and back, then to the red line and back, the far blue line and back, and finally all the way to the other end and back. Three or four of those, and I was breathing so hard I couldn't talk. Ten of them, and most guys had a hard time standing. Hockey players have lots of names for that drill: suicides, mountain climbers, gassers. We called them Herbies.

When we got off the ice, we put on shorts and running shoes and ran from the Fieldhouse to our hotel—a quarter mile straight uphill. We walked down and did it again. We walked down once more, and we were done—for the moment. We showered, walked back up the hill and had lunch, and then most of passed out in bed or on the grass. Later in the afternoon, we had another on-ice practice—for another two hours. Then we ran that hill two more times. We used the last bit of energy we had left to eat dinner and fall into bed. We did that for fourteen days.

On the ice, Herb pushed and pushed for more effort, more work, and never in a gentle way. Silk, you're too damn slow. Strobel, you've got a million-dollar set of legs and a ten-cent fart for a brain. Christoff, Christian, Pavelich, Eruzione, Wells, Verchota, Suter, you're playing worse and worse every day, and right now you're playing like the middle of next week. Or the middle of next month. Ramsey, you're an eighteen-year-old prima donna, and next year you're going to be a nineteen-year-old prima donna. Jack Hughes would skate with the puck in practice, and Herb would blast him for not passing quicker. One time, Herb walked up behind John Harrington on the bench before practice and said into his ear, "You're the worst defensive player I've ever seen."

I would be skating in practice thinking, working as hard as I could, and Herb would snap, "Eruzione, I'm going to send you back to Port Huron."

I'd correct him. "I played in Toledo, Herb."

"Whatever."

Sometimes he didn't even have to say anything. I'd notice him just staring at me, no expression, those blue eyes of his looking right through me. In my head, I'd be wondering, Oh, no, what did I do now? Nobody ever heard "Good job." Herb never told anyone he was getting better. He just pushed and pushed and pushed, day after day. I felt like saying "Screw you," but I wasn't going to quit. So I just kept working. Practice was only two hours. I had played football for Bob DeFelice and hockey for Jack Parker. I'd painted bridges in the hot sun. I could put up with Herb's crap for two hours.

Fifteen of the twenty-six guys on the initial roster were from Minnesota. Two of them—Bill Baker and Phil Verchota—had played against me and Jack O'Callahan in the Minnesota-BU brawl in 1976. Several more had been in the brawl at the 1978 National Sports Festival. Jack had fought Steve Christoff in that one. It wasn't just us eastern guys who were cautious with the players from "the U"—that was what they called the University of Minnesota. Mark Johnson and Bob Suter had played for the University of Wisconsin—"the U" was their hated rival. The animosity between Badger Bob and Herb didn't make things any easier. But Herb worked us so hard that we didn't have energy left over to fight each other or settle scores. After a week in Lake Placid, we found out that they were actually pretty good guys. We also discovered that everyone had something in common: we were all going to have to go through hell to make it on this team.

Our team had speed, a lot of speed. Mark Johnson, Rob McClanahan, Eric Strobel, Neal Broten, Buzz Schneider—all of those guys could fly. Dave Christian, Jack O'Callahan, Mark Pavelich, John Harrington, Mark Wells, Steve Christoff—were excellent skaters. All of them could stop and start, change direction, transition from forward to backward and back again without losing a step. Herb wanted a skating team. He had studied the Russians and their fluid, swirling skating and passing. He'd played against them in the 1964 and 1968 Olympics. He was convinced that we had little chance if we played hockey the traditional up-and-down NHL style: wings staying on the wings, center in the center.

Above all, he wanted us to keep the puck. No throwing it into the other team's end and then trying to get it back. "You work so hard to get the puck. Why would you just give it back to them? In football, you don't punt on first down." If you dumped the puck into the corner against the Russians, you'd never get it back. Instead, we'd pass and skate the puck up ice, weave in unpredictable patterns, always moving to open space. If we found no way to keep moving forward, Herb wanted us to turn, pass the puck back to our defensemen, skate back around the D, and try it all over again, weaving and moving. Herb's plan was to take the European-style game and throw it right back at them. It made sense: if you always have the puck, the other team can't score. And if we didn't have the puck, Herb wanted us to play more of the aggressive North American style: jump on the guy with the puck right away, get in his face, don't give him time to make a pass, force him into throwing the puck away.

It wasn't easy to learn. At first I wasn't sure where I was supposed to go. I was so used to skating up and down, north-south. Herb would scream, "Weave, weave, weave, and don't just weave for the sake of weaving!"

Nobody knew what he meant by that, but he said it over and over.

Other times, he would draw up some complicated drill, and I'd think, Jeez, where's he going with this? So I'd get behind some of the Minnesota guys and just do what they did. With all the movement and changing of positions, sometimes I would end up doing the center's job, the right wing would take over on the left wing, the center would move to the right. So you had to think and anticipate and improvise, and you had to know where you were going and where everyone else was going, too. We played basketball and mimicked the motion Herb wanted. He took us out to soccer fields to walk through the weaving patterns. It was confusing, but it was fun to have the puck all the time.

The style was perfect for Olympic-sized rinks, which are one hundred feet wide, compared to eighty-five feet for NHL ice. That's a lot of extra room to weave and swirl. The problem was that it wasn't going to be easy practicing it. There were very few Olympic-sized rinks in the United States back then. So Herb planned a three-week tour in Europe, with games in the Netherlands, Finland, and Norway and as many practices as he could schedule. All twenty-six players went, plus Herb and the man he had chosen to be his assistant coach, Craig Patrick.

We played our first two games against the Dutch national team and won both. As we traveled around, I got to know some of the western guys better. Eric Strobel and I both liked to play backgammon. So we played game after game in the back of the bus with all the gear. He won most of the time, and I probably still owe him about $1,200. As we went from one rink to the bus to a new hotel to the next arena, I found that the western players were really talented and actually pretty good guys. I loved the whole tour, despite Herb's continuing to skate us into the ground. I visited places I would never have dreamed of seeing—and I didn't have to pay a dime for anything. Every day, I thought, How does a kid from Winthrop get to do this?

In Finland, we had games against six club teams and won four; then we moved on to Oslo for two games against Norway. We were going to face the Norwegians in the Olympics, and Herb wanted to make a statement now. "Let them know we are going to be hell to deal with," he told us. By then we'd been on the road, away from home, wearing the same clothes, for twenty days. We were training and playing hard, going from buses to hotels to games over and over. Herb sensed it, and in the locker room he said something about "If we don't skate in the game, we'll skate after." Herb was always saying off-the-wall things. I didn't think anything of it, and nobody else did, either. Norway was one of the weakest teams we would face in the Olympics, yet as time was winding down, we were trailing 4–3. Thankfully, we got a late goal to salvage a tie. After the teams shook hands, we skated to our bench. Herb was there at the door, steaming. "Get on the line," he said, and I knew exactly what that meant: Herbies, the drill wherein we skated to the blue line and back, red line and back, far blue line and back, far end and back.

After we skated the first one, the Norwegian fans clapped, thinking it was some kind of skating demonstration. Then after we went up and back, up and back, a couple more Herbies, they realized it was some kind of punishment. It went on and on. We skated in groups of five. We'd get back to the end, Herb would let us skate circles to catch a couple of breaths and then stretch, and he'd blow his whistle again. Up and back, up and back. We skated another Herbie, then another. The rink attendant turned off the lights to get us off the ice, but Herb kept blowing his whistle. Buzz Schneider and Mike Ramsey had gotten kicked out of the game for fighting and were watching from the stands in street clothes. They asked Craig Patrick if they should put their gear on and get out there, too. No, Craig said. The rink attendant handed over the keys so we could lock up when we were done. Blue line, red line, blue line, far end and back, on and on. Guys would stop and fall to their knees. Out of frustration, Mark Johnson slammed his stick against the boards. Herb exploded. "If I hear another stick hit the boards, I'll skate you until you die!"

Finally it ended. "If you play like that tomorrow night, you'll skate again," Herb snapped. I had no doubt he would make us do it. It wasn't the final score that had ticked him off; it was that we hadn't take the game seriously. We hadn't respected our opponent or all the work we had done over the past three weeks. In hockey, you can be the best team in the world, but if you think you're going to win just by showing up, you're playing with fire.

We played our second game against Norway the next day. We won 9–0.

After we got back from Europe, Minnesota became our home base. I had to leave Donna back in Winthrop and got an apartment with Ralph Cox, a right wing from the University of New

Hampshire. He had a Fu Manchu mustache and an incredible shot. He wasn't the fastest skater, but he could put the puck into the net. He was from Braintree, Massachusetts, and I'd played against him in college but didn't know him that well. He hadn't been at the tryout at the National Sports Festival. He had broken his leg and could not participate in the tryout, but Herb had taken him anyway, because of the way he could score.

Three of the other New England guys—Jack O'Callahan, Dave Silk, and Jack Hughes, a defenseman from Harvard— moved into an apartment complex about six miles away. Jim Craig bunked with the team doctor. Several of the Minnesota guys were from the area and lived at home, with their parents, or in the apartments they'd had since getting out of college. Buzzy Schneider was married and had a home of his own. We practiced at a suburban rink and were scheduled to play games at the Metropolitan Sports Center in Bloomington— but only a few. Herb had an exhibition schedule of sixty-one games—against college and minor-league teams, four against NHL teams, a pre-Olympic tournament in December against teams from Sweden, Russia, Czechoslovakia, and Canada. Of the sixty-one, forty-eight were on the road. We were going to be spending a lot of time in buses and airports.

We kicked off our four-month exhibition schedule by playing four NHL teams: the Minnesota North Stars, St. Louis Blues, Atlanta Flames, and Washington Capitals. Thirty-five seconds into the North Stars game, a defenseman sucker punched Phil Verchota and kept punching even after Phil fell to the ice. The 13,000 fans in the building booed, and Phil skated to the bench with a couple of loosened teeth. I had a fight in the second period, Bill Baker had fights with two different North Stars, and Mike Ramsey exchanged punches in the third. We lost 4–2. The next day we played the Blues in a small arena in Des Moines, Iowa. There were no fights, but we lost 9–1. The Flames beat us 6–1. The final game was in Lake Placid, on the big Olympic ice, which was suited to Herb's style and our speed. We played better but lost 5–4. We had a long way to go to compete against older, more experienced teams. Then came games against minor-league teams. Against the Maine Mariners of the American Hockey League, there was a scuffle, and before I knew it, the Mariner bench emptied and punches were flying. Jack O'Callahan got belted in the face, and his eye swelled shut. On the bench, I'd see blood trickling down his cheek, yet he kept taking shifts. It didn't help them. We won 4–2. When we played the Birmingham Bulls, a player named Dave Hanson jumped Mike Ramsey. Mike skated away with a cut under his eye and took six stitches. If those pro teams thought they had something to prove, it wasn't working. We beat Birmingham, 5–2. Hanson was fairly well known, too. Two years before, he had played one of the Hanson Brothers in the movie *Slap Shot*. He had been the inspiration for the name.

The western guys had very different personalities from the eastern guys. They weren't quick to offer you their opinion and tell you how it is. They stayed at home most nights, and several—Neal Broten, Mike Ramsey, Dave Christian—weren't even of legal age to drink. The western guys who did go out were usually in before midnight. For Jack O'Callahan, Dave Silk, and Jack Hughes, midnight was when the party was just starting. Jack O'Callahan always had an opinion about everything and didn't mind telling you that his opinion was the only one that counted. While the western guys observed speed limits, O'Callahan and Silk were notorious for driving like maniacs to catch flights, weaving in and out of traffic, passing cars in the breakdown lane. Buzz Schneider's wife heard about one white-knuckle ride and told Buzzy he wasn't allowed to get in a car with those guys again.

We had so many exhibition games on our schedule because we had to raise money to cover our team's expenses. Back then, Olympic teams didn't have multimillion-dollar budgets the way they do now. Each exhibition game raised money for our travel, equipment, and lodging. When we played the North Stars, their fan club gave us a donation of $1,024. We had fund-raiser luncheons and dinners along the way. We'd be on the road for two weeks, come home for three days, and then go back out again. We went from Birmingham to Houston, Cincinnati to Boston. We were eating, playing, and traveling together, almost like a family. Today's Olympic teams don't get that kind of camaraderie and experience. They show up at the Games, play, and go home. We had to be a team on the ice, but we also had to be a team off the ice.

In truth, though, we became something more than just a team. Looking back now, there are so many pieces of this story that would never happen today—amateurs scraping by to represent the United States in Olympic hockey, for one thing—but playing all those games and spending all that time together were among the most important and the most special. Because we had to be together and support ourselves as a team, we had no choice but to become a family. Sure, there were squabbles and tensions just like in any family, but we were all playing for something greater than ourselves; we were playing for the group. Sometimes in quiet moments, I found myself thinking not of hockey but of my family back home in Winthrop, with everybody living in that house together—three families' worth of people. Growing up, I hadn't known how unique that was, to be surrounded by family like that, but out there with those teammates, with everyone feeling that sense of purpose, I knew right then how special that was.

Of course, the bond between us didn't change the fact that on the ice most of us were still hearing it from Herb all the time, especially about keeping possession of the puck.

"Morrow, don't dump the puck! That went out with short pants!"

Kenny heard that over and over. Herb constantly pushed and challenged. "I dare you to be better than you are," he often said.

Off the ice, Herb didn't say much to us players. He'd walk past me outside the locker room without looking at me or saying a word. It was hard to tell if you were doing well, if he liked you as a player. He mixed up the lines almost every game. I usually played with Neal Broten at center, but we had a bunch of different guys on the right wing. When you play with new guys, you get to know them, too, and after two months together I was hanging out with Steve Christoff and Phil Verchota one night, Ken Morrow and Mark Wells the next. Ralph Cox and I didn't have a car in Minnesota. Steve Christoff picked us up for practices. Ken Morrow helped get us some wheels. His brother sold us a Mustang for $400. When winter came to Minnesota, Billy Baker took me ice fishing. I was from Winthrop, not Minnesota, so I showed up in a light jacket, almost a windbreaker, no gloves, no boots. We sat out on a frozen lake for hours, the wind blowing snow into the air. I nearly froze to death. Billy had his insulated boots, heavy coat, and big mittens on and laughed the whole time.

We beat the college teams—Minnesota, Wisconsin, Colorado College—pretty easily and had tough scraps against the Canadian national team. Against the minor-league teams scattered around the Midwest, we won more often than we lost. The fluid, European style Herb had taught us was coming together, and we were playing more and more like a team. Our top line had Mark Johnson at center and Rob McClanahan on left wing, and they had real chemistry. A Badger and a Gopher. A year before, they would have been enemies. Mark Pavelich centered the second line. He was from Minnesota's Iron Range, the sparsely populated northeastern corner of the state where playing hockey is about the only thing there is to do in winter.

Mark was a very quiet guy, but on the ice, he was fast and shifty, a great passer. He had an incredible sense of where other players were going to be, and he never seemed to get off the ice. After practices, he'd stay and shoot one puck after another or just skate around and around, working on his stick handling, lost in his own mind. He played with John Harrington, another guy from northern Minnesota. Both of them had played at the University of Minnesota Duluth, and they both had the strangest way of playing. Nobody could skate with them. I was on their left wing a couple of games, and I was completely lost. I had no idea where they were going. The only guy who clicked with them was Buzz Schneider. They became a line, and we started calling them the Coneheads—from the *Saturday Night Live* skits. As a team, we sometimes struggled to move the puck out of our zone, but otherwise our defense was very strong, with Billy Baker, Mike Ramsey, Ken Morrow, and Jack O'Callahan getting a lot of minutes.

By then I was hearing fewer and fewer first names. It wasn't Jack, it was OC. It was Bakes and Sutes. Coxie, Wellsy, and Silky. Brots, Pav, Rammer. Dave Christian's father and two uncles made Christian Brothers hockey sticks, so he became Koho—which was the name of a competing stick company. I was Rizzo or Rizzy. John Harrington was Bah, but that wasn't a nickname from us. He had gotten that growing up and never shook it. No one called him John. Mark Johnson was Magic because he was so good and so skilled—like Magic Johnson, the basketball player. Another thing was happening, too: anytime I mentioned BU hockey, guys would cut me off. "Hey, hey, don't get regional." If Magic started going on about Wisconsin football, it was the same reply. If the western guys started joking around about the Beanpot—"What's that tournament you have, the Teapot?"—they'd hear it, too. "Don't get regional."

We developed our own ritual, too. Before each game, Jimmy led the team out of the locker room. Bah was always second in line, and I was always last. It had to be that order every game. It was our superstition. Late in October, we had a game in Michigan against the Flint Generals of the IHL, my old league. An old friend from Toledo was playing for Flint then: Paul Tantardini. It wasn't the greatest evening for Tanner. We were weaving and moving the puck in high gear, and the minor leaguers struggled to keep up. At one point, Tanner found himself standing still at center ice, looking right, left, right as we buzzed around him, totally confused. "What the hell is going on?" he shouted. The final score was 15–0.

While in Flint, we had a banquet to raise money. Ken Morrow had grown up nearby in Davison, Michigan, and at the dinner, his uncle sat next to Herb. Kenny's uncle and Herb got to talking about our sixty-one-game exhibition schedule, and Herb started going down a list of games, pointing to each date: this is a skating team, this team's a physical team. Herb had a purpose planned for every game. The last game was on February 9 in Madison Square Garden against the Soviet Olympic team, a friendly exhibition right before we headed to Lake Placid. "And that's where we get our butts kicked," Herb said. For some reason, he planned to have us get blown out by the Russians right before the Games. Somehow he thought that would be a good thing.

About that time, Herb had us vote for a team captain. I voted for Buzz Schneider. He was the oldest guy on the team—a month older than me—and he had played in the 1976 Olympics. He was also a great guy and a great player and would make a great leader for the team.

At the end of practice on November 2, all of us circled around at center ice for a few last words from Herb, same as always. He said something like this: "We skate again tomorrow, be on the ice at ten, Mike's captain, and our next game is against Birmingham." Just like that. Like it was a detail—Mike Eruzione is captain. I was amazed. I figured the twelve Minnesota guys would have voted for one of the Minnesota players, and I didn't see how I could have gotten the votes. I could have gotten only five votes from the eastern guys—less if not all of them voted for me. But I had always worked hard, and I got along well with everybody. I was always upbeat and positive, just like at the

World Championships when I had kept saying we could beat the Russians, when Badger Bob had laughed at me. Maybe that's what the guys wanted, a captain who was positive.

The joke in the locker room was that it was a Russian election: Herb hadn't counted the votes and just named the guy he wanted to be captain. Maybe because he wanted to balance the East-West thing and didn't want it to look like too much of a Minnesota team. Whatever the case, it didn't matter, and being captain didn't make me any more of a leader than the other guys. There were plenty of guys who would have been great captains and would be leaders for us whether they had a C on their jersey or not. Buzzy for sure. Billy Baker had been Herb's captain the year before at Minnesota when they had won the national championship. Jack O'Callahan had been BU captain in both his junior and senior seasons and had led the Terriers to a national title. Practically every player had been a captain in college or high school. So I was captain, but it felt like I was just a captain among captains.

As the weeks went on, the main thing I did was listen to Herb. He'd call me into his office, I'd sit down, and he'd start talking—about hockey, the team, the schedule. It wasn't a conversation. It was just Herb talking and me nodding and listening. Sometimes he'd explain what he was trying to accomplish in practice, what he was trying to get across to the team. "There's a method to my madness," he'd say. I'd go back to the locker room and tell the guys, "Herb's got a reason for this stuff."

Herb rarely talked to players individually, and he didn't spend time with us or mix with us off the ice. You never knew where you stood with him, whether he liked your play or was about to cut you. One game, you got lots of ice time, and the next you were sitting in the stands. Plenty of times I called home and said I'd probably be cut in a week. Herb was very distant, and you couldn't just walk into his office and ask, "Hey, how am I doing?" At some point or another, every player reached a point where he thought he hated Herb.

The person we could talk to was Craig Patrick. Craig had played eight seasons in the NHL, knew a lot about hockey, and was easygoing. At thirty-two, he was ten years younger than Herb but still older than us players. We could go to Craig to vent—about Herb's incessant bitching and criticizing and the constant switching of lines and ice time. Craig would give you a fair hearing, and if you needed it, he'd pick up your confidence. Sometimes he'd take complaints back to Herb—not that it ever made a difference. But with Craig, at least you had someone to talk with to keep your sanity. Herb had said he wouldn't be anyone's friend. He was the bad cop. Craig was the good cop.

I called my parents the night after Herb announced I was the captain. The Winthrop newspaper got wind of it and wrote a story about Jeep and Helen, the proud parents. By then four players had been cut and the roster was down to twenty-two. There were still two more guys who weren't going to make it to Lake Placid. I was scoring goals and working hard, and now that I was captain—well, what coach would cut his captain?

A day or two later, in practice, we were practicing the weave and Eric Strobel and I weaved right into each other. I broke my left hand, my shooting hand, and would have to miss ten or twelve games. For my family, it was a big disappointment. We were in Boston to play Harvard. It was going to be a chance—maybe the only chance—for my parents and Donna to see me play in the USA jersey. Now that wasn't going to happen. While the team was in Boston, I took Bill Baker, Eric Strobel, Mark Johnson, Bah Harrington, Buzz Schneider, and Dave Christian to my house for dinner, just like I used to do in my BU days. My mother made big pans of lasagna, meatballs, sausage, and three or four kinds of pasta—an Eruzione feast. I introduced the guys to Donna and my family. Then the cousins started to drop in. A few more came from upstairs. Then my aunts and uncles showed up. And more cousins. The guys couldn't keep track of the names. Billy wanted to know how all those people could live in one house. To make room for everyone who was staying for dinner, my parents had moved their bed out of the living room. They had put three tables together, and we all squeezed in to fit everybody. Thirty people were laughing and eating and passing plates, going for seconds. It was so loud you had to shout to talk to the person next to you. The next night, Jeep and my mother went to the Harvard game, and they got to see me in red, white, and blue. Herb let me skate in the warm-ups.

When I got back into the lineup, I was out of sync and stopped scoring. By then it was obvious that certain guys were locks to make the team. Magic, Pav, Brots, Steve Christoff, Rob McClanahan—they were playing almost every game. Billy Baker, Rammer, and Ken Morrow were sure things on D. Jim Craig was set as our starting goalie. Steve Janaszak was the backup. OC was getting a lot of minutes and was piling up assists. Everybody loved the way Jack played. He was intense. He was tough as nails in the corner. He was vocal in the locker room. He got other guys pumped up. As intense as he was, he didn't take himself too seriously. He used to say that in

Charlestown, the tough section of Boston where he had grown up, you became either a hockey player or a bank robber. If you asked why he had chosen BU over Harvard, he'd say, "Well, I wasn't going to get any smarter at Harvard."

Another guy who had to be a sure thing was Koho—Dave Christian. Dave had grown up in a hockey family. One of his uncles had won an Olympic silver medal in 1956. His father and another uncle had been on the US team that upset the Soviet Union and Czechoslovakia in Squaw Valley in 1960 to win the United States' only gold medal in hockey. His father had scored the winning goal that sealed the gold. Dave was a forward and a dynamite skater. He had a way of seeing the ice and finding open lanes to get the puck to other players. Herb wasn't happy with the way we were moving the puck out of our zone. Our passes didn't always connect. We got bottled up sometimes. Then, in November, Bobby Suter broke his ankle, and Herb needed another D. So in December, he switched Dave Christian to defense. Right away, the breakout became quicker, crisper. We became a faster team. Herb wasn't going to cut Davey. Not now.

I felt good about making the team because we had four left wings and Herb was going to keep four. On the right side, we had five guys fighting for four spots. Surely it would be a right wing that would be cut. The forwards who worried most were Silky, Phil Verchota, and Ralph Cox. Silky had been on edge about getting cut since day one, and Herb was still riding him about his skating. Phil was maybe a little faster, but not by a lot. Then there was Ralph. If there was one guy I'd want to take the shot if we needed a goal in the last minute, it was Ralph. But he wasn't that fast to begin with, his leg wasn't 100 percent healed, and Herb was obsessed with speed. For the new style of Herb's to work, we had to be able to skate with the Swedes and the Czechs. And the Russians—well, nobody could skate with the Russians. One of the defensemen would probably be cut, and it was looking like it would be either Bob Suter, if his ankle didn't heal, or Jack Hughes. One of them would make it but not both. For two guys it was going to be crushing, to come all this way, to put in all this work, and then to be sent home.

Right before Christmas, we played in a warm-up tournament in Lake Placid. Canada, Sweden, and Czechoslovakia sent most of the players they were sending to the Olympics. The fifth team in the tournament was the Soviet Union. It didn't send its Olympic team. It sent its "B team." The tournament wasn't enough of a challenge for its real Olympic players. They were warming up against the Rangers, the Islanders, and the Montreal Canadiens.

By that time, we were playing good hockey on the ice. Off the ice, it was like being locked up with the most immature group of juveniles. The locker room was a circus. You couldn't do anything or say anything without two or three guys busting your chops. Sometimes on the road, you'd get 3:00 a.m. wake-up calls. Ice cubes in your shoes. Talcum powder in your gloves. Dave Christian was the worst. If he was bored at a fund-raising banquet, he'd sneak under the table and try to light guys' shoes on fire.

A few weeks before we arrived in Lake Placid for the Christmas tournament, we had a birthday party for Billy Baker at a hotel. The beer was flowing, and somewhere long after midnight the inevitable happened: pieces of cake and the remains of a couple pheasants started flying through the air, sticking to the walls. Then Bobby Suter thought it would be funny to pour a beer on the captain's head, and Mark Pavelich decided to help him. Donna was visiting, and I was standing there with beer running down my face, soaking my clothes. "Donna, we're outta here," I said, and we left. Of course, the next day, that was all I heard: constant imitations of me in my Boston accent saying, "Donna, we're outta here."

At the Christmas tournament, Mark Johnson and Rob McClanahan got a small tree for their room and decorated it. But almost right away, the tree disappeared. Someone spotted it in my room, and then it was gone. Then it appeared other places in the hotel, but Robby could never find it. Whoever was behind the joke knew it would get to Robby. He was very meticulous. His sticks had to be taped just so, and he seemed to spend an hour preparing them before games. The business with the tree annoyed him for days. One night in Lake Placid, Silky and I were hanging around at the hotel, laughing about all the things Herb said over and over—the Brooksisms. Bah started rattling them off one after another, doing a pretty good imitation of Herb.

"You look like a monkey screwing a football out there."

"Passing comes from the heart, not from the stick."

"We were damned if we did and we're damned if we didn't."

Silky suggested we make a list. Bah got a little spiral notebook. "Brooksisms," he wrote on the first page, and below it, "As told by Coach Herb Brooks of the 1980 US Olympic Hockey Team and retold by John Harrington & Dave Silk & Mike Eruzione."

"Let's be idealistic, but let's also be practical."

"In front of that net, it's bloody-nose alley."

"You can't be common, because the common man goes nowhere. You have to be uncommon."

"For lack of a better phrase . . ."

"Don't dump the puck in. That went out with short pants."

"Fool me once, shame on you. Fool me twice, shame on me."

"We went to the well again, and the water was colder and the water was deeper." To this day, I have no idea what that's supposed to mean.

And of course: "Weave, weave, weave, and don't just weave for the sake of weaving."

There was one that everyone understood: "Gentlemen, you don't have enough talent to win on talent alone."

What Herb was saying was that we would need more than speed. To beat the older, more experienced European teams, we would need to do more than skate fast and shoot the puck hard. If we were going to make it to the medal round, we would have to draw on other things: the crowd for energy; our team spirit, determination, pride, desire—all things you can't measure with a yardstick or a stopwatch. Maybe the biggest thing, though, was our youth. Buzzy Schneider and I were the old guys—but we were just twenty-five. The next oldest guys were Ken Morrow and Bill Baker, both twenty-three. Neal Broten and Mike Ramsey had just turned nineteen— still teenagers. The average age was twenty-two. About half the team would still have been in college if they hadn't been on the Olympic team. Herb used to joke with reporters, "Some of them are so young they still believe in Santa Claus." Herb thought that could be an asset. Twenty-year-olds have more energy than thirty-year-olds, more stamina. They get more excited and pumped up. "Use your youth," he would say. "Use your enthusiasm."

In this Christmas tournament, we beat Sweden, Canada, and Czechoslovakia, dominating in the third period in each game. Against the Soviet B team, we trailed 3–2 in the third period, but thanks to all those Herbies, we still had gas in the tank. Magic scored two goals, Eric Strobel got one, and we took the gold medal. Everyone had to wonder if maybe it could be a dress rehearsal for something bigger.

Before we left Lake Placid, we had a Christmas party. Each guy had been given the name of another player to buy a present for, and I passed them out. Mark Pavelich, the outdoorsman, got a fishing rod made from a hockey stick. Jim Craig, who talked nonstop, got a giant jawbreaker to put into his mouth and earplugs to give to whoever was standing near him. Eric Strobel and I each got a hard hat with a headlamp—so we could see better next time and not crash into each other. OC got a pair of giant sunglasses to go with his Hollywood personality. We had a present for Herb, too: a big leather bullwhip.

In January, we hit the road again—Oklahoma City, Tulsa, Houston, Tulsa again, the University of Wisconsin, Fort Worth, Dallas. Seven games in ten days, planes and buses and hotels. We were tired and just wanted to get to Lake Placid, and we played like it. We lost two games we should have won, and even when we came out on top, we didn't look good. Herb still had to make the last cuts, but instead of sending two guys home, he brought two new players in—both from the U. One was Tim Harrer, a senior, one of the top scorers in college hockey. The other was Aaron Broten, Neal's younger brother, a freshman sensation for the Gophers. Herb said that if they played well, he might take one or both to Lake Placid. Nothing against Tim or Aaron. They were both good guys and damn good hockey players, but the twenty-two of us had been busting our butts and sweating it out day after day for months. We had done the Herbies. We had run the hill. We had taken all of Herb's badgering and mind games. And now, just a few weeks before the Olympics, he was bringing in two new guys? Guys who hadn't gone through all that? And he was going to cut a couple of our guys instead? It was BS. Every single guy in the locker room thought so.

After Harrer arrived, Craig Patrick found me in the locker room one morning. "Herb wants to see you." I thought it was just another routine talk with Herb, like all the others we'd had over the last four months, when Herb had talked about hockey and the team and the schedule and I had mostly nodded and listened. But this time, I sat down and Herb said I wasn't playing well, my hand was hurting my play. "I don't see you making this team," he said.

I wasn't sure I was hearing this.

"You don't think I'd cut the captain? The way you're playing? I never should have taken you." He said he wouldn't embarrass me. He'd tell the press I hurt my back and I was going to Lake Placid as an assistant coach. "You'll be right behind the bench with me. But you're not going to play." Part of me said he was messing with me, he's not going to cut the captain. But part of me said he just might.

I went back to the locker room and told OC. The word spread, and by the next day, all the guys knew Herb had said he was going to cut me. I would have to fight to keep my spot on the team. The next day, we played Fort Worth and lost 5–3, but I scored two of our goals.

For months, all of us had taken Herb's act. But now, with these new guys coming in, a group of us decided to speak up. Silky, Billy Baker, a few others, and I went to Herb and told him enough was enough. You can't just pull some guys out of college hockey. You can't cut guys who've been on this team for five months. Not now, not with the Olympics three weeks away. That isn't fair.

"If you're going to cut me, cut me," I told him. "But pick the team from the guys who've been here all along."

Herb snapped back: Nobody had ever been guaranteed a spot. No promises had been made. The process had been open and fair. The players who had been playing best would make the team.

"But we're a family now," I told him. "This shouldn't be happening."

Herb listened, and we talked a bit more, and finally, he said, "You want to be a family? That's the way you want it?" He paused a moment and said, "Okay."

Tim Harrer and Aaron Broten went back to the U. A day or two later, the eastern guys and a few other players were hanging out at the apartment Coxie and I shared. The phone rang. Herb wanted to know where he could find Jack Hughes. "He's right here," I said and handed the phone to Jack. It was the call none of us wanted to get. A few minutes later, another call. This time Herb wanted Ralph.

Herb asked Ralph to meet with him in person. Ralph later said that Herb's eyes had been red. He said he needed the best skating team possible to keep up with the Europeans on the big ice surface. Ralph's leg, Herb explained, was holding him back. In 1960, Herb had been the very last man cut from the Olympic team, the one that had beaten the Soviets and Czechs and won the gold medal in Squaw Valley. He knew how crushing it would be.

"It's all right. I understand," Ralph told him. "I'm going to go on and play pro hockey. And you're going to go on and win the gold medal."

The roster was set. In a week we'd be in Lake Placid for the real thing. But first there was one more exhibition game to be played.

CHAPTER 9

SPIT IN THE TIGER'S EYE

The Madison Square Garden crowd booed when they skated onto the ice wearing those plain red-and-white jerseys with "CCCP" across the chest. Their faces were the same as ever— cold, expressionless. I never saw them smile, ever, not at the World Championships, not against the NHL, not in the Olympics. When they scored a goal, they just patted each other on the head once or twice. No celebration, no laughing, no emotion, no enthusiasm.

Before the game, there had been some concerns about security. Anti-Soviet sentiment was running high in the United States in February 1980. The Soviet Union had just invaded Afghanistan, and the United States couldn't do anything about it. President Jimmy Carter was threatening to boycott the Summer Olympics in Moscow. Outside Madison Square Garden, some protesters demonstrated as the Soviet team arrived. The Cold War wasn't the only issue weighing on people then. The mood of the whole country was down. Forty-four Americans were being held hostage in Iran, and we had no way of getting them out. The economy was bad, inflation was high, unemployment was rising, gas prices were high. The Vietnam War and Watergate were still on people's minds. No one seemed to feel good about where we were as a country.

By that time, we had played sixty games in our pre-Olympics schedule and had a record of 42–15–3, but now we were going to see how we measured up against the Soviets, the team that not even the NHL could beat. It would be a final challenge. Then, three days later, we'd play our first Olympic game, against Sweden. When the Russians skated out onto the Garden ice, a lot of us couldn't help but stare. For years, everyone had heard about the Soviets, how good they were. Nobody thought we had a prayer of beating them. They had won four Olympic gold medals in a row. They hadn't even lost an Olympic game in twelve years, not since the '68 Games. These were the guys who had beaten the NHL. And we were college players, amateurs, average age twenty-two. We watched as they skated circles in their end, passed pucks back and forth.

"That's Mikhailov, the captain."

"There's Kharlamov, that guy's fast."

"Look, it's Tretiak." It was almost like we wanted their autographs.

The puck dropped, and they moved it around, *bing-bang*, from one guy to the next. They'd circle back into their own zone, the puck would ping back and forth among three or four different players, and then suddenly there would be a long pass and one of them would be flying down the wing into our zone. The Soviets would make a play, and on our bench, we would turn and look at one another. "Did you see that move?" We were just standing around like spectators. "How did he do that?" On the ice, we were scrambling around, missing easy passes, mishandling the puck, even crashing into one another.

After four minutes, a Russian passed from behind our net to Alexander Maltsev, all alone in front of Jim Craig, and he banged it in. A penalty on the Soviets gave us a power play, but we didn't get a single shot on Tretiak. We had a second power play and a third, and it was the same. We had five skaters against their four but couldn't manage even one shot on goal. The Soviets had a couple of new guys who were supposed to be good, players most of us had never seen. One was Vladimir Krutov, just nineteen, tough and stocky. He was known as "the Tank" because he was so hard to knock off the puck. A pass came to Krutov in front of Jim Craig, and he just flicked it with his skate. It went right to his stick, and he immediately snapped it between Jimmy's legs. A couple minutes later, Krutov got one of those sudden long passes. He skated in and deked Jimmy—left, right, then back to the left—and finally tapped the puck into the open net. At the end of the first period, the score was 4–0. Jimmy had made a lot of good saves; otherwise it might have been 6–0 or 7–0.

In the second period, though, we were quicker, faster. We intercepted their passes, we connected on our passes, we were able to weave and move up the ice. We forechecked and chased the Soviets and forced them into a few mistakes. About halfway through the period, Steve Christoff skated down the right boards and stopped. I was trailing and skated down in the middle of the ice, with no one on me. Steve slid me a pass; I took a quick look and saw an opening at the left post. I snapped a shot off. There was some traffic in front of Tretiak, a screen. And before the best goalie in the world could slide over, it hit the back of the net. They scored two more goals, and the period ended 6–1. We skated with them in that period. At times we controlled the puck and kept it away from them. They got two goals, and we got one. For those middle twenty minutes, it was actually a pretty even game, nothing like the first period. The second period wasn't all good news, though. A Russian checked Jack O'Callahan in open ice, took out his knee. OC flipped up in the air, helicoptered around, and slammed back down onto the ice. Jack had to be helped off the ice. Jack always had a fire about him. In our locker room, he was always pumped up more than anyone else, walking around patting guys on the head or shoulder. "C'mon, boys! Let's go, we can take these guys! We can do it!" Anytime we needed a shot of energy, OC had plenty to spare. Now his knee was pretty messed up. He was out for the rest of the game and, it seemed, out of the Olympics, too.

Early in the third period, Phil Verchota scored another goal for us. That must have pissed off the Soviets, because in the next three minutes they scored three goals. One minute it was 6–2, the next it was 9–2. Just like that. That was how the Soviets played. You scored a goal against them, and they seemed to wake up, kick into high gear, and put the game out of reach. Fall behind those guys, and they would bury you. I'll never forget one of the goals they scored, and neither will anyone else who was in the building. Maltsev, the guy who'd scored their first goal, streaked down the right side into our zone and then cut to the middle of the ice. For a split second, Dave Christian, back on defense, seemed to have Maltsev stopped. But the Russian suddenly spun around backward, completely—he did a 360. And without looking, he whipped a backhander into the net. All in one motion. I had never seen anything like it. Nobody had. I think everyone in the arena except the Russians stopped and asked, "Wait, what just happened?" On our bench, even Herb asked, "Did you see that?"

Later in the period, Steve Christoff got us a third goal, and Krutov, the Tank, got a third, giving him a hat trick. The game ended 10–3. It could have been 15–3—the Soviets definitely hadn't played as hard as they could for the whole game. When Herb came into the locker room, I thought, here goes. But he wasn't mad. He didn't yell.

"Don't worry, don't panic," he said. "It's our last game of spring training, and we've played sixty training games and none of them mean anything." Tuesday, when we would face the Swedes, he said, "it means something." Later, when we tromped onto the bus, Herb said one other thing: "Gentlemen, if you ever get to play the Soviets again, remember how you played in the second and third periods, and not the first."

In front of the press, Herb put the blame on himself. He said he had given us a bad game plan and should have let us play more aggressively.

"Sometimes a real butt kicking is good for a quality team or a quality athlete," he said. He also said he wasn't too concerned about the Soviets, anyway. "I'm worried about the Swedes and the Czechs, the teams we've got a chance to beat, the teams we have to beat."

A reporter asked the Soviet coach, Viktor Tikhonov, if the game had been more like a practice for the Soviets. "You are quite correct," he answered. "We showed what we can do, and they didn't. To know the real strength of a team, you must play strong opposition."

He didn't say, "We can beat the Americans without even try-ing." But that was what he meant.

The Olympic Village was located about six miles outside Lake Placid. It was out in the woods and was designed to become a federal prison after the Games ended. It consisted of a big main building and five others in an odd shape, almost like the letter *S*. There was an open area in the middle, and the whole place was surrounded by a tall chain-link fence with razor wire coiled along the top. There weren't enough rooms for all the athletes inside, so the organizers set up a few dozen mobile homes on the grounds in the middle. We stayed in those. I shared one with Bill Baker, Jim Craig, and Phil Verchota.

Some countries didn't like the idea of housing their ath-letes in a place that was going to become a prison. I was told that the rooms were cramped and gloomy. They were going to be cells someday and had narrow, barred windows designed to stop prisoners from escaping, not to let the sunshine in or provide scenic views. But there was logic to it at the time. The Lake Placid Games took place just eight years after eleven Israeli athletes had been taken hostage and killed at the Sum-mer Games in Munich. Security was a concern. And for the Olympics, it wasn't set up like a prison. Four or five cafeterias served all kinds of food, whatever you wanted, day and night. There was a movie theater, disco, and game arcade, with pin-ball machines, pool tables, foosball, and video games. You could just walk up and play as much as you wanted. Never had to put in a quarter. I spent a lot of time there. I met ath-letes from all over the world. We traded Olympic pins and souvenirs. The first days there, I took the shuttle bus into town, too. Lake Placid is a tiny village, but it was all dressed up with flags and there were all kinds of entertainment. There were mobs of fans wearing their countries' colors. It was like a giant open-air festival. I found a bar that I liked called Chair Six. It had a singer I liked, and I got to hang out with fans and hear what was going on around the games. The big talk was Eric Heiden, the American speed skater, who was the best in the world by far and had a chance to maybe win five gold medals.

When OC got back to the Olympic Village after the Madison Square Garden game, he and Herb conferred with some doctors. Herb had to decide whether to bring Jack Hughes back to replace O'Callahan or keep OC and take a chance that he would recover enough to play, and the deadline for submitting the final roster for the Olympics was just a day away. OC was devastated. Playing in the Olympics was his dream. He was an important player. He had been our top-scoring defenseman over the course of our exhibition schedule. He was a big part of our locker room, too. One knee specialist who was in Lake Placid was known for some radical treatments that had worked well for other athletes. The doctor gave Jack some rehab exercises to do and told him he'd have to do them every three hours, even through the night. And that's what he did. OC would do an hour of rehab, ice the knee, get some sleep, then get up two hours later and do it again. He barely slept for thirty-six hours, but his knee ligaments tightened up. And just hours before the roster deadline, Herb had one last talk with the doctors and then called OC into the medical trailer.

"I don't know if you're going to be able to play," Herb said, "but I'm sticking with you."

*   *   *

Maybe it was because our team was so young. Or maybe it was our lack of experience. No one except Buzzy had played in an Olympics. A lot of our guys had played in World Championships, but the Olympics were a much, much bigger deal, a whole different ball of wax, with media from around the world, bigger crowds, and many more distractions. Maybe it was pressure. Twelve teams were in the Olympic hockey tournament, divided into two divisions. The Soviets, Finland, Canada, Poland, the Netherlands, and Japan were in the red division. We were in the blue division with Sweden, Czechoslovakia, West Germany, Norway, and Romania. Our first two games were against the two toughest teams in our division: Sweden and Czechoslovakia. In the standings, teams would get two points for a win, one for a tie. We had to win at least one of those games, get at least two points, to have a shot at the medal round, and maybe we'd win a bronze medal. To get a medal, any medal, with a team that young would have been awesome. What a thrill it would be to win a bronze medal at the Olympics, here in the United States, on home soil.

But if we lost both of those games, the tournament would be over for us before it even really got started. So there was a lot riding on the first game. If we lost, we would have to beat Czechoslovakia, and they were head and shoulders above everybody else but the Soviets. Sweden had an older team, with a number of players in their thirties who'd played in the 1976 games. They were quick skaters and moved the puck well. One young kid on their team was the goalie, Pelle Lindbergh, just twenty. He'd been drafted by the Philadelphia Flyers. The crowd might have had something to do with the way we played, too. The game was played the evening before the opening ceremonies. A lot of fans hadn't even made it to Lake Placid yet. The brand-new Olympic Fieldhouse seated 8,000, but it was only half full. The American fans cheered for us, but there wasn't much energy coming from the crowd. And there wasn't quite the same energy in our room, either. OC was on the bench—in red ski overalls and a white turtleneck. His knee wasn't ready to go.

Whatever it was, when the game with Sweden started, we weren't weaving or connecting on passes. We tried to hit the Swedes, and we put so much effort into trying to lay a body on them that we stopped playing our game. Instead of carrying the puck and making plays, we blasted slap shots from the blue line. Big shots from sixty feet out might have looked good for the fans, but they weren't effective. Lindbergh had plenty of time to see the puck, and when we missed the net, which was often, they were totally harmless. When the Swedes got the puck, we backed off and let them come up the ice. I think all of us were worried about not making any mistakes, so much so that we weren't playing our game at all. And when we had a chance, Lindbergh was there. At one point we seemed to have a goal. Buzzy Schneider scored. But the referee said no. Off-sides. Then, eleven minutes into the game, a Swedish defense-man fired the puck high, over Jimmy's shoulder, and it caught the top corner. Fortunately, Jimmy stopped everything but that one shot, and we headed to the locker room down only 1–0.

Back in Winthrop, a crowd was jammed into my living room on the second floor. My father was sitting on the brown-and-tan shag carpet, leaning on the coffee table, my mother next to him on a stool. Behind my mother, three cousins had squished themselves onto a single chair. On the other side, my two aunts, my sister Nanci and a cousin sat on the sofa. My brother, Vinny, my sister Connie, and other cousins stood at the back, with nowhere to sit. Seventeen people in all, all of them cheering at a small, fuzzy color TV set with rabbit ears on top, following the action taking place 250 miles away in the Adirondack Mountains. Jeep and my mother would not watch another game on TV. They made plans to come to Lake Placid themselves in a couple days. My mother was flying to Albany, with Donna, and then they'd take a bus the rest of the way. Jeep wouldn't fly. He couldn't get himself to board an airplane, not even for the Olympics. So Jeep, my cousin Tony, my football coach, Bob DeFelice, and five other guys cooked up another way to get there: they rented a Winnebago. It was going to be eight guys and probably eight cases of beer on a road trip to the Olympics. They planned to stay at a campground outside Lake Placid and see all the hockey games I would play, however many that turned out to be.

When I got to the locker room after the first period, Robby McClanahan had his skates and most of his gear off and an ice pack on his thigh. He'd gotten checked pretty hard and had gone to the locker room before the end of the period with a charley horse. We were all settling on the benches when Herb came in and started bitching out the whole team. "This is what we've been working for, and this is how you're playing?" He was pissed. Then he noticed Robby, and that's when it started. "You gutless son of a bitch! No one's going belly up now! Get your gear back on, you candyass!" Robby threw off the ice pack and yelled back at him. The two of them were nose to nose, screaming, swearing. "You can take your team and shove it!" Robby yelled.

I was sitting there stunned. Harrington was next to me. "He's lost it," Bah said. "Twenty minutes into the Olympic Games, and Herbie has lost it already."

Herb and Robby just kept screaming, both red in the face. Robbie was crying. OC—in regular clothes because of his knee—grabbed Herb from behind and dragged him out into the hall, where cops on security and USA Olympics officials stood listening to the pandemonium in our room. Robby followed Herb to the hall, yelling that he was going to play. "I'll show you! I'll show you!" Robby came back, but Herb was right behind him. "It's time you grow up, you big baby!" The two of them were yelling in each other's faces, everybody was swearing at Herb. I thought they were going to start throwing punches. Magic shouted, "Mike, get him out of here! Get him out!" It was bedlam, total chaos.

Herb finally left the room. Here it was again, Herb flipping out, like in Norway, like when he had threatened to cut me. We all had the same thoughts: What the hell is wrong with him? This is messed up. The guy's a lunatic. That prick, what an asshole. Everybody pulled together to back Robby, to support him. Robby put his gear back on, and the other left wings—Buzzy, Bah, and I—gathered around him. "We'll cover for you," we told him. "Skate if you can. If you can't, we'll pick up the slack." We still had two periods to go, so I tried to settle myself down after that insanity, but it had been such a rush of adrenaline. When I stepped onto the ice, my heart was still pounding, my blood was still boiling.

In the second, we were weaving again, attacking again. Dave Christian hit the post. Mark Johnson swept in on a breakaway, but Lindbergh got a piece of it and the puck went wide. Buzzy and Steve Christoff both had good chances. On the bench, Robby couldn't sit down. He stood to keep his thigh from tightening up. With less than a minute to play in the period, Mike Ramsey chipped the puck ahead and Magic and Silky slipped behind both Swedish defensemen. It was just the two of them bearing down on Lindbergh. Magic, cutting to the middle, passed to Silky on the left. They nearly collided, but Silky gave Lindbergh a deke and then went upstairs—snapped the puck over Lindbergh's shoulder from ten feet out. Everyone piled off the bench and raced to Silky, who was dancing with his stick in the air. Herb had told us he wanted everybody off the bench for every goal. He wanted us to celebrate every goal like it was New Year's Eve, to get the crowd into the game, to get some of the youthful excitement and energy he thought we would need.

In the locker room at the next intermission, there was relief. We had our game back. Now we just had to keep playing it. Five minutes into the third, Sweden chipped the puck into the corner, and that's when we made a mistake. A Swedish defenseman had been left all alone in front of our net. When the pass came, he simply knocked it past Jim Craig. Again we were behind. We had good chances down at the other end, but Lindbergh was tough to beat. When we got a power play, Herb sent Magic's line out, and guess who hopped over the boards to take his regular shift? Rob McClanahan. Even with a sore leg, Robby got off a good shot, but we remained a goal behind.

Then, with forty-one seconds left, the Swedes iced the puck. There was a face-off back in their end. Herb waved Jimmy to the bench and sent out an extra attacker. Jimmy had stopped thirty-four shots. He'd held the Swedes to just two goals. He had given us a chance. Now he was on the bench for the final forty-one seconds, heaving big breaths, head down, sweat dripping from his face.

Herb put Buzzy and Mark Pavelich onto the ice with Magic at center. Rammer and Billy Baker were on the points. Silky was the extra skater. Magic won the face-off back to Rammer. His slap shot was blocked, but he gathered the puck and slid it across to Billy on the right side. Billy rimmed the puck along the boards, and it went behind the Swedish net. Buzzy and Pav battled three Swedes, and somehow Pav came up with it on the left boards. Then he slid the puck to the middle of the ice—right where Billy was coming in from the blue line. Lindbergh had been on his right post, and now he had to move to the middle of his crease. There were less than thirty seconds left in the game. The puck was forty-five feet from the net when Billy hammered it. It was low, a missile, and when it hit the back of the net, it was like a giant bomb went off in the Fieldhouse. The crowd roared. All of us on the bench jumped up, sticks in the air, then hopped the boards and charged onto the ice. We mobbed Billy, all of us fell down. It was a dog pile of blue jerseys, with the big blond kid from Minnesota at the bottom.

It was a 2–2 tie. We had hoped to get two points from that game. We got one.

The opening ceremonies took place the next day, in a temporary open-air stadium set up about two miles from the center of town. It was about 20°F, but I was pretty warm in the outfit all the American athletes wore: a sheepskin coat and matching sheepskin gloves, winter boots, and a white cowboy hat. It was a spectacle like nothing I'd ever seen. Hot-air balloons floated overhead, parachutists dropped from the sky. The athletes from all the different nations marched in one after another. The Canadians were greeted with loud cheers because Canada had just sneaked six American hostages out of Iran. There was polite applause for the Soviet Union. As each nation marched in, thousands and thousands of balloons floated up to the sky. White doves were released and fluttered around the stadium over the heads of the crowd. There were fireworks and music and a hundred ice dancers twirling on a sheet of ice in the infield. And when we finally marched in, that was it for me. That was the most moving moment at Lake Placid. I had made it. I was here with athletes from all over the world. I was representing my country. I was an Olympian.

Billy Baker's goal changed a lot of things. We weren't supposed to beat Sweden, and we hadn't played our best game. Yet we had tied them. Before the Olympics, the Swedes had been ranked third in the world, but on the ice, they weren't faster than we were. They weren't better than we were. What would have happened if we had played a good game? What could happen if we played well in the next few games? If we came out fired up? If Jimmy was able to keep the games close for us? If we limited our mistakes, played with our usual energy and intensity? If we did those things, we could beat a lot of the teams in this tournament, maybe even the Czechs. That's what was in my head when I left the arena after that game, and I wasn't alone. The team wasn't down because we hadn't played well. We walked away from that tie with more confidence than when it had started.

Hardly anyone outside of our team thought we could beat

Czechoslovakia, though. The Czechs were a much bigger mountain than Sweden. Like the Russians, they were amateurs in name only. They were actually professionals. In 1976 and '77, they had beaten the Russians in the World Championships and taken the gold medal. The next two years, they had taken the silver medal in the worlds. They had medaled in the last four Olympics, two silver and two bronze. The Czechs were second only to the Soviets.

Before the game, Dave Christian took some tape and made a pair of wings that he attached to the side of his helmet. We were sitting there in the locker room, and he said, "Guys, something tells me that I'm really going to be flying tonight." Everybody cracked up. We weren't tight like we had been against Sweden. For this game, we were loose. When Herb came in, he told us not to be in awe of the Czechs.

"So they've got seven guys from the 1976 Olympics. So they have an average age of twenty-six. So they've got some guys thirty-two years old," he said. "So what?" Any man can shoot a tiger, he said. "But a man of character will walk up to the tiger, spit in his eye, and then pull the trigger."

Well, the tiger scored first. Two minutes after the puck drop, we left a Czech uncovered ten feet from our goal. A pass came from the corner, and before Jimmy could react, it was in the net. But even with the Czechs scoring first, we were in high gear, weaving, skating with the second-best team in the world, stride for stride. We were in their face when they tried to move out of their zone. When we had the chance, we slammed them into the boards. Two minutes after the Czech goal, my line was on the ice—Neal Broten at center and Steve Christoff on the other side. The face-off was outside their blue line. The Czechs actually won the draw, but Brots was so quick. He jumped on the puck and carried it into their zone. I went with him to the left, and Neal slid me the puck. It was a little behind me, but I was able to kick it ahead with my right skate. Just before I got to the bottom of the circle, I fired a wrist shot. It pinged off the right post—and the game was tied.

It was another one of those on-ice New Year's celebrations, with every guy hopping the boards, patting Neal on the back, me on the back. The Fieldhouse was packed, and the chant "USA! USA! USA!" boomed around the arena, flags waving everywhere. Only a minute later, the Coneheads—Pav, Buzzy, and Bah—swirled their way into the Czech zone. Buzzy threw a backhander at the Czech goal, and Pav chipped the rebound into the net. The Czechs evened the score before the end of the period, but I think they realized that they were in for a tough game. College guys or not, the US team was fast and good. Our locker room was the total opposite of the scene during the Sweden game. Everybody knew we had it going, everybody was upbeat. "It should be four–two, not two–two," I said, but that wasn't news to anyone.

We had them on their heels in the second, too. Then Pav drove down the right wing with the puck, stopped, spun around, and threw a backhander to the front of the Czech goal—just as Buzzy arrived to tip it in. The game was now ours. A Czech player carried the puck to our blue line, and Kenny Morrow leveled him. He lay on the ice looking at the ref, arms out, like he was asking, "Is that legal?" Billy Baker rammed another Czech player right at their bench and flipped him over the boards. The guy landed on his head, and his legs and skates were sticking straight up in the air.

Then, Magic, taking a pass from Robby, dangled through two defenders and put a backhander into the top corner. It was a Magic goal. Only he could make that play. USA 4, Czecho-slovakia 2. The place was going crazy. The home crowd was behind us.

The third period was more of the same. Davey Christian got tripped heading for the goal, but Phil Verchota followed and flipped the puck past the netminder. Bah took the puck coast to coast, curled behind the Czech goal, and centered to Buzzy, who one-timed it, his second goal of the night. The Czechs cut the score to 6–3, but then came Magic again. He darted between the two Czech defensemen, slid a pass to Robby. Robby got knocked down, but as he was falling, before he hit the ice, he reached out and poked the puck in. It was everything we had been working toward for the last six months. It all came together. We controlled the puck. We harassed the Czechs into turnovers. We were faster, we had more energy and enthusiasm, and we had the conditioning to skate away from them in the third period. All those Herbies paid off.

The Czechs didn't like getting blown out and decided they were going to do something about it. With three minutes left, Magic was skating out of our zone. Didn't have the puck, wasn't near the puck; he was looking ahead at the puck and had his head turned. A big Czech defenseman, Jan Neliba, wearing the number 3, plowed into him, blindsided him, put his shoulder into him up high, a total cheap shot. Magic fell to the ice and lay on his back, his left hand holding his right shoulder. The game stopped. Our trainer went to look at Magic.

Neliba stood on the ice, and Herb had a message for him. "I'll bury that goddamn stick right down your throat, number three. You'll eat that goddamn Koho, three." It was picked up by a television camera. That was a time when "goddamn" was as bad as an F-bomb on TV, and the whole TV audience heard it. Herb Brooks was backing up his players, telling Jan Neliba he was going to get a hockey stick rammed down his throat. And the Americans watching loved it.

Right before the end of the game, there was another incident, involving Anton Stastny, one of three Stastny brothers who were the stars of the Czech team (they would later defect and play in the NHL). He rammed me from behind in front of their bench. I turned and swung my elbow at his head as hard as I could but missed. Before I could make another move, Steve Christoff came in and cross-checked Stastny in the throat. Stastny and I kept pushing and jawing, and I said plenty of things my mother wouldn't have liked. He started to move closer to me when Rammer grabbed him and held him back. You mess with one of us, you're messing with all of us. Finally I pointed upward. "Scoreboard, sucker: 7–3."

Time ran out a minute later. To get to the medal round, we'd figured we would need two points in the first two games. Instead, we had three.

CHAPTER 10

"I JUST HAVE A FEELING"

The other players and I were still celebrating our upset of
Czechoslovakia in the locker room when Herb walked across
the street to Lake Placid High School. Its auditorium had been
taken over temporarily and turned into the media center for
the games. Herb took a seat at a table on a stage in front of
a microphone and five hundred reporters from around the
world. The questions came in bunches. The world suddenly
wanted to know about the college kids who had pulled off this
incredible win. Who are they? Where did they come from?
They wanted to talk to us, the players, too.

Where's your star, Mark Johnson? Can you bring him out?
And the goalie, we want to interview him. What about the
captain?

No, Herb replied. He was going to do the talking for the
team. The players would not be made available. He knew we
had won by playing as a team. We hadn't relied on just a few
guys. It hadn't been just Mark Johnson or Jim Craig or the
captain. It had been twenty guys all pulling for one another.
"You start singling out players, and you have a star system,"

Herb said. "We have a team rule that we play as a team and as a family."

He also worried that we would relax amid the sudden fame and media attention. We had come to Lake Placid hungry, with something to prove, with an edge, and he wanted to keep it that way. He didn't want us to start feeling pleased with ourselves because we had pulled off one big upset. There was still a long way to go toward getting a medal, and we could still blow it. He didn't want us thinking we were a bunch of "big doolies," which was a name Phil Verchota used for guys who were big shots, big wheels. I didn't really care about not talking to the media, and I don't think anyone else did. We were focused on trying to make the medal round. No one was thinking about being in the spotlight.

The next day, though, it was a frenzy. When a couple of the guys and I left the Olympic Village for practice, reporters were waiting for us at the gate. When we got off the shuttle at the arena for that day's practice, more were waiting there with all kinds of questions.

"Do you have a girlfriend?"

"Do you have hobbies?"

"How many kids in your family? How old are they?"

"Do you own a dog?"

"Does your roommate snore?"

I kept getting asked if I was going to turn pro after the games. No teams were calling Bob Murray, my agent, so I wasn't sure. I felt that I had shown in my time with the Olympic team that I could play hockey at an elite level, but the NHL didn't seem interested.

"If I don't get an offer after the Games, that'll be it," I said.

"I'll retire. Maybe I'll go home and find a college coaching job somewhere. I don't know." How could I know then what would happen in just a couple of days?

After beating the Czechs, we suddenly became the talk of Lake Placid. When I walked down Main Street, everybody wanted to shake my hand. Total strangers hugged me. But Lake Placid is a little village way up in the mountains, closer to Montreal than to New York City. There were no out-of-town newspapers. You could get only a local station on TV. We had no idea what was going on across the country. We didn't know we were on the front pages and all over television. We didn't know that people who knew nothing about hockey were now tuning in to our games. The day after we beat the Czechs, the *New York Times* said we were now "America's Team"—we had no idea. The reaction around the country came as a shock when we finally experienced it later.

That afternoon, a Saturday, we faced Norway. Instead of the new Fieldhouse, we played the game in the old Olympic Arena that had been built for the 1932 Winter Games. It's shaped like an aircraft hangar and seats maybe 1,000 people, a totally different atmosphere from what we'd had against the Czechs. The Norwegians were true amateurs. Their players were plumbers, taxi drivers, doctors, salesmen. They played hockey part-time. We took them lightly once and skated Herbies for hours. When we put out our best effort, we destroyed them 9–0. And we had two other reasons to be fired up. Magic Johnson was playing, despite some lingering pain in his shoulder. And OC was in uniform. He wasn't going to play, but we had him on the bench.

Herb came into the locker room before the game and said, "You guys aren't good enough to beat Norway." He was trying to remind us not to repeat the mistakes of September. Yet four minutes into the game, it was 1–0 Norway. We were behind in the first—again. How could this be happening? Between periods, Herb stormed into the locker room. "Who do you guys think you are? You guys are playing like a bunch of damn individuals! If somebody makes a good play, tell him he made a good play! If Jimmy makes a good save, tell him, 'Good save!' Stop carrying the puck. Start passing the puck. Play like a team." Then he stormed back out. For a minute we just sat there, silent. Then Dave Silk spoke up.

"Why don't we all say something nice to each other?" he said, trying to lighten the mood. He turned to Eric Strobel, the guy with the golden locks. "Eric, you have beautiful hair." It went on from there—you've got nice eyes, you do a wonderful job taping your stick—until we were all laughing so hard we couldn't say anything more. When we finally settled down, somebody said, "Let's win the damn game," and we were ready to get back to hockey.

Forty-one seconds into the second period, we were on the power play. A slap shot came at the Norwegian goal; I picked up the rebound and flipped it into the net. Four minutes later, Magic gave us the lead. Then Pav passed to Silky from behind the net. Bang, it was 3–1. We got more goals from Mark Wells and Kenny Morrow. We weren't happy with the way we played, but we shuttled back to the Village winners and still unbeaten. We had two games left: Romania and West Germany. Romania was the weakest team in our division. They wouldn't have been a match for a middling college team, and for once we scored first and kept the goals rolling. The game ended 7–2. That wasn't the only good news. OC suited up for the Romania game and played, and he even picked up an assist.

The toughest moment for me came a day later on Wednesday, February 20. We played West Germany, and we might have lost—because of something I did before the puck was even dropped. West Germany wasn't going to be a pushover. US teams had struggled against West Germany in the past. A year before, in the World Championship in Moscow, West Germany had beaten the US team twice, even with Jim Craig in goal. In the 1976 Olympics, the United States had seemed assured of a medal, but West Germany had pulled off an upset. The US team had gone home with nothing.

A few hours before the West Germany game, we found out we were going to the medal round no matter what, win or lose. Sweden had just beaten Czechoslovakia, knocking the Czechs out. But the West Germany game still mattered a lot. Sweden and the United States would finish as the top two teams in our group. The question was whether we would finish first in our division, ahead of Sweden, or in second, behind them. Whoever got the top spot would play the Finns next. The second-place finisher would have to face the team no one wanted to play: the Soviets.

Since we had tied Sweden, first place would be decided by who had the greatest goal differential. It's pretty simple: You add up all the goals your team scored and all the goals you allowed. Subtract one number from the other, and you get the goal differential. It came down to this: if we beat West Germany by seven goals, we'd have a better goal differential than Sweden did, and we'd end in first; win by less than seven or lose, and the Soviets would be our next opponent.

Seven would be a lot of goals, but we were the better team, no question. The West Germans had lost to Romania, and we had trounced Romania 7–2. When we skated out onto the ice, I thought we could pull it off.

As captain, I had the job of warming up Jim Craig. While the other players skated and stretched to get loose, I stood in front of the net and gave Jimmy five shots to his glove, five to his blocker, five low to the glove side, five low stick side. Then I fired some harder shots to get him used to seeing and feeling the puck. I was probably a bit too pumped up. I accidentally fired one high on Jimmy, and it hit him in the throat. He fell to the ice, and it seemed like he was out cold. He lay motionless for several minutes. Steve Janaszak, our backup goalie, started to get ready to start the game.

Jimmy came to. He said he was okay, that his windpipe had swelled up and he'd just had trouble breathing. He skated around and said he was ready to go. Two minutes into the game, a West German defenseman, Horst-Peter Kretschmer, wound up for a long slap shot from outside the blue line, seventy feet away, normally an easy shot for Jimmy to block. He barely moved. He thought it was going wide, but it whizzed past and caught the corner of the net. We got our legs going and started pumping shots on the West German goal but couldn't get one by their netminder. Late in the period, with frustration building, Mark Johnson, who was about the cleanest player around, threw an elbow. When the West German player went after Mark, Dave Christian threw him to the ice. All three went to the penalty box, giving the West Germans a four-on-three power play. They won the face-off and threw the puck at the net from the blue line with fifteen seconds left. It went in.

I was pissed. We had been on a roll. We had tied Sweden. We had dominated the Czechs. We had beaten Norway and Romania handily. Now we had gotten to West Germany, a team we should have had no trouble beating, and the captain had pinged our goalie in the throat and we were down 2–0 after the first. Fortunately, there were still forty more minutes of hockey to play. There was a consensus in the locker room: screw the seven goals thing and first place. "Let's just go out and win the goddamn game," I said, expressing what everyone else was thinking.

In the second period, Robby McClanahan took a pass from Dave Christian, went around the German goalie, and scored on the backhand. A little later Neal Broten whacked a loose puck into the German net, and we were tied. In the third period, we came out flying. Robby got his second of the game, and Phil Verchota iced it with a fourth goal. I walked into the locker room relieved.

It was another game where we dominated the third period. We were so young and Herb had worked us so hard and gotten us into such incredible condition that every third period was ours. Every team we faced was out of gas by the final twenty minutes, but we were still flying. Herb had always said, "You don't have enough talent to win on talent alone." Well, we had conditioning to go along with our talent, and it made us a dangerous team as the games wore on. The Russians, though, might be a different story. We might have outskated the Czechs and the West Germans in the third period, but nobody ever outskated the Russians.

We would find out in two days. We'd play the Soviets on Friday in the early game, at 5:00 p.m. Sweden and Finland would play at eight. Our final game would be Sunday morning against Finland, followed by the Soviet Union against Sweden. But those weren't normal semifinal games where the winners simply play for the gold. Back then, the medal winners were determined by a complicated point system: two points for each win, one for a tie. If two teams had the same number of points, the tiebreaker was the goal differential. In calculating points, the preliminary game counted. So we had one point because of our tie with Sweden. Sweden also had one point. The Soviets had two because they had beat Finland in the preliminaries. The Finns had none. It looked like we had a good chance at the bronze. If we lost to the Soviets but beat the Finns, we would get a bronze or maybe a silver, if we were lucky. And gold? We'd have to beat the Soviets for that. No one outside the team thought it could happen, but in one game, anything can happen.

I left the rink after the West Germany game and headed back to the Olympic Village, six miles outside Lake Placid off a winding two-lane highway. The following day was a day off, but it was pointless to go out on the town. It had been crazy after we had beat Czechoslovakia, but now it was off-the-charts crazy. So I headed back to the Village.

One guy who still went into town quite a bit was Steve Janaszak. He met an interpreter working at the Games and liked her. A lot. Janny had the hardest job of anyone on the team. As Jimmy's backup in goal, he had played in only seventeen of the sixty-one exhibition games before the Olympics, and so far he hadn't played at all in Lake Placid. I know it was extremely frustrating for him. Steve is intensely competitive and a damn good goalie. He had been the MVP of the college hockey final four in 1979, leading Minnesota to a third national title under Herb. But he never let the frustration get to him. He worked as hard as anyone in practice and worked to contribute in any way he could. He sharpened skates for the other guys. He sat on the bench during games, a white towel around his neck, always upbeat and positive and cheering for

Jimmy, cheering for everyone. His doing so had an extremely important impact on the team. If I was mad about getting less ice time than I thought I deserved, how could I complain? How could anyone complain? If the guy who's not playing in the Olympics is still working hard and helping out, you better keep working, too, including Jimmy. If he didn't stay on top of his game, Steve would be right there to take the job.

Nobody outside our locker room thought we had a prayer against the Soviets. Why would they? The Soviets had won the gold medal at the last four Olympic Winter Games. They hadn't lost a game at the Olympics in twelve years. A year before the Olympics, the same lineup of Soviets had embarrassed the team of NHL All-Stars in the Challenge Cup. The third game had been a 6–0 blowout, and Tretiak hadn't even played. The Soviets had used their backup goalie, a blond kid named Vladimir Myshkin. A team of future Hall of Famers couldn't even score a single goal on the Soviet backup goalie. We weren't just underdogs; we were under-underdogs.

No US team had won against the Soviets since the 1960 Olympics, when the Americans had taken the gold in Squaw Valley. In the 1975 and '76 World Championships I had played in, we had been no match for them at all. And of course, they'd pounded us once already, 10–3, in that exhibition in New York right before the Games in Lake Placid had started. The hockey writers and columnists and experts had all but awarded the gold to the Soviets. When I had first arrived in Lake Placid, there had been stacks of *Sports Illustrated* all around the Village, with a preview of the Games. The hockey article said we might win bronze, but it said the Soviets were virtually assured of gold. *Boston Globe*, same thing: "Nobody's going to touch the Russians."

By now I knew something about the Soviet players. Mikhailov, Petrov, and Kharlamov—they skated circles around NHL teams. Those guys were among the top scorers at every World Championship and Olympics. When those three guys played Canada in the Summit Series in 1972, ten of our players were still in peewee hockey. The Soviets had another guy, Helmut Balderis. He was actually Latvian, not Russian. Whatever he was, he was fast as hell. And they had Maltsev, who had scored that spinning-360 goal in Madison Square Garden. And Tretiak, of course.

Regardless of who they had, though, I thought we had a chance. Two days before the West Germany game, I called home and talked to my sister Nettie. "I feel really good," I said. "I like the way we're playing. We could beat them"—meaning the Russians, not the Germans. That had always been my attitude going into any game in any sport—football, baseball, or hockey—going back to Winthrop High, Boston University, the 1975 World Championship. If you think you are going to lose, you probably will. If all you think is negative thoughts, guess what? Nothing but negative thoughts will stay in your head. I wasn't thinking, I hope we don't get embarrassed again. Not at all. For days I had been saying "With heart and enthusiasm, anything can happen." With the way we were playing, I believed we could win.

Jack O'Callahan and Mark Johnson felt really good, too. Once we knew we would be playing the Soviets, OC kept telling other players how it could happen. Score early, he said. Get incredible goaltending from Jim Craig. Get some breaks. Don't take penalties. No bad mistakes. Keep the game close.

My high school graduation, with *(left to right)* Auntie AT, my cousin Linda, Uncle Tony, me, and my parents. I was awarded a trophy for most outstanding hockey player that year.

Me and Ricky in the locker room at Boston University.

At the opening ceremonies, in our Olympic outfits: cowboy hats and sheepskin coats.

Relaxing in my trailer in the athlete's village.

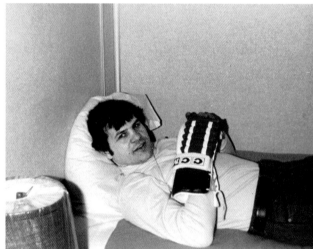

The night before we played the Soviets, visiting Jeep and my mother at the Winnebago in Lake Placid.

Celebrating behind Tretiak after Buzzy Schneider tied the game 1–1 in the first period. *(Photograph courtesy of Joe Lippincott)*

Standing on the bench in the final minute, hoping the guys on the ice can clear the puck out of our zone. *(Photograph courtesy of Joe Lippincott)*

Piling on Jim Craig in jubilation. *(Photograph courtesy of Joe Lippincott)*

"I can't believe we beat the Russians." Bah Harrington *(left)*, Dave Silk hugging Craig Patrick *(center)*, Jack O'Callahan and Mark Wells *(foreground)*, and Neal Broten *(right)*.

Postgame handshake with the Soviets.

The Soviet team watching our celebration from their end of the ice.

274 Bowdoin Street, with banners welcoming me home from the Olympics.

Being honored in the governor's office. *Left to right:* Governor Ed King, Nanci, Massachusetts speaker of the House Tom McGee, me, Connie, and my father and mother.

Me and Donna.

Ricky and me with his father, Al Meagher, and Jeep. Both dads were born on the Fourth of July.

Me with Jeep, the "famous father."

My son, Michael, and his wife, Megan, with Trey—Michael A. Eruzione III—and my granddaughter Rayley Marie.

Tim and LeighAnn with their boys, TJ, Leo, and Mikey.

The fourteen cousins from the house on Bowdoin Street. *Front row from left:* The downstairs cousins, Karen, Bubba, and Geraldine. *Middle row from left:* Me and my siblings, Connie, Jeannie, Nettie, Nanci, and Vinny. *Back row from left:* The third-floor kids, Gail, Laurie, Linda, Tony, and Richard.

My three children, Paul, LeighAnn, and Michael.

My family today. *Front row from left*: Michael's wife, Megan; Rayley Marie; TJ, and LeighAnn's husband, Tim. *Middle row from left*: Michael, Trey, Donna, and me. *Back row from left*: LeighAnn, Mikey, Paul, and Leo.

Magic knew Russians better than any of us. He had been to Russia several times with Badger Bob and had studied the Soviet game. He knew about all the players, Mikhailov and Kharlamov and the others. When he was in high school, he had had their jerseys and posters of them in his bedroom. As the game crept nearer, Mark kept saying the same things as OC: Keep the game close—tied or down by only one. The Russians scored in bunches. "We can't get down two," he said. "If we get down two, we'll be down four."

After practice that day, Jimmy told Herb, "We're going to do it. Just watch."

The one thing everybody on the team believed in was one another. By that time, we had been a team for six months and had been through a lot. You weren't best friends with every guy on the team, but you respected each guy. We had a level of trust in one another that when the game was on the line, we were there for the team, for the group. We were a team, not individuals. We were twenty guys living together and taking care of one another.

And we were a different team from the one that had been embarrassed by the Soviets in Madison Square Garden two weeks earlier. We'd come back to tie Sweden. Czechoslovakia was supposed to be the only team that had a chance against the Soviets, and we had dominated them. Our confidence was sky-high. We had been outskating every team since the Sweden game. Why wouldn't we have a shot against the Russians? It was only one game. We wouldn't have a chance in a seven-game series. But in one game, anything can happen.

I went to bed that night feeling relieved that we'd come back to beat West Germany and looking forward to the next challenge. It was the biggest we'd ever face.

* * *

The following day, Thursday, February 21, the day before we played the Russians, would end in a pretty unusual way: drinking beer in the woods. But it started off in typical fashion: hanging out, relaxing in the Olympic Village. I might have been one of the few people who liked the Village. I played *Space Invaders*, the video game, every day. Singers came in and performed for us. I saw Tanya Tucker one night. I met athletes from other countries. We traded Olympic pins, hats, jackets. Sometimes I'd see the Russians, but they mostly kept to themselves.

I never talked to any Soviet players. A few guys did. Buzz Schneider would say hello to Tretiak, the goalie. Buzzy had played against him many times—in the 1974, '75, and '76 World Championships and the 1976 Olympics in Innsbruck. Buzzy sort of had Tretiak's number. In the game we had lost 10–5 in the '75 World Championship, Buzzy had gotten a hat trick. Tretiak respected Buzzy for that. When they crossed paths in the Village, they'd say hello and exchange a few words. After we had beat the Czechs, the bitter rival of the Soviet team, Tretiak had given Buzzy a hug and a handshake. It wouldn't be their last encounter at the Games.

The afternoon before playing the Soviets, we had one final practice. Before I caught a shuttle to the rink, awesome news started spreading through the Village: Eric Heiden had won the 1,500-meter race, his fourth gold medal. Two days before, I had cheered in the cold at the speed-skating oval as he had crushed the field to win the 1,000 meters. Now he had a fourth gold medal after previously winning the 500, 1,000, and 5,000 meters. I was in awe of the guy. He had thighs like tree trunks. He was a machine. He could explode out of the start and win the sprint races, then turn around and blow away the field in the long distances. Imagine a runner who could win a 100-meter dash and two days later win a marathon. That was essentially what Eric was doing. In two days, he'd go for gold in the 10,000 meters. No one had ever won gold in five speed-skating events before. At that point, he was the story of the Games, the star of the US team.

Before practice that Thursday, Herb started talking about something he'd been talking about a lot in the previous few days. He'd been saying it a lot—he'd noticed something about the Russians.

"I don't like the way they're playing. They look sloppy. They're bored. They're not here to play hockey. They're here to have a vacation and buy jeans."

And when I watched them play, Herb seemed to have a point. Their line changes were kind of lazy. They hadn't looked sharp in Lake Placid so far. They had scored seventeen goals against Holland, but they'd given up four. They could shut out the NHL's best but then give up four to the *Dutch*? Against Canada, the Soviets had been losing 3–1 before they had finally woken up and won 6–4. Finland had almost beat them. The Finns had led 2–1 with five minutes to play. But the Soviets had erupted for two goals in seventy seconds to pull out the win.

And their top guys: the captain, Mikhailov, was thirty-five; Petrov and Kharlamov were thirty-two. All three were on their third Olympic Games. "How much do they really want to win?" Herb kept asking. "How much do they care?" It was true; those guys had two gold medals already. They had played in nine or ten World Championships. They had played in the 1972 Summit Series against Canada. And here they were in Lake Placid beating Japan 16–0 and Holland 17–4 without even trying.

"They're not serious," Herb said over and over in the locker room, in the Village, on the shuttles. "They're ripe. Somebody's going to beat these guys. You watch. Somebody's going to beat them."

Then Herb started talking about Mikhailov again, making fun of the guy. Boris Mikhailov was one of the most accomplished players in international hockey. But he had a longish face and nose and a grin that made him look just like Stan Laurel, the silent-film comedian. "Look at that guy Mikhailov. Ya know who he looks like?" Herb had been saying occasionally the last few weeks. Now he was at it again. "Can't play against Stan Laurel? Stan Laurel can't skate. Piece of cake, guys."

He went after the Soviet coach, too. Viktor Tikhonov had a pretty impressive head of hair, and he combed it back in a big wave that rose up on his head. "Look at Tikhonov," Herb said. "Look at that guy. Look at his hair. He looks like a chicken." I admit it got a laugh out of me.

Herb kept our practices closed—no media, no visitors. He didn't want distractions. That day, we were skating at the old rink, the smaller Olympic Arena that had been built for the 1932 Lake Placid Games. I skated out onto the ice, and I heard someone whistle—loud. I looked over, and there were two guys at the glass in the corner. One of them was Deefa, Bob DeFelice, my high school football coach. Jeep was next to him, waving like crazy. "Hey, Mikey!" Then I noticed something else: my dad had a six-pack in one hand and an open beer in a brown paper bag in the other.

I thought Herb would kill me. I skated over and started yelling at them. "I can't believe you brought a six-pack to practice!

You're not even supposed to be in here! How'd you get in here?"
I turned to my football coach. "Deef, get him out of here!" My
father just laughed and waved. He stayed and watched the
whole practice. The truth was that Jeep had gotten in by walking up to a state trooper and offering him a beer. They had
gotten to talking, and the trooper had just let them go in.

It was the last practice before the biggest game we'd ever
play, and it was short. We just worked on some breakouts and
power plays. Herb didn't want to do anything different. Just
stick to the normal routine. The whole time I was thinking
that any minute Herb was going to pull me aside and talk to
me about Jeep, but he never said a word. Herb and Jeep had
similar backgrounds. Herb came from a working-class city
neighborhood, East Saint Paul, Minnesota. His parents were
Irish immigrants. Jeep had never thought he was somebody
special, never thought he was better than anybody else. Jeep
was definitely from the East Coast, but he definitely wasn't an
elitist or a preppie. Herb liked that kind of person.

By then so many media people were pushing for interviews
that Herb decided to have me and Jim Craig talk to some reporters after practice. "Do you college guys have a chance against the
Russians?" I gave an honest answer. I said the game could go
two ways. "One is that the Russians just come out and blow us
apart," I explained. "The other is that we hang on. We hang on
and hang on, and then at the end, well—anything can happen."

Other questions came, and I kept talking. "You look at a guy
like Mikhailov," I said. "What does he care? I was watching
him in 1972 when I was a senior in high school, and he was a
champion."

That was the kind of stuff Herb had been putting in our
heads, and now I was saying it to reporters.

"He was with the best team then. He's with the best team now. He's done everything, won everything. Doesn't there come a time when it doesn't matter anymore whether you win again? What do you have to prove? If you're the Pittsburgh Steelers and you've won four Super Bowls, do you have to win a fifth to prove that you're good? I don't know. I'm only wondering. I've never been on a team like that."

A reporter from my hometown paper, the *Winthrop Sun Transcript*, said the Russians were so much older and more experienced than us. They were basically professional players, and we were amateurs. "But that doesn't mean that on any given day we couldn't beat them," I told him. "I believe we can. If Jimmy Craig comes up with the great game, we get a break here and there, and the crowd gets behind us, anything can happen."

If you don't believe you're going to be successful, you probably won't be.

The game was scheduled for Friday at 5:00 p.m., dinnertime for most of the country. ABC, which was broadcasting the Games, didn't put its Olympics show on the air until later and was trying to have the game moved to 8:00 p.m. I didn't care. The other guys didn't care, either. We just wanted to get onto the ice and play. But the question hung in the air.

That evening I went to see my parents. Jeep and Bob, my football coach, my cousin Tony, and five other guys had rented a Winnebago and driven it to Lake Placid from Winthrop—because Jeep didn't like traveling by plane. They had parked the Winnebago at a KOA campground near Whiteface Mountain, about fifteen miles from Lake Placid. They were having a blast. They'd build a campfire and drink beer and Jeep would get out his guitar and sing, and before they knew it, other campers would be wandering over to join in. Of course, Jeep was still Jeep. To keep warm, he had brought a heavy army coat and a big fur hat—almost like a Russian fur hat. But on his feet, he wore leather dress shoes and thin black dress socks. Everybody else was marching around in the snow and slush in winter boots and thick socks. Jeep's feet were cold and wet every day.

My mother was staying with a bunch of other parents who'd rented a house together. There were forty people jammed into the place. They called it the Hostage House because it was so cramped and also in honor of the fifty-two American hostages who were being held in Iran. My mother was in a bunk bed in a room with seven other women. The bathroom was a constant fire drill, people coming and going and waiting their turn all hours of the day and night. If you left your toothbrush in the bathroom, forget about it; it would be hours before you could get back in there. They took turns cooking. Each parent had to cook one meal for the group, and they ate a lot of hot dogs. My mother made lasagna, although it almost didn't happen. She couldn't find ricotta cheese out there in Lake Placid, in the sticks. But she and Dave Christian's father drove around from store to store and finally found some.

My mother was going over to the Winnebago that evening to see my father. I had no way to get to the campground, but the security gate was always manned by several New York State troopers. We'd become friendly with them. They'd taken an interest in the hockey team and would wish us luck as we were coming and going. A few asked for autographs. I went up to one. "Could you drive me somewhere?"

"Hop in," he answered.

At the campground, I sat down at the table in the Winnebago and opened a Miller High Life. There was some chicken and hamburgers going on the campfire. My mother and father filled me in on the family news. Donna had been there for several days and had seen us beat Romania and West Germany, but her boss had insisted he needed her back to work. She'd hopped onto a late bus to the Albany airport and gotten there after midnight. Her flight was one of the first to leave in the morning, so she had slept there on a chair in the waiting area.

Back home, my sisters and Vinny and my cousins were watching every game, usually in a mob crowded around a television in the house on Bowdoin Street. Winthrop had gone crazy. A banner wishing me luck hung outside the ice rink. My sisters had made a banner from a bedsheet and tied it to the second-floor porch. "Good Luck Capt. Mike" it said. The day before had been Ash Wednesday. My mom told me my sister Nettie had lit a candle, put two dollars into the offering box, and prayed that we would win.

At the house, the phone was ringing off the hook, my mom said. Everyone was calling: neighbors, school friends, former teammates, parents of friends, high school buddies, college teammates, coaches. Even strangers. They called the house to wish me luck, to say they were proud—people who didn't even know me. My sister Nanci took a call from Mrs. Franklin, my second-grade teacher. She was the one who had told me all those years before that there were other things in the world besides hockey. She must have been ninety by then. Mrs. Franklin said she didn't stay up late much anymore but she'd been staying up to watch us play every game.

It's funny to think about today, the way professional sports teams and even college teams now have special diets and a training table and high-protein meals before games. The night before the biggest game of my life, the night before we played the Soviets, I was drinking Miller High Life in a Winnebago out in the woods.

After an hour or so and a few beers, I had to get back to the Village.

"I have a feeling," I told my parents. I'm not sure what it was or where it came from, but I had a feeling of confidence, a sense that good things were going to happen. "We've played these guys once already," I said. "This time, we're going to beat the Russians."

I kissed my mom good-bye and gave Jeep a hug. The trooper who had driven me out to the Winnebago had waited in his cruiser the whole time. We drove off. Jeep got out the guitar and threw some more wood onto the fire.

CHAPTER 11

MAGIC

The Fieldhouse in Lake Placid has seats for 8,700 people. For the game played on Friday, February 22, every one of them was filled. Another 1,000 or so must have gotten through the doors, because the aisles and rafters were jammed. People crowded in anywhere there was a place to stand and see the ice.

It would become known as the greatest sporting event of the twentieth century. Millions of people would watch it when it was finally broadcast. And over the years hundreds of millions have seen the game, watched the highlights, read about it, talked about it, even cried about it. They've given it a name, called it a miracle. People would remember where they were when they heard the score, what they were doing, who they were with, who they hugged.

Yet when it was played, the game was witnessed by not even 10,000 people. Hardly anybody, when you think about it.

By the time I was up and out of my trailer that morning, the game-time question had been resolved. We were told that the Soviets had said *nyet*. So we'd play at five o'clock and ABC would air it later on tape at eight. Fine. We could have played at midnight, for all I cared. I just wanted to play. That morning I called Donna. She had made it in to work after her exhausting trip home. She had looked so tired that her boss had told her she didn't have to stay in the office. She'd been floored. A few days before, she was going to lose her job if she wasn't there by Friday morning. Now she was going to have to watch the game on TV instead of being there in Lake Placid, watching it live. I was disappointed for her, but I was confident about the game.

"I just have a feeling," I told her. "I have a good feeling about this."

In the Olympic Village, the game was on everyone's mind. Americans and athletes from other countries slapped me on the shoulder, shook my hand, wished us luck. Hockey players, skiers, figure skaters, speed skaters. Especially athletes from the Eastern Bloc. "Beat the Russians," they said quietly. "Please."

When we arrived that afternoon at the Fieldhouse, we got a taste of the mood in the rest of the country. The wall outside our locker room door was covered with telegrams. Plastered with them. Not dozens—hundreds. Messages to the team from California, Michigan, Arizona, New Jersey, New Mexico, Massachusetts, Minnesota. From all over, not just hockey states. Illinois, Alabama, Virginia, Oregon, Ohio, Georgia, Colorado, Iowa, Wisconsin, Vermont, New Hampshire. People who had never watched a hockey game were rooting for twenty college players no one had ever heard of, and they wanted us to win. "Go for the gold!" one said.

They wanted us to beat the Soviets. One telegram actually said, "Save us from the cancer of communism." A lady from Texas wrote, "Beat those Commie bastards."

I always felt pride putting on the USA sweater, playing for my country. But this was something I'd never imagined.

* * *

In our cramped locker room, we started pulling on skates and socks and shoulder pads. Normally it was like a circus in there: twenty guys with the maturity level of twelve-year-olds talking, joking, teasing. OC was up walking around, too wired to sit. But that night, you could hear the *riiiippp* as guys wound tape around their shin pads, the clinking of the buckles as the goalies strapped on their pads. Nobody complimented Eric Strobel on his flowing golden hair. Once everyone was dressed, we just sat there, like in church. Over to my right, Billy Baker was sitting next to Steve Janaszak, our backup goalie. Billy looked at Steve, and, without making a sound, he mimed the words "What do we do now?"

Steve mouthed back one word: "Pray."

I was sitting there trying to get myself ready to play smart, to play the way Jack Parker had taught me. If we were going to have a chance, we couldn't make any costly mistakes. We couldn't give the puck away and give the Soviets two on ones or three on twos. So I was telling myself not to take chances. If you have a wide-open opportunity to score, fine, go for it. But be more defensive than offensive. Get back to our zone so it's not just our two defensemen alone back there. Don't give the Soviet forwards space to wheel around and make their bang-bang pass plays. I was thinking that if I got the puck in our zone, I'd better not try to make a fancy play. Don't skate the puck through two Soviets. If you have no open space and no one to pass to, bang the puck off the boards and clear it. Play smart. Defense first.

This, too: don't hit Jimmy in the throat.

* * *

Twenty years before we went to Lake Placid, the 1960 US Olympic hockey team had pulled off a miracle in Squaw Valley. That was the last time a US Olympic team had defeated the Soviets, a 3–2 upset. The first goal had been scored by Bill Cleary, a center from Cambridge, Massachusetts, who now coached at Harvard. He had defended me months before, and he now strode into our quiet locker room that night with a message: "There is no doubt in my mind—nor in the minds of all the guys on the 1960 team—that you are going to win this game."

So there actually was someone outside the team who thought we had a chance.

Cleary stepped out, and then Herb moved to the middle of the room. He wore a tan jacket, light blue shirt, blue USA tie, and plaid pants—a fashionable look back then. He glanced down at a yellow scrap of paper in his hand and started talking.

"You were born to be a player. You are meant to be here. This moment is yours. You're meant to be here at this time."

As Herb said it, I looked around the room, and guys were nodding. Janaszak remembers feeling like he was ready to run through a wall, even though he wasn't going to play. Buzz Schneider felt it. Ken Morrow remembers it as the best motivational speech he ever heard, and he heard a lot over the course of his pro career and four Stanley Cups. OC was pumped. "Herb's right!" he was saying to himself. "Screw these Russians."

I didn't have that reaction. Maybe it was because I was a little older. Maybe it was because I was the captain and I'd heard Herb go off on crazy tangents so many times. Whatever it was, I was sitting there asking myself "What the hell is Herb talking about? Born to be a player? What's that supposed to mean? I wasn't born to be here. I'm here for a hockey game. Let's just get out there and play."

The speech is now legendary in sports. But at the time, I thought it was just Herb being Herb.

I didn't need to get jacked up for the game. We were playing the Soviets. In the Olympic Games. In our own country. For a chance to win a medal. In front of my mother and father and family and friends. It was all the things I'd dreamed about growing up. How could I not be fired up for that?

Until we had beat the Czechs, I had never imagined I'd play for a chance to win a gold medal. I'd worked hard for so many years. To get a scholarship. To make the BU team. To stand out in Toledo. To make the Olympic team. I'd put in all the work without knowing what the end would be, if I'd make it to the next step, the next level. I wouldn't have gotten to this point, to this game, without some lucky breaks. Meeting Jack Parker. Playing with Rick Meagher. Keeping my amateur status—by accident. When I think back on Herb's speech now, maybe he was right. Maybe each of us really was born to be a player, born to be right there, in this moment.

It was a buzz. A hum. You could hear it as we walked down the hall and turned right to the ice. Ten days before, when we had played Sweden, the building had been half empty. But now we got to the bench and we had to stop and look: fans in every seat, the upper deck filled, people standing. And throughout the crowd, flags. Big ones, small ones, the Stars and Stripes waving back and forth. When we stepped onto the ice, it started. "USA! USA! USA!" I felt as if I were ten feet off the ground.

Mark Johnson's line—Magic, Dave Silk, and Rob McClanahan—started the game. Ken Morrow and Mike Ramsey were on defense. The Russians sent out their top line: Vladimir Petrov, Valeri Kharlamov, Boris Mikhailov—and damn, it really was Stan Laurel.

Mark and Robby were both twenty-two, Dave twenty-one. Each had played three seasons of college hockey and were playing their second game together as a line. The three Russian forwards had been playing for the Soviet national team for eleven years, since 1969. They had been skating together as a line for nine years. When they had started playing together, some of our guys had been in sixth grade.

What no one knew then was that each of our starting five skaters would go on to long pro careers. Robby would play five seasons in the NHL, Dave eight. Ken would spend ten years with the New York Islanders and win four Stanley Cups. Rammer was a first-round draft choice by the Buffalo Sabres, eleventh overall, and ended up playing nineteen years in the NHL. Mark was the best player we had. He had a sixth sense of where to be, where the puck was going to go. He knew where his linemates were going to be before they knew where they'd be. That's why we called him "Magic"—he was our Magic Johnson. Mark played eleven seasons in the NHL.

And there were more on the bench. Neal Broten, center on my line, had had twenty-one goals and fifty assists the year before as a freshman at the University of Minnesota. Neal, Jack O'Callahan, Mark Pavelich, Dave Christian, and Steve Christoff would all go on to play in the NHL.

We were young and unknown. At the time, people thought of us as "the college guys." But we were much better than people thought and much better than the Soviets realized.

On the TV broadcast, Al Michaels was calling the game with Ken Dryden, the great Montreal Canadiens goalie. Just before the opening face-off, Dryden said, "In the next two and a half hours the US players will go through the most demanding and difficult and perhaps exhilarating game of their lives. They will be playing against a very good team, a team that is better than they are. And after that time, after it's all over, this team will know an awful lot about themselves." He was right.

Right away, everyone knew it was going to be different from the last game against these guys. Just after the opening face-off, a Russian center, Viktor Zhluktov, got free about twenty feet from our goal and fired a wrist shot. Jimmy came out at him to cut down the angle. He blocked the shot with his pads and covered the rebound. Jimmy was on. A moment later, Eric Strobel slammed a Russian into the boards. The college guys weren't spectators this time.

About three minutes into the game, Billy Baker got the puck behind our goal and skated it up the right wing. He cut around one Russian, then another, then carried it deep into the Soviet zone and backhanded a pass toward the goal. Phil Verchota redirected it, and Tretiak had to dive to make the save and cover the puck—a good scoring chance for us. The Soviets weren't skating rings around us; it was an even game.

That brought the crowd to its feet and we heard it for the first time in the game: "USA! USA! USA!"

A minute later, Mikhailov was called for hooking and we had a power play. Mark Johnson scooted between the Soviet defensemen but didn't get a shot off. Still, there was another scoring chance for us. My line—with Neal Broten at center and Steve Christoff on right wing—hopped over the boards. A defenseman, Vasili Pervukhin, went to get the puck, and I ran him into the end boards—my first hit of the game. I ended up with the puck in the corner. I waited and waited and finally spotted a chance: Jack O'Callahan open just above the face-off circles. I slid a pass, hoping OC would hammer it at the net. A Russian tipped the puck before he could get his stick onto it.

It was incredible that Jack was even playing with the knee injury he had. But he was as tough and intense and gritty as any player as you could find, the kind of guy we needed in a game like this. That was why Herb had kept him on the team even with a bad knee.

Minutes later, Sergei Makarov, one of the Soviets' young stars, took the puck down the left wing. Mike Ramsey, just nineteen years old, crushed him with a body check. A moment later, Valeri Kharlamov was picking up speed through the neutral zone. Ken Morrow stepped up and belted him, knocking the Russian clear off his feet. Another Russian got pushed into the boards by Dave Christian. Bill Baker slammed Alexander Maltsev. Our defensemen were setting the tone: come across our blue line, and you're not going to get much open space.

Heading into the game, I'd felt confident that we could score some goals on the Soviets with the forwards we had. But the Soviets had scored fifty-one goals in five games—an average of more than 10 goals a game. In my mind, the bigger question was how we could keep them from scoring five or six. We obviously had to have great goaltending by Jim Craig, but we would need incredible play by our defense, too.

Soon I was out for my third shift of the game, and I barely touched the puck. Hockey is like that. You have to be patient. You're not going to score on every shift or even get a shot on every shift. But you have to keep playing, and when a chance comes along, you have to make it count.

About nine minutes into the game, Buzz Schneider carried the puck from behind our goal, chased by Vladimir Krutov, "the Tank." Krutov swung his stick with one hand and whacked Buzzy across the forearm. I saw it from the bench and thought it had to be a penalty, but there was no whistle. The slash caused Buzzy to lose the puck, and it skidded right to a Soviet defenseman, Alexei Kasatonov. He slapped it at the net. Krutov reached out and tipped the puck on its way to the goal. Jimmy was in a good position, but the puck skipped past his left foot.

Krutov made a good hockey play. He got away with a slash and scored. Later, though, he wouldn't have the same luck.

On our bench, there was no panic. We had given up the first goal in four of the five games we'd played. That was no big deal. Being down 1–0 was normal.

For the next few minutes, the game seemed to slow down. Maybe the Soviets thought they now had the game under control. Maybe the crowd thought the Soviets would take over. But neither team was making plays or getting shots. We were behind, but no one was panicking. We had played those guys before, in Madison Square Garden. This time, here in the Olympics, we knew their moves. We knew how they could erupt for goals in bunches. We knew we had to play every minute as hard as we could.

Then Mark Pavelich stole the puck at our blue line. He carried it to the right side, then passed it back to the left wing— right to the stick of Buzz Schneider, the guy who'd had Tretiak's number in the 1975 World Championship. Buzzy carried the puck over the blue line and blasted a slap shot from the top of the face-off circle, fifty feet from the goal. It wasn't a high-percentage shot, but he caught Tretiak off guard. The puck whizzed past the goaltender's glove hand and caught the top corner.

I jumped up off the bench and hopped over the boards. Everyone did. The Olympics had no rule against leaving the bench to celebrate a goal, and Herb wanted us to do that. Herb thought it would fire up the crowd, and he figured we needed every bit of energy and excitement we could get. One time early in the tournament, we had scored and Janaszak had stayed behind. "Janaszak," Herb had barked at him, "get out there!"

We skated to the corner and patted Buzzy on the back, on his helmet. It wasn't a wild celebration, though. The game was far from over. Buzzy wasn't even smiling.

After that goal, the Russians woke up a little and buzzed around our zone. Off a face-off, Kharlamov fired a hard, quick wrist shot. Jimmy flashed his glove and snared it. After the whistle, Jimmy noticed that the knob of tape at the butt end of his stick had come loose. I took his stick and skated to the bench to get a replacement. I usually said little to Jimmy during games, just a tap on the pads after a whistle or a save. Jimmy had an incredible ability to concentrate. When he was focused, you didn't want to mess with that. As I skated back with the new stick, I saw his blue eyes behind his white mask. We were in the Olympics playing the Soviets with a chance to win a medal. He'd just made a dazzling stop on one of the best hockey players in the world. But his eyes looked like he was playing a pickup game back at BU. I handed him the stick without saying a word.

With about three minutes left in the period, Makarov, the young guy, came across our blue line again—and got leveled. It was Kenny Morrow using that big body of his. Later on in the same shift, Makarov was back in our zone. He tried to thread a pass through the slot, but the puck hit Kenny's skate—and came right back to Makarov's stick. It was a lucky bounce. Jimmy didn't have a chance to react. Makarov snapped it over his glove.

Now the Soviets were back in front, 2–1. We had to keep it close. *If we get down two, we'll be down four.* Right after the center-ice face-off, the Soviets fired off another shot and Jimmy kicked it out. The Soviets got the rebound and fired again, but Jimmy knocked it into the air with his glove—and then whacked the flying puck away with his stick. A minute later, Mikhailov snapped off a shot from right in front, but Jimmy got his left skate on it.

The highlights of the game always focus on the goals, but that sequence of saves was one of the most important points in the game. The Soviets had a couple of prime scoring chances. If Jimmy hadn't stopped those shots, it would have been 3–1. I can't imagine the pressure Jimmy faced. If I made a mistake, I had five guys to bail me out. If he made a mistake, the game could be over.

In the final minute of the period, my line was back on the ice and Neal Broten carried the puck into the Soviet zone. Neal tried to slide a nifty pass across to me on the left side of the goal. I was ready to slap the puck into an open net. I was about to tie the game up. But the puck never got there. It caught Tretiak's skate and then trickled just wide of the post.

As the time wound down, it looked as if we were going to end the period behind by one goal, a pretty good outcome.

The Soviets chipped the puck up the boards, and I dived at their blue line to try to keep it in. I didn't get it. As the puck slid toward our end, Neal went to the bench for a change and Mark Johnson hopped on. I picked myself up and looked at the scoreboard.

Ken Morrow picked up the puck at our blue line but was met right away by Mikhailov. In a normal hockey game, a player in Kenny's position would probably dump the puck into the Soviet zone, and that would waste the last few seconds. But that's not what Herb had taught us.

"Morrow, don't dump the puck in. That went out with short pants."

Kenny threw it back to his defensive partner, Dave Christian. Before the Olympics, Dave had played two years at right wing for the University of North Dakota and racked up twenty-two goals as a sophomore, an impressive total. But now he was playing a new position. There's no way I could have made that move to defense, but Dave flourished. He quarterbacked the breakout as well as anybody.

Dave skated the puck to the red line and wound up to slap it from center ice. I saw the scoreboard showing seven seconds left. I started skating to the bench. I thought the period was over.

Just about the same moment as Davey blasted his slap shot, I saw Mark Johnson. He was flying, turning into the Soviet zone. I was wondering, Where the hell is he going?

Dave's shot was right on. The puck hit Tretiak square in the pads. But instead of controlling the rebound, the Soviet goalie let the puck bounce twenty feet away. The two Soviet defensemen thought the period was over. They were standing flat-footed. They had stopped skating.

But Mark Johnson never stopped skating in any game, on any shift. He blew past the Russian defensemen and scooped up the rebound. I was almost at the bench, and I couldn't believe what I was seeing. The two Soviet defensemen were trying to hook Mark, but he was gone. Tretiak was fifteen feet out of his crease. Magic dipped his shoulder to fake a shot. Tretiak bought it. He dropped to his knees.

I still wasn't sure this was really happening. Mark cut to the left. Tretiak was down, helpless. The net was wide open. Mark flicked a wrist shot.

The bench exploded. All of us leaped up, arms and sticks in the air. People in the stands were screaming and jumping. The guys on the bench hopped onto the ice, and we charged over to the corner, where Mark was standing with his stick in the air. He was barely smiling, as surprised as everybody else at what had just happened.

Then I looked up at the clock. Everybody did.

0:00

No time left.

But had he scored before time ran out? The red light was on, signaling a goal. If time had run out, a green light would have come on and the goal judge wouldn't have been able to activate the red light.

As we headed back to our bench, the Finnish referee conferred with the official scorer. It was deafening. "USA! USA! USA!" The Soviets had left the ice. They'd gone to their dressing room. Maybe that was their way of showing that they didn't think the goal should count. Maybe they were disgusted with the final play. Whatever the case, Bill Baker and I went to the referee. "Good goal," he said. The puck had been in with one second left.

The ref also said we would have to have a face-off to end the period. If Mark's goal was good, there was still a second or a fraction of a second left in the period. Play would have to restart to run out the last fraction of a second that was left on the clock. When we lined up for a face-off, only three Russian skaters returned from the locker room, not five. They didn't bother sending five guys for a half second. Then there was another surprise. I looked over from our bench and saw a netminder skate out to the Russian goal. It wasn't Tretiak's number 20. The number on the jersey was 1.

It was Myshkin, the backup.

I turned to Herb. "Does this mean Tretiak is out of the game?" He shrugged.

CHAPTER 12

ONE MOMENT IN TIME

In the locker room, there was no hooting and hollering, no celebrating. There were still forty minutes of hockey to go. But we had energy. I could feel it. Our confidence level was off the charts. Two weeks before, we had trailed 4–0 after one period against those guys. This time we were tied. We were even. I knew that if we worked hard in the next two periods, we would have a chance. Magic's goal was the second biggest of the Olympics, after the one Billy Baker had scored against Sweden. We would have felt good if we had trailed only 2–1 at the end of the first period. But Mark had made a play, an incredible play, and now we were on an entirely different emotional level.

I leaned back against the wall and caught my breath. OC was up walking around, talking to the guys, and patting them on the shoulders, fired up as usual. Jimmy was going through his between-periods routine: taking off his gear and then strapping it all back on again. In my mind, I kept going over what we needed to do: Keep skating. When they have the puck, chase them, forecheck them. Don't give them room to breathe.

When the Soviets came out for the second period, the best goalie in the world was sitting glumly on the bench.

Fifty-eight seconds into the second period, John Harrington was called for holding. A power play for the Soviets. We looked good for a minute. Rob McClanahan blocked a shot and cleared the puck. Mark Johnson broke up a play and skated it to the Soviet end. But then a Russian stole the puck at the red line and fed it to Maltsev, who was skating in full stride. He didn't need to do a 360 this time. He streaked between our defense, cut left around Jimmy, and calmly slid the puck into the net.

On the bench, Herb said nothing. He paced back and forth, stone-faced, with that intense, blue-eyed stare of his. Again, it was no big deal. We had been down before. That was the way every game had gone. Just keep playing, keep skating. Maybe somebody will make a play.

For the next several minutes, the pace slowed. We iced the puck. They went offsides. Lots of whistles and face-offs, few clean shots. Then Mark Pavelich got the puck along the boards in our zone and chipped it out to center ice—just as Bah Harrington slipped behind the Soviet defense. I jumped up to my feet. Everyone on the bench did. Bah had a clean breakaway, a chance for us to tie the game.

He shot wide. Missed the net.

Play continued up and down the ice. The puck ended up behind our net. Jimmy went behind and covered it. Petrov jabbed at Jim, and Ramsey slammed him into the boards. Watching from the bench, I was thinking, Careful, don't get a penalty. But one had been called. The Finnish ref gave one to Jimmy for covering the puck, for delay of game.

Mark Johnson, Buzz Schneider, Ken Morrow, and Mike Ramsey went out to kill the penalty. Off the face-off, Mark chipped the puck past the Soviet defenseman and had a two on one. He slid a pass to Buzzy on the left, but Buzzy shot it wide—another good chance with no shot on goal. The Soviets came back the other way. Petrov was open right in front, but Mark dived and blocked the shot with the blade of his stick. Magic wasn't just an offensive player.

The Soviets slowly began to pile up shots: Fetisov, Kharlamov, Makarov, Valeri Vasilyev all put shots on goal. Jimmy stopped each one. With about three minutes left, my line was out. A Russian wound up for a slap shot from the blue line. He was my man. I went out to block the shot, but it got through. Jimmy stopped it. As he covered the rebound, Krutov jabbed for the puck. Ken Morrow plowed into him from behind, and the Russian fell, his helmet knocking into Jim's mask. I grabbed one of the Soviets. Mike Ramsey locked up with another.

If I'd gotten to the point quicker, if I'd blocked that shot, I would have had a clean breakaway. It would have been a scoring chance for us. Instead, Jim lay on the ice, shaken up. He was okay, though, and after taking a minute, he was ready to go.

The crowd, once so loud, had become hushed, tense, nervous. They probably figured we'd put in a good effort but anytime now the Soviets were going to kick into gear, score two or three goals, and take over the game. I wasn't nervous. I had spent six months playing for Herb Brooks, and every single week I'd thought I was about to be cut. Every time Craig Patrick had said Herb wanted to see me, I had felt a jolt of fear. You want pressure—that was pressure. Playing the Soviets, that was a hockey game.

With under a minute left, my line was back out. Krutov stole the puck in the neutral zone and broke down the right side. Dave Christian raced over to angle him off, and Krutov slid a pass to Yuri Lebedev, who seemed to be all alone in front of our net. But Mike Ramsey was hustling back and dived to knock the puck away. We needed a defensive play. Rammer made a play. Steve Janaszak had played with Rammer at Minnesota. He knew how fearless Mike was. "Mike," Steve told me once, "would block a shot with his face if he had to."

When the horn sounded ending the second period, the Soviets had gotten twelve shots on Jimmy. We'd put only two on Myshkin. They'd gotten the better of us in the period, but we'd had a couple good chances, like Harrington's breakaway. In the locker room, Herb told us to break the third period into four five-minute segments. We don't have to score in the first or even the second segment, he said. We're down by only one goal, anything can happen. Just keep playing your game and take it five minutes at a time. We were itching to get back onto the ice.

I liked our chances. We knew we had played well in every third period so far. Maybe this would be the same. "Let's work harder than those guys and see what happens," Bah Harrington said. It wouldn't be long before some hard work by Bah would pay off.

Back in Winthrop, the whole town was going crazy trying to follow the game. Since it wasn't broadcast live on TV, neighbors and friends were calling my house to find out what was going on.

Up on the third floor, my cousin Laurie had found a radio station giving updates on the game. All the cousins, my sisters, my aunts and uncles, nieces and nephews gathered around to listen in. Then they fanned out around the triple-decker house to other radios to try other stations for any news. Soon they had four or five other radios going, checking different stations in case one had further news. The phone was ringing every few minutes. People driving around the neighborhood pulled up and honked their horns to ask for updates or shout the latest news to my sisters up on the second-floor porch.

A few minutes into the third period, Makarov was back again, skating the puck into our zone with speed. He and Krutov had been the most dangerous Soviet forwards throughout the game. I had played against Petrov, Mikhailov, and Kharlamov and knew what they could do. We seemed to be holding up pretty well against them. But Makarov was twenty-one, Krutov a teenager. Each had a goal at that point. Every time the Soviets got a scoring chance, it seemed that one of those guys was involved.

Makarov came over the blue line, deked one way, and slipped past Mike Ramsey, giving him an open lane to our goal. Jimmy slid to his right and covered the net. He gave Makarov no opening, nothing to shoot at. Makarov lost the puck and didn't even get a shot off.

A goal then would have been tough to bounce back from. We would have been faced with scoring two goals just to tie. But Makarov didn't score. Jimmy was there. Soon the first five-minute segment of the period was over and it was still a one-goal game.

About seven minutes into the period, Neal Broten picked up the puck and wheeled around our net. Krutov chased him, carrying his stick up high. Krutov whacked Neal with his stick. Earlier in the game, Krutov had slashed Buzzy Schneider, gotten away with it, and scored a goal. This time, though, the Finnish referee blew his whistle. Two minutes, high sticking.

At that point, it was almost seven thirty in the evening on a Friday. The almost 10,000 people in the building never imagined what they were about to witness. Hardly anyone in the country was even aware that the game was going on.

The twelve most incredible minutes in US sports history, in Olympic history, were about to unfold in an ice rink in a small town in the Adirondacks, and no one had a clue it was coming.

With the man advantage, we got the puck into the Soviet zone and Mike Ramsey fired off a hard slap shot. I was battling to get into position in front of the net. I chopped at the rebound, but it went wide. It was the second time I'd had a scoring chance but hadn't made good. How many more would I get?

The Soviets twice iced the puck to kill the penalty. Broten, Christoff, and I headed for the bench. Herb sent out Magic Johnson, Dave Silk, and Robby McClanahan. Both the power play and the second five-minute segment were winding down.

We had twenty seconds left on the man advantage when Billy Baker skated from behind our net and passed to Dave Silk. Silky carried the puck over the Soviet blue line and was checked by a Soviet defenseman. As he was falling, he managed to sling the puck toward the goal. In front of the net, it hit the stick of Sergei Starikov, a defenseman. Then it hit his skate. And it went right to the stick of guess who? The guy who always seemed to be in the right place at the right time.

Mark Johnson.

Magic whipped the puck at the goal. Myshkin couldn't get his pads down in time. The crowd erupted. Mark jumped into the air. All of us on the bench jumped into the air. Starikov slammed his stick onto the ice. It was 3–3. Now it was a hockey game, a game anyone could win.

Mark danced in the corner, running on the toes of his skates. We swarmed off the bench and mobbed him. The fans were jumping up and down, hands in the air, as jubilant as the Soviets were shocked. Even Herb couldn't keep up his stone face, and he raised his fists and let out a cheer. The crowd, nervous and tense moments before, was now insane, full of electricity. The chant went up again, louder than ever: "USA! USA! USA!"

In an instant, the game had taken on a whole new perspective. It wasn't the Soviets skating circles around the college guys. It was tied. It was anybody's game. Anybody who's ever played sports knows the danger of letting an underdog believe. When a team that's supposed to have no chance suddenly sees that victory is possible, the chemistry changes. Intangibles take over—pride, heart, commitment, things you can't measure. It becomes a game of emotion. Talent, speed, and experience suddenly don't matter as much. The underdog is skating faster, running on adrenaline and energy. Small plays become magnified. Even a blocked shot or a good check fires up the team to make more plays. The other team, the one that should be winning, tightens up, feels the pressure. When that happens, destiny sometimes trumps talent.

Steve Janaszak must have had a sense of destiny. As the crowd was still screaming and celebrating Mark's goal, he leaned over to our equipment manager, Gary Smith. "If we get another goal, the roof is going to come down on this place," Janny said.

He'd have to wait only eighty-one seconds to find out.

In the stands, sitting in section 3, row G, Jeep turned to my mother. "Helen, Michael's not done nothing yet. C'mon, he's due."

On the Soviet bench, the coach, Viktor Tikhonov, was chewing out the players. On the ice, the Soviet players were chewing each other out. When play restarted, the Soviets iced the puck. Off the face-off in their end, they iced the puck again. When did those guys ever ice the puck? How many times had they iced the puck while embarrassing the NHL All-Stars? I don't know the answer to that. But I do know the answer to this: Which team was rattled?

After the second icing, the Coneheads—Mark Pavelich, John Harrington, and Buzzy Schneider—hopped over the boards. The Soviets won control of the puck and quickly moved up the ice. Jimmy Craig stopped a wrist shot from the circle, but the rebound lay free and a Russian pounced on it. He threw it back at the net. That time Jimmy went down sliding and kicked both legs out to his right—he stacked the pads—blocking the shot. Two good scoring chances, and Jimmy stoned both.

Dave Christian, the forward converted to D, picked up the puck behind our net, moved to the left, and passed up the wing to Buzzy Schneider.

At that point, Buzzy had been on the ice for thirty-six seconds, not that long. It would not have been crazy for him to carry the puck into the Soviet zone and try to make a play, maybe score. A lot of players do that when the game is on the line: they stay on the ice, they want the puck, they want to make a play, make something happen, win the game. But if you trust your teammates, if you believe in one another, you don't really care who scores a goal. You just care about doing the right things so that your team scores the winning goal.

Buzzy skated across the red line, slapped the puck at Myshkin. Harrington and Pav stayed out and charged into the Soviet zone. But Buzzy raised his stick and turned to our bench. He cut his shift short to get fresh legs onto the ice. It was the smart play. And it was lucky for me.

I hopped over the boards to replace Buzz. The puck rebounded from Myshkin to the left boards. A Soviet defenseman went to retrieve it, but Harrington, the guy who talked about working hard in the locker room, went hard on the forecheck. He slammed into the Russian, scrapping, not willing to let him have the puck. The puck squirted up the boards, where Pav raced after it. He slipped but managed to tip the puck. It was heading to the middle of the ice.

Just as I crossed the blue line.

I gathered the puck and turned toward the net, putting the puck on my forehand. I was in the high slot—the exact same spot I had been in when I had scored in Madison Square Garden two weeks before, when I'd fired at the left post and beat Tretiak. Here I had a Soviet defenseman, Pervukhin, between me and Myshkin. Out of the corner of my eye, I saw both Harrington and Billy Baker crashing toward the net. The options came to me in a split second. If Pervukhin came to me, I was going to pass to Billy or John. If the defenseman stayed, I'd use him as a screen to block the goalie's view.

Pervukhin dropped to his knees to block the shot. I had a screen. I had an opportunity to make a play.

Moving to my right, I pulled the puck a bit and fired it back the other way.

Toward the left post.

"Just get it on net," I said as I followed through on the shot.

I lost the puck. I couldn't see it. What I saw was the net. The back of the net suddenly bulged out, punched back by something. It took a moment to realize it. But then I saw the fans behind the goal leaping up out of their seats, hands in the air, and I knew.

The roar was deafening. My legs took over, and I just started running on my skates, high-stepping in the corner like some crazy drum major at a halftime show. In the stands, Jeep leaped out of his seat, his glasses went flying. "Oh, my God! That's it!" he shouted. My mother jumped up, and the two of them started kissing each other and hugging. Then they turned and hugged Tony and Deefa and everybody else who was within reach, fans they didn't even know.

Baker and Harrington got to me first. Then Pav and Dave Christian. It was so loud, I couldn't hear anything, the scream-ing and cheering at jet-plane decibels.

The first thought I had was: I have to get out of this cor-ner fast or I'll be mobbed and trampled. Coming at me from the bench was a wave of white jerseys. This time it wasn't the friendly tapping on the helmet we'd given Buzzy back in the first period. The first bodies to arrive pinned me against the boards, the second group jumped into the red, white, and blue mob. OC threw his arm around my neck, put me in a headlock. The rest were slapping me in the head and grab-bing my jersey and each other.

The people in the stands weren't the only ones going crazy. Back in Winthrop, my sister Connie, who was married by then, was in her own house, trying to get news of the game on the radio, when the phone rang. "Your brotha! Your brotha!" a friend of hers said, in a panic. "Your brotha scored!"

"Oh, that's great," Connie replied. She just thought it was nice that I had scored. She didn't know the full picture. She had no idea what was going on, what the goal had meant.

"No!" her friend explained. "Your brotha scored! And they're ahead! They're winning! They're beating the Russians!"

Connie hung up. She later told me she had been so stunned she thought her heart wouldn't be able to take it. In a panic herself, she called Nanci. Nanci had left her job at Logan airport. She had heard on the radio that the game was tied 2–2, and her stomach was in knots. The tension had just been too great, so she had gone home early. Now Connie was on the phone. "You're pulling my leg," Nanci said. "He did not. Cut it out." To everyone in Winthrop, it seemed too incredible to be true. Cars drove by my house, honking their horns. The phone was ringing again. Friends and strangers were calling in hope of getting updates on the game. Within minutes, people started to gather outside the house: neighbors, friends, strangers. For the final minutes of the game, they wanted to be at 274 Bowdoin Street.

On the ice, the guys were still hugging and shoving me. The impossible had happened. We had scored. *I* had scored. We were *leading—the Russians!* "USA! USA! USA!" thundered through the arena. Steve Janaszak looked up and the roof wasn't coming down, but he could see the rafters shaking.

For us guys on the team, our celebration ended almost as quickly as it started, though. Yes, we had the lead, but how much time was left? I glanced up at the scoreboard.

Ten minutes. Exactly. An eternity. How many goals could

the Soviets score in ten minutes? Just ten days before, they had scored three goals on us in three minutes. In 1975, they had scored ten in ten minutes.

Neal Broten, Steve Christoff, and I stayed on for the center-ice face-off. We were excited, and we had energy. We had played fifty minutes of hockey against the best-skating, best-conditioned team in the world. This was usually when the Soviets would take over, score some quick goals, and put the game out of reach. But nobody on our bench was tired. All those Herbies were paying off.

The Russians got the puck into our zone. I rammed Maltsev against the boards. But he slipped away, darted to the net, and tipped a shot as it was heading toward the goal. The puck glanced off the post. A Russian slid it back through the crease, and Maltsev was there, at the right post, with an open net, but he tipped it wide. In less than a minute, two good chances for the Soviets. We scrambled to get the puck and finally cleared it out. Finally, a whistle. The Soviets were offsides, giving us a break in play. We went to the bench. Herb was pacing the bench, telling us to relax, but God couldn't have gotten us relaxed. We were wired.

Play restarted with Magic's line out. The Russians got the puck into our zone, but we cleared it. Mark picked up the puck and hit Robby McClanahan on the left wing. His shot went wide. Back the Soviets came to our end. Alexander Golikov tried a backhander. Jimmy sticked it aside. The puck got tied up along the boards. Another whistle. And an incident. I still remember it as clear as day. In the scrum for the puck, Buzz Schneider ended up with Golikov's stick in his hand. Once play stopped, Golikov reached out to take his stick. Buzzy didn't even look at him or his outstretched hand. He just tossed the stick onto the ice in front of Golikov and skated away. Pick it up yourself. I loved it. Way to go, Buzzy. That right there was the attitude we needed.

Eight minutes to play. "USA! USA! USA!" On the bench, guys were telling each other to relax, don't go crazy, play smart. Over the roar of the crowd, I leaned over to Neal. "We can't run around in the defensive zone!" I shouted. I didn't have to tell him. He knew it.

Mark Wells went out with Strobel and Verchota. The Soviets again got control of the puck. Kharlamov had it along the boards in our zone, and Mike Ramsey leveled him. Mike was just nineteen years old. Two years before the Olympics, he had been a senior in high school. Yet here he was, barreling into one of the best hockey players in the world. Rammer hit Kharlamov so hard that the Russian's head bounced off the ice.

The puck slid up to the point. Zinetula Bilyaletdinov fired a slap shot, and Jimmy gloved. Another face-off. Now there was 7:30 left. Herb sent Neal, Steve, and me to replace Wells's line. Herb was calling for short shifts—twenty to thirty seconds. There was no reason to stay out longer. Go balls out, and get back to the bench. Our team doctor, George Nagobads, kept track with a stopwatch. "Twenty-five seconds, Herb," he'd say, and Herb would wiggle his hand above his head to call for a change.

None of the guys minded taking short shifts. We all were happy to take short shifts because no one wanted to be on the ice when the Soviets tied it up.

On our shift, the Soviets had the puck in our zone, but we managed to keep them from getting a shot on goal. After twenty-five seconds on the ice, the puck came to me in the left circle. I started skating, but there were two red jerseys in front of me. Neal was on my right but covered. I had no play. I iced it. That's what I'd told myself before the game: Be smart in the defensive zone. If you don't have a play, dump it out.

Back on the bench, I looked up: 6:47 left. Only twenty-eight seconds gone. How could that be? It was like time was standing still.

A face-off to Jimmy's right. The Soviets won it, and Viacheslav Fetisov, a defenseman, fired from the blue line. Ken Morrow charged out at him and slid on the ice to block the shot. To go down in front of a ninety-mile-an-hour slap shot takes guts. Or a real desire to win. Kenny had both. The puck hit him in the thigh and bounced out of the zone.

The Soviets regrouped and came back at us. Kasatonov blasted a slapper. Jimmy caught that one, too. Another whistle.

6:26 to play.

Herb was pacing up and down the bench. "Play your game," he was saying. "Play your game. Play your game. Play your game." We were playing our game. We were blocking shots, we were battling. When the Russians had the puck, we hounded them.

In the stands, my mother pressed her hands together and started saying Hail Marys over and over and over. "I must have done a hundred of them," she told me later. She had a grip on Jeep's arm. Jeep held his St. Anthony medal tight in his hand. "This is for Michael," he prayed. "Make this thing end four–three. No more, no less."

With 5:46 to go, a face-off. The Wells-Strobel-Verchota line jumped onto the ice. Mark, Eric, and Phil were supposed to be our fourth line, but they were all tough, smart, gritty players.

And fast. Herb didn't hesitate to send his fourth line out with the game on the line. He had as much confidence in them as he did in any of us. Mark, Eric, and Phil had earned Herb's trust and respect.

The Soviets got control of the puck and dumped it into our end. Strobel won a battle on the boards and cleared it. Petrov picked up the puck at the red line, but he had nowhere to go—Wells, Strobel, Christian, and Baker were lined up across the blue line like a picket fence. With nowhere to go, he took a desperation shot—a slapper from seventy feet away. Jimmy came out and deflected it into the stands.

Neal, Steve, and I lined up for the face-off, with 5:21 left to play. Neal pulled the puck back toward our goal, a crucial face-off win. Dave Christian whacked it out of the zone. The Soviets dumped it back in. They *dumped it.* Those guys were famous for their swirling, intricate pass patterns, their weaving, their deception, misdirection, and drop passes, their head-spinning offense. And here they were resorting to dump-and-chase hockey. They were off their game.

Jimmy was yelling to the defense not to tie up the puck, keep the clock moving. Dave Christoff got to the puck and iced it. 4:55 left. Only twenty-six seconds had ticked off. Was the clock even running?

We stayed out for the face-off to the left of the goal. Herb was telling the players on the bench, "Poise. Poise. Puck control."

The Soviets won the face-off and fired, but the puck was blocked in front. It never reached Jimmy. Neal got the rebound, skated the puck to center ice, and threw it into the corner. I got to it along the boards and chipped it behind their net to kill time. The Soviets regrouped. Maltsev carried the puck over the blue line, but Neal and Steve converged on him and knocked the puck away. We cleared it. Herb was wiggling his fingers. I headed to the bench. Buzzy hopped the boards to take my place.

Krutov chased the puck into our zone, but he was checked by Dave Christian. Buzzy sent the puck back into the Soviet zone. Pav stole it and fired it behind their net. A Russian tried to clear, but John Harrington deflected into the stands. Face-off in the Soviet zone, more than 160 feet away from our goal.

Now there was 3:53 to play. Every minute seemed to last a week. "You'd look up at the scoreboard and say, 'They forgot to turn on the clock,'" OC said once, years after the game.

With every stop in play, the cheering revved up again. "USA! USA! USA!" There was incredible energy in the building, and it was going from us on the ice to the crowd, and they gave it right back to us in the chants and cheers. It was strange, though. When I was on the ice, I was so focused on playing that I couldn't hear the crowd, I couldn't hear anything. But when I was on the bench, the crowd, the "USA!" chant, was the only thing I could hear.

The Soviets gained control of the puck off the face-off and threw it into our zone, but Mike Ramsey cleared it. Harrington took the puck at center ice, skated in, and fired a wrist shot on Myshkin. He gloved it, forcing another whistle and another face-off in their zone, with 3:23 left. Each face-off in their end was good for us. The more ice we could keep between the Soviets and Jim Craig, the better.

Magic, Silky, and Robby went over the boards. They lined up against Petrov, Mikhailov, and Kharlamov, the three oldest guys the Soviets had. Krutov and Makarov, the two young guys who'd given us the most trouble, were on the bench. This late in the game, I liked the matchup.

The Soviets again took the puck into our zone, but they couldn't even get a shot off. They were gasping for air. Bill Baker stole the puck and carried it out. At the far blue line, a whistle. We went offsides, but it was another chance to catch a breather and change lines.

There was 2:31 left to play. Herb kept rolling four lines. Wells, Verchota, and Strobel were out for the draw. The Soviets got control of the puck, but those guys swarmed them, bottled the Soviets into their own zone. Frustrated and tired, the Soviets iced it.

Now there was just 1:59 to play and another line change. Wells's line came to the bench, and my line went out for the face-off, to the right of Myshkin. They got control and threw the puck out to center ice. Billy Baker threw it right back in. Steve Christoff chased the Soviets on the forecheck—and they did it again. The Soviets iced it. The greatest hockey team in the world was behind by a goal in the Olympics, and they were panicking.

Only 1:29 to play now. The crowd was going insane, on their feet, cheering as loud as ever. "USA! USA! USA!" No one was sitting. Mark Johnson's line replaced us. Again they lined up against the same guys: Petrov, Mikhailov, and Kharlamov. Herb held one finger up in the air to remind Mark, Dave, and Robby to send only one forward into the Soviet zone on the forecheck. The other two should stay back. Be smart. Be defensive.

I sat on the bench, my chest heaving after my shift. I was thinking that the Soviets would try to get the puck into our end and then pull Myshkin for an extra attacker on this shift. That's what you do when you're down by a goal with a minute left: you pull the goalie. If we had been trailing, Herb would have brought Jimmy back to the bench and tried to get Mark Johnson on the ice as much as possible. We had a plan for this situation. But had the Soviets ever been down with a minute left? Had they ever had to pull their goalie?

The Soviets won the face-off. Petrov carried the puck to our blue line and slid the puck into the zone. It had barely enough steam to reach the net, and Jimmy just pushed it to the corner. But it counted as a shot on goal. In fact, it was incredible. It was the first shot on goal the Soviets had gotten in more than four minutes. This was the high-powered Soviet team that had averaged ten goals a game. In the most crucial part of the game, we held the Soviets without a shot for almost five minutes.

We cleared the puck out, the Soviets threw it back in. And there was an offsides whistle. Only 1:12 to play now. Down at the far end of the ice, Myshkin was still in his goal. Mark, Dave, and Robby stayed out for the face-off. They weren't gassed. They were young. They'd done all those Herbies in the dark in Norway. The Soviets? They stayed with Petrov, Mikhailov, and Kharlamov, the oldest guys they had.

Magic won the face-off, and Mike Ramsey, the teenager, cleared it into the Soviet zone. Petrov got to it and passed up to Kharlamov, who chipped the puck into our zone. Mikhailov got to the puck behind the net and centered to Petrov, but Petrov's backhander went wide. Ken Morrow got the puck on the right boards. Mikhailov checked him hard, but it didn't matter; Kenny had already chipped the puck out of our end.

My line was due up next, and I was itching to get out there. You always want to be on the ice for the last minute in a big game. But Herb left Mark, Dave, and Robby out there. He made the right call. The right guys were out there.

Thirty seconds left. Petrov got the puck at the red line and fired a slap shot at Jimmy—again from seventy feet away. It might as well have been from 170 feet away. Jimmy saw it all the way, came out, and kicked it to the boards. We didn't realize it then, but that would be the Soviets' final shot on goal of the game. In the final six minutes, they got three shots on Jimmy—one was actually a dump-in that barely amounted to a shot. The other two were slap shots by Petrov from outside the blue line. Herb had told us to think of the game in five-minute segments. In the last of those segments, the Russians didn't get a single shot from inside our zone.

I was standing up on the bench now, yelling to the guys on the ice. "Come on, get it out!" OC and Pav were shouting the same thing. We were all yelling, banging our sticks on the boards. Herb was just behind us, still staring with no hint of emotion.

Dave Silk got to the puck on the right boards and poked it out of the zone. Kharlamov picked it up, but he was out of gas. His legs were rubber. He dumped it into the corner. At a moment when the Soviets were desperate to score, their best skater and playmaker dumped the puck—he gave it back to us. Mark Johnson got to the puck behind the net and shoveled it into the right corner, where Mike Ramsey leveled another Russian. Mark pushed it back the other way, behind the net again, to the other corner. Mikhailov and Kharlamov were standing now, barely moving their feet, exhausted.

Ten seconds left. I wasn't ready to celebrate yet. We had scored against Sweden in the last minute. "Get it out! Get it out!" I was saying to myself. "It's not over until we get it out."

Ken Morrow got to the puck along the boards. On the broadcast, Al Michaels described the final play: "Morrow . . . up to

Silk, five seconds left in the game . . . " The puck slid over the blue line.

"Do you believe in miracles? Yes!"—one of the greatest calls in sports.

OC, Pav, me, Neal, Buzz, Bah, Janny, Bobby Suter, Wellsy, everyone charged over the boards. Dave Christian and Billy Baker got to Jimmy first and knocked him to the ice. Neal flung his stick straight up into the air. I whipped mine around and let it go to the rafters. Somehow Neal and I came together behind the pile and hugged as sticks clattered back down. OC and Rammer hugged and fell to the ice, Rammer on his back, Jack kneeling with his arms thrust into the air, shouting out in jubilation, revealing his missing teeth. It is that scene, with OC and Rammer in the foreground and the pile on Jimmy in the background, that would become the picture everyone remembers, the picture that comes to everyone's mind when they hear "Miracle on Ice."

It was delirious. Christoff hugged Pav. Baker swung his arms around Craig Patrick. I left Neal and found Robby. Rammer got up and hugged Janaszak. OC turned to find someone to grab and shake. Herb wasn't on the ice with us. The second the game had ended, he had left the bench and disappeared down the tunnel.

On the ice, I looked at the scoreboard, and one thought ran through my mind.

I can't believe it, I said to myself even as I hugged one teammate and the next and the next.

I can't believe it.

I can't believe we beat the Russians.

The Russians. They watched, stared, from their blue line. They were probably asking themselves the same thing: Did this really just happen? Finally we got ourselves together and lined up for the postgame handshake. I think maybe the Soviets were somehow relieved. Maybe they could finally go back home and relax and be just another hockey team, not have to be perfect all the time. Maybe it was a relief to them, because I swear, a couple of the Soviets in that handshake line were almost smiling.

Then the four of us found one another. It wasn't planned, it just happened. OC got to Jimmy first. Dave Silk joined them, throwing his left arm around Jimmy's shoulders and his right around Jack's. I was the last to arrive. A photographer caught the moment. The four of us are practically nose to nose. Silky is on the right, reaching behind Jimmy, grabbing my jersey, pulling me in. I'm on the left, shouting with joy. Jimmy's back is to the photographer, his face obscured, but the blue nameplate with "CRAIG" in white letters stands out on his jersey. Jack, in the center, is smiling, a gloved hand patting my head.

The BU four.

You ask any one of us about that photo, and I guarantee you'll get the same response: "Sometimes you gotta get regional."

CHAPTER 13

"HELLO, MR. PRESIDENT"

In Winthrop, Nanci turned on her TV. It was 7:25 in the evening. Walter Cronkite was near the end of the *CBS Evening News* when he informed his viewers of a breaking story: In a shocking upset, the US Olympic hockey team had defeated the Soviet Union, 4–3. Almost in disbelief, Nanci called Bowdoin Street and passed the news on to my sister Nettie. Everyone at home had been listening to different radios, trying to find some news on the game. Nettie hung up the phone, ran up the stairs, stubbed her toe, tripped over the dog, and then told the upstairs cousins what had happened. A roar went up on the third floor. Then Nettie ran downstairs. On the first floor, she grabbed Jeannie, and the two of them started jumping up and down, hugging, crying.

Just around the corner, Donna was having dinner with her family—her mother, father, and brothers and sisters. When the Aliotos heard the news, the house erupted.

Horns began blaring in the street in front of the Bowdoin Street house. Neighbors, friends, and strangers standing outside began singing "The Star-Spangled Banner," then roared with delight when Jeannie and Nettie appeared on the second-floor balcony, waving and cheering. Newspapermen appeared on the steps, TV trucks, TV cameras with their bright lights and reporters with microphones trailing long cables. And that was only the start of it.

Thirty miles away, at Phillips Andover Academy, Vinny, my brother, was on the ice at hockey practice when a friend ran over from the dorm. "They won! They beat the Russians!" his friend said. He added that I had scored a goal, but he didn't have any more details than that. Vinny left practice, hopped into his friend's car, and raced for Winthrop.

We galloped and hollered our way down the corridor to the locker room. New York State Police troopers on security duty in the hallway were wiping away tears. In the dressing room, we hugged and laughed, shook hands and whooped. It was still hard to believe that it had happened, that we'd done it. We were beyond being surprised. We had just beaten the best hockey team in the world. A team made up of a couple minor leaguers, a couple teenagers, and a bunch of college guys had beaten the Soviets. Had there ever been an upset like this? Ever? This is what Bah Harrington said: "I've got to bite myself to make sure it's true." When we finally settled down on the benches and the room got quiet for a second, somebody started it: "God bless America, land that I love . . ." All of us, all twenty guys, were singing like drunken fools. We got to ". . . and guide her," and realized we didn't know all the words. We hummed and mumbled the rest.

The one person who was missing was Herb. I hadn't seen him on the ice, and he wasn't in the locker room. Later I found out he had left the bench as soon as the game had ended. He didn't come on the ice to celebrate with us, with the team he'd just led to the most incredible victory. He did go up to where ABC had a camera to be interviewed by Al Michaels and Ken Dryden. While he was with them, a call came from the president of the United States. Jimmy Carter told Herb that our team had made the American people very proud and the victory reflected the ideals of America.

"And he invited us to the White House for a couple cases of Coke," Herb said.

All of the US Olympic athletes were invited, in fact, not just us hockey players. Our win over the Soviets wasn't the only reason to celebrate. Eric Heiden had won four gold medals and was poised to win a fifth. He was the greatest speed skater ever.

None of us was in a hurry to get out of the locker room. The feeling in there, with all these guys I had lived with and trained with and played with—I didn't want it to end. Finally Herb appeared in the locker room. His eyes were red and welling up. Somebody had brought a case of champagne into the room, but it remained untouched. It had to sit for two more days. It would be opened only if we beat Finland for the gold medal.

In Winthrop, Vinny arrived at the house, and before he got to the door, he was stopped by reporters. "What do you think about your brother scoring the winning goal?" they asked. He had left Phillips Andover knowing only that we had beat the Russians. So that was how he found out I had scored the fourth goal, the one that had put us ahead—in front of bright lights and a TV camera.

In the midst of all the hoopla, my Uncle Jerry sat serenely on the couch, watching TV, observing the hysteria and celebrating going on around him. He was never a man of words, but when a reporter approached, he spoke from the heart: "This is really something. Coming from a small town like Winthrop, my nephew is captain of the US team and scores the biggest goal of his life. I'm very happy. I can hardly express my feelings."

When Jim Craig stepped out of the Fieldhouse into the cold winter air, he was immediately mobbed by fans and reporters, pinning him against a wall. I followed him out, and half the mob turned and pinned me against the glass door. People were patting me on the back, reporters were shouting questions. All around, people were shouting, "We're number one!" and waving flags, hugging strangers, laughing, a few crying. Some were singing "The Star-Spangled Banner." I heard one question: "How does it feel, is it ecstasy?" "That's not strong enough! It's a human emotion that's indescribable!" I shouted back. People climbed onto the roof of the Fieldhouse and were shouting, standing with their arms in the air. Fireworks—which had gone off every night during the Games—lit up the sky. I had never seen people this proud to be Americans. When had people ever felt this patriotic—when World War II had ended? When I found my parents, my mother couldn't settle down. "Michael, you're going to give me a heart attack!" she said. "This thing tonight is more exciting than my wedding!"

Most of the guys on the team went over to the Hostage House to watch the game on tape delay. Jim Lampley of ABC grabbed me and my parents, plus Jim Craig and his father,

Don. He wanted to interview us after the game aired and took us out to dinner. It gave me a chance to correct him. ABC had been pronouncing my name "Er-roots-ee-oh-nee." There's no *T* sound. After dinner, we went out onto Main Street. A crowd gathered around us and sang "God Bless America" and waved flags. Jim Lampley introduced Jeep and my mother, and he got our name right. Jeep was wearing his big fur hat and his patent leather shoes. It was quite a moment. We didn't have a TV until I was almost in high school, and now here were Jeep and Helen Eruzione on national TV. How does an Italian couple from Winthrop end up doing that? Never in their wildest dreams had my parents ever thought they'd experience a moment like that. When Jim asked me about the game and the goal, I said what I had felt at the time, what was in my heart, and what had gotten me here. "It was a big thing for me and my family and my town and parents." That's how I felt. Without the family I had, and the town I had come from, I wouldn't have been able to be there in that moment.

The next morning, Saturday, the second-to-last day of the Lake Placid games, I awoke at 10:00 a.m., and it still hadn't sunk in. But as I ate my usual breakfast—steak and eggs—at the Olympic Village, reminders were all around. Other US athletes and even some from other nations had put up posters and signs in the cafeteria and around the main building congratulating us on beating the Soviets. We would have a practice that day at 1:45. It would be our final practice—not just the final practice before the gold medal game but our final practice ever. The twenty of us had been together practically every day for the last five months, and we had developed an indescribable bond built on the respect, trust, and love we had for one another. And now, we would be on the ice together only two more times—once for this day's practice and then for the final game against Finland with the gold medal on the line. That thought was beginning to sink in: this magical ride will come to an end soon.

Hundreds more telegrams had arrived overnight. A wall outside the locker room and another inside were completely covered with telegrams, almost two thousand of them. One was from Terry Bradshaw, the Pittsburgh Steelers quarterback. Another simply read, "Congratulations on kicking the Soviets butts. What's your secret?" It was signed "The Afghan Rebels."

As we were getting ready for our last practice, all kinds of people wandered in to ask for autographs and pictures: security guards, US and Olympic officials, fans. A few guys were signing sticks and other souvenirs when Herb burst in. "You're not good enough for all this attention! You're too young to win! You don't have enough talent to win on talent alone!" he exploded. He was trying to rile us up again. All of us had heard this kind of thing before. I just rolled my eyes. "What's he so pissed off about? We just beat the Russians!"

The Finns were no pushovers, though. They had almost beat the Soviets themselves. They had a lot of good players, including a speedy young wing named Jari Kurri, later to become part of the Edmonton Oilers' dynasty and a Hall of Famer. On top of that, we might have taken down the Soviets, but we weren't guaranteed a medal. Win, and we would take gold. That was clear. But if we lost, the goals-for/goals-against formula would come into play. If we lost by two goals and the Soviets and Swedes tied, there would be a four-way tie, and based on goal differential the Soviets would still win gold.

When we got onto the ice, we circled up around Herb, and he said we were too young. "You can't win this." He made us skate our asses off. It was the hardest practice we'd had in months. The whole time, he kept saying it: "You guys are just too damn young!" He was trying to tell us that if we let ourselves become caught up in all the media attention, all the celebrating, we could blow it. He said it over and over, and soon all of us were sick of hearing it. And he was right; lose to Finland, and no one would care that we had beat the Russians.

I didn't go out to the Winnebago that night. I stayed in the Village. The singer Dionne Warwick was going to do a show with Jamie Farr, the actor from the TV show *M*A*S*H*. He was from Toledo. I wanted to tell him that Toledo was my second home.

The gold-medal game was scheduled for 11:00 a.m. on Sunday, February 24, 1980. There'd be no tape-delay broadcast this time. Americans all across the country could tune in live. As we got dressed in the locker room, we were excited. We were anxious. We couldn't wait to get out and play. Herb walked into the locker room, looked at us, and said, "If you lose this game, you'll take it to your fucking grave." Then he turned, walked a couple of steps, stopped, turned again, and repeated, "Your fucking grave."

He didn't need to tell us that. Each of us knew we couldn't let down in this game. We had come too far. We had been through too much. Everyone gets opportunities in life. It's what you make of them that counts. We had an opportunity to win a gold medal, to achieve something no one had thought was possible. There was no way we were going to relax after beating the Russians.

The Fieldhouse was again jammed to capacity. We could hear the "USA! USA!" chants even before we left the dressing room. Before the opening face-off, I skated to center ice to shake hands with the Finnish captain, Jukka Porvari, and exchange token gifts, an Olympic tradition. It was a friendly encounter, but I knew we'd have to keep an eye on him. He was my age and was the Finns' top scorer, fifth overall in the Olympics, in fact.

When the game started, we weren't tense as we had been in the Sweden game, and we weren't sloppy as we had been in the Norway game. We were playing our skating game and putting shots on their goalie, a thirty-three-year-old veteran named Jorma Valtonen. But sometimes in hockey you can dominate a game and still lose if your opponent has a hot goaltender. Valtonen was stopping, gloving, or kicking out everything we threw at him. We had a chance to win the gold medal, and their goalie picked that day to have the game of his life. From right outside the crease, Steve Christoff tipped a shot toward the goal, but Valtonen deflected it into the air, and, while falling to the ice, he reached up and snatched it away with his glove. Valtonen got the better of Steve on that play.

Halfway through the first period, Ken Morrow was looking to move the puck out of our zone, and he sent a pass up the middle of the ice and across our blue line. Normally, one of the three forwards would weave into that spot just as the puck arrived. This time, there was no weaver there, and the pass went right to a Finnish forward. The Finns moved the puck to the left and then slid a cross-ice pass back to the right side, into an empty space fifty-five feet from the goal. Porvari was right there to hammer the puck at our goal. Jim Craig moved from the right side of the net over to the left but didn't have time to get set. The puck flew over his left shoulder.

We continued pressuring the Finns, but that was how the period ended, 1–0. Once again, we were behind. We had trailed Sweden, we had trailed the Czechs, the Norwegians, the West Germans, and the Soviets. It was nothing new. I knew, and all the other guys knew, that we could outskate them. We'd had fourteen shots in the first period; they'd had only seven. We were the better team; we would just have to break through and put the puck past Valtonen. No reason to panic. Just keep working.

Neal Broten wasn't a great player just because he could score goals; he was a great player and a great teammate because he scored goals and also did so many of the little things that put the team into a position to score. A few minutes into the second period, Mike Ramsey was sent off for roughing. We kept the Finns from getting any good chances, and as the penalty was winding down, the Finns were trying to move out of their zone. But Neal, with his speed, hounded one of the Finns into losing the puck. Christoff was right there to pick it up. He skated in and threw a backhander at the net. The shot was tipped by a Finnish stick, and it slid between Valtonen's legs. Tie game.

A minute and a half later, the ref called another penalty on us: Buzzy for slashing. Another power play for the Finns. They brought the puck into our end, and our defense left the front of the net uncovered. When a Finnish defenseman fired at the net, Mikko Leinonen was all alone to tip it behind Jimmy. Now we trailed again. We kept battling and putting shots on Valtonen, but we went into the locker room still down by a goal. We had trailed Sweden, Czechoslovakia, Norway, and West Germany. We had trailed the Soviets going into the third period, too. But in each of those games, we had dominated in the third period. I wasn't nervous. Mark Johnson wasn't nervous. Mark Pavelich wasn't nervous. And OC definitely wasn't nervous.

Jack hadn't played much in the first two periods, so he wasn't winded and had a lot of energy bottled up. As the rest of us sat back in the locker room, Jack got up and started pacing back and forth. "There's no way Finland is keeping a gold medal from us!" he snapped. "We are not going to lose to a bunch of friggin' Finns!" He kept pacing and yelling it over and over: "We are not going to let Finland keep us from the gold medal!"

Then Phil Verchota spoke up. "Jack's right! We are not losing to Finland!" Soon everyone was standing and talking. "We've got one period of hockey to win the gold medal. This is going to be our best period. We are not going to lose to these guys!"

Herb opened the locker room door, and we charged out to the ice. Two minutes into the period, Dave Christian, the forward who'd become a smooth-skating defenseman, slithered past two Finns and slipped the puck to his left—right where Phil Verchota was heading. Phil wristed it before Valtonen could move. Tied 2–2. Again it was "USA! USA! USA!" and the rafters were shaking.

Everyone always knew that Mark Johnson was our best player. He'd shown that in the Soviet game. With a little more than half gone in the period, a Finnish player was trying to gather the puck behind their net, but Magic flew in and took it away. Then Mark spun around backward to get away from a defenseman and fed a pass right to Rob McClanahan, at the corner of the net. Robby waited a second, and when Valtonen started to go down, Robby zipped it between his legs.

Everyone in the building leapt to their feet. "USA ! USA! USA!" It felt like the whole building was shaking. In the stands, my mother and father kissed each other. Then both of them hugged Vinny, who'd driven out to see the game, my cousin Tony, and Coach DeFelice. On the ice, Robby raised his stick and just stood there; no running away on his skates, no celebration. Just stood there with his mouth open. It seemed as if he couldn't believe what he'd just done. As if he couldn't believe he'd just put us ahead in the gold-medal game.

There were still fourteen minutes to play, and just thirteen seconds after Robby's goal, Neal Broten was sent to the penalty box. We killed that penalty, but as soon as it was over, there was another penalty: Dave Christian for tripping. We held off the Finns and killed that penalty, too. But with under six minutes remaining, the referee called a third penalty: roughing on Phil Verchota. Phil got to the box and threw a glove down onto the bench, pissed. How many penalties were we going to have to kill off? Off the face-off, we gained control of the puck, Kenny Morrow iced it, and Steve Christoff took off after it. He was flying into the Finnish zone. One second he was at the blue line, the next he was all over the Finnish defenseman behind the net. Steve bodied that player off the puck, fended off a second Finn, and threaded a pass to Mark Johnson, who was cruising toward the Finnish goal. Mark took the pass and backhanded the puck at Valtonen. The veteran goalie stopped the shot with his right pad, but Mark pounced on the rebound and slammed it in.

Again the building erupted. Herb, wearing a plaid jacket for this game, threw his arms into the air. All of us, for the last time, hopped the boards and mobbed Magic. Three minutes and thirty-five seconds were left, and we had a two-goal lead.

Everyone in the building was standing. They sensed what was about to happen. With sixty-one seconds left, we lined up for a face-off. The puck came to me near the red line, and I passed it back to Billy Baker. He fired into the Finnish zone, and Mark Pavelich flew in after it. Pav took the puck away from a Finnish defenseman in the corner and slid the puck to the middle of the ice, between the face-off circles—right where I was heading. I hammered it. It was one of the hardest slap shots I've ever taken, and the puck got past Valtonen. But it pinged off the right post, slid right across the goal mouth, hit the other post—and caromed out. I'd remember that.

Seven seconds left. Another face-off. The crowd was roaring now, waiting to count down the final seconds. I looked over at the bench, and guys were hugging and shouting. Brots and Christoff banged their sticks on the boards. Bah Harrington stood on the bench, arms and stick in the air. The puck dropped, and a Finn fired it the length of the ice as the crowd chanted, "Four . . . three . . . two . . ." On television, Al Michaels made another memorable call: "This impossible dream comes true!"

Then it was deafening. Bill Baker flung his stick, javelin style, over the glass. Buzzy whipped his into the corner. I tossed mine over the glass. I didn't know it, but my cousin Tony's football buddy, one of the guys in the Winnebago, wrestled it away from a fan. Weeks later I was surprised when the stick turned up at my house, shortened a few inches by my brother.

Eric Strobel got to Jim Craig first, then Buzzy, Bobby Suter, Silky, and the rest of the mob. The celebration was actually less delirious than the one after the Soviet game. I was overjoyed that we had beaten Finland, but I had expected us to win. It wasn't a surprise to me. We lingered on the ice after the hand-shake line, hugging each other and waving to our families in the stands. That's when Jimmy, in that famous scene, draped an American flag around his shoulders and looked into the stands to find his father, Don. Eventually Olympic officials made us leave the ice. There was another game to be played, Sweden against Russia, to decide who would get silver and who would get bronze.

Vice President Walter Mondale came into the locker room and congratulated us. A phone was brought in, and Herb took another call from Jimmy Carter. The president said he and the cabinet had the TV on in the Oval Office and couldn't get any business done because everyone wanted to watch the game. Then the president of the United States asked to speak to the captain.

"Hello, Mr. President," I said.

"Tell your whole team how much I love the team. They played like true champions. We're so proud of you, and I'm looking forward to seeing you all tomorrow." He wished me good luck, and I replied, "Good luck to you, too."

Vice President Mondale took the phone for a moment, then turned to Jim Craig. "The president wants to know what you'd like for dinner." Jimmy told him, "Two lobsters, sir. Oysters. The kind of seafood you get back home." A New Englander to the end.

The players who weren't part of the celebration were OC and Mark Pavelich. They had been randomly selected to take the drug tests after the game and had had to report to a room down the hall. For the test, you have to pee into a cup, but after playing, you're dehydrated. So there was an assortment of things to drink, including Kirin, a Japanese beer—a fine selection if you're in the mood to celebrate winning a gold medal. OC and Pav started pounding down one after another.

Back at my house on Bowdoin Street, those present counted down the final seconds, too. My sisters, aunts, cousins, and uncles—twenty-one in all—were glued to the TV in my living room. A few reporters had come over to watch the game with my family. One of them noticed a newspaper story tacked to the wall. It was the one with the headline "Mike Eruzione— He's Pete Rose on Skates." My mother was so proud of that one. She still had it in her kitchen six years later.

Donna was standing in front of the house on the lawn when a woman TV reporter approached. "You're the girlfriend, right?" A cameraman quickly snapped on his light, and the reporter shoved a microphone at Donna. "What's the first thing you're going to do when you see your boyfriend?"

"I can't say that on TV!" she blurted out. All these years later, and she still can't believe she said that.

Everyone watching on TV at my house saw me toss my stick into the stands. Nanci opened bottles of champagne and filled plastic cups for Jeannie, Nettie, Cousin Gail, Cousin Richie, Connie, Auntie Ann, Auntie AT. Outside, about two hundred people were singing "God Bless America" and chanting "USA! USA!" It was kind of funny. When I was a kid, the neighbors would call the cops on us because of the noise. Now everyone was part of the noise.

When they put me on the phone with Jimmy Carter, the house erupted again. My Auntie AT could hardly believe what she was seeing, and then she said one of the sweetest things:

"Who would ever dream—Michael talking to the president. It'll never come down for us. It'll never get out of this house. This thing will always be here with us." I'm sure she didn't realize how true it would turn out to be.

Some of the people outside just walked into my house, grabbed a beer, sat down in the living room, and watched TV with my sisters and cousins, like a big party, an open house. One guy helped himself to some of the ravioli on the stove. Nanci was coming down the stairs when she noticed an elderly couple walking up. "Do we know you?" she asked.

They said their names were Tom and Mary, and they had watched the game in Kenmore Square and just had to come by and say hello. It had taken them an hour and a half to get there by subway and bus, so Nanci welcomed them in and Connie poured them some wine. They sat in the kitchen talking for a while, and then they went upstairs to Uncle Tony's and had coffee and cake with him. Around eleven that night, somebody gave them a lift back home.

Back in the locker room in Lake Placid, we left all our gear on—jerseys, pants, shin guards, everything—and only took off our skates and put on shoes. Then Herb led us across the street to the high school auditorium. For this press conference, he brought the whole team. By then, a few of the guys had dipped into the champagne that had been waiting for us for the last two days. When we walked in, the media applauded. The guys slumped into chairs on the stage, hair still wet from sweat, some still swigging champagne. For the first time in six months, all of us could finally let go. I took a seat at the table. Looking back at us were what looked like a thousand reporters with notebooks and pens, microphones and cameras. Herb, still in his plaid jacket and tie, took the microphone. He admitted he'd kicked our butts along the way. "You're watching a group of people who startled the athletic world— not the hockey world, the athletic world," he said. "I love this team." Loved this team? That was the first time we had ever heard that.

Somebody asked if there was one word to describe our victory. "I guess we're all a bunch of big doolies now," I answered. Laughter. What's a doolie? they wanted to know. "Phil Verchota will explain what a doolie is," I said. Phil stepped forward from the back of the stage. He had made up the word. "A doolie is a big wheel, a big gun," he said. "I scored a goal today, so I'm a big doolie." Another round of laughter.

Another reporter wanted to know if we wanted to stay together as a team. Jimmy answered that one: "This is it. We couldn't stand each other another week."

Of course, it wasn't true. I tried to explain what we were: "We came together six months ago from all different parts of the United States, all different kinds of backgrounds, and all kinds of beliefs. We gelled into a team, and I don't think there's a coach or anybody in the country right now who can say they've experienced the kind of thing we have here. We are twenty guys playing on the US Olympic hockey team. We are not from Boston or Minnesota. We're a US team. A family."

Hearing that, Silky couldn't help himself. "Yeah," he yelled from the back. "But there are a lot of guys who wished they could say they were from Boston."

Jimmy got a lot of questions about the Finland game, the Russian game. He gave a lot of credit to the guys in front of him and the defense we had played. Then he went on to something else: "I want to say something about a man here who never played in these Olympics and deserves a gold medal as much as all of us put together." Steve Janaszak was the only player out of the eight teams in the hockey competition who had not seen a minute of action. "If ever a guy who didn't play in a game deserves a gold medal, it's Steve," Jimmy said. "He pushed me for six months. He busted his butt even though he knew he wouldn't play. He's somebody I really love. I want to thank him publicly for making me a better person and a better player." Janny, eyes welling up, walked across the stage and threw his arms around Jimmy.

Then there was a noise from the back of the auditorium—a door opening. OC, his drug testing completed, swaggered and staggered down the aisle. In his right hand was the seventh or eighth bottle of beer. The guys started laughing and clapping at his arrival. "OC! Jack O'Callahan! He's here!" OC hopped up onto the stage, then hopped up onto the table and, standing tall, arms in the air, saluted us and the media with his beer.

A foreign reporter wanted to know where Charlestown is. "Charlestown?" OC said, "Charlestown is in the shadow of Bunker Hill." Then he added, "Americans won at Bunker Hill, and Americans won at Lake Placid!"

Another reporter pointed out that, well, actually, the Americans lost the Battle of Bunker Hill. "I don't want to hear that! What do you think there's a monument there for? Right in front of my house. We won, I tell you we won!" After that, OC lay down on the table on his side, his hand propping up his head.

The next day, newspapers all across the country reported Jack's comments. The US hockey team's wiseass defenseman who had grown up at the foot of Bunker Hill didn't know who had won the famous battle there. At least that's how it was portrayed.

"What are your favorite Brooksisms?" someone asked. Bah went into his Herb imitation: "We were damned if we did and damned if we didn't. We went to the well again, and the water was colder and the water was deeper. We reloaded and went up to the tiger and spit in his eye, then we shot him. Fool me once, shame on you; fool me twice, shame on me. It's a good example of why we won the game. And for lack of a better phrase, that sums it up!" Everybody in the place doubled over in laughter.

When the questions started winding down, we all had to face some reality. The next day, we would visit the president at the White House, and then it would be time to go our separate ways. It was over. This incredible moment in time was about to come to an end. "Who knows if I'll ever see Harrington or Christian or any of them again," I said. I paused a second. "On the other hand, that may be a good thing." Laughter again.

There are so many good memories I have of that team, and it's so hard to describe to anyone what it was like being part of that special group. That press conference was probably the best public example of what it was like. It showed the world who we were and what we were.

Around Lake Placid, word had gotten out that the hockey medal ceremony was going to be later that afternoon. Back then, the medal ceremonies were an open event, no tickets needed. It would be our last appearance in the Fieldhouse. We walked out onto the ice and lined up on the blue line. The jerseys and pads were gone, replaced by our light blue warm-up suits. The

Russians had defeated the Swedes 9–2 to take the silver. They were still in their uniforms. The stands were as packed as they had been earlier that morning for the game against Finland. People were cheering, singing, waving flags. My mother and father, Vinny, Cousin Tony, Coach DeFelice, and other friends were in the corner of the arena, to the left of the giant flags of the medal-winning nations. The Swedish players were called up one by one to receive their bronze medal. Then the Russians were awarded the silver.

Finally it was our turn. We accepted ours in the same order in which we had always marched out to the ice. Jimmy went first. He stepped up onto the platform, bowed down. The president of the International Olympic Committee, Lord Killanin, draped a gold medal around Jimmy's neck. He waved to the cheering crowd, stepped down, paused to kiss his medal—and it slipped off the ribbon and clattered onto the ice. Didn't matter. Nothing could wipe the smile from his face. Bah, as usual, was next, and the other guys followed. Then it was my turn. I stepped up onto the five-sided platform, accepted my medal, and turned to face the three flags, the American flag in the middle. On my right was the Swedish captain; on the left, the Soviet captain, Boris Mikhailov. I put my hand over my heart, the music started, and I sang our national anthem out loud. The other nineteen guys sang on the blue line, arms around each other and gold medals around their necks. I looked up, and I could hardly believe what I was seeing: the American flag, the Stars and Stripes, was rising to the rafters, just a little higher than the Soviet flag and higher still than the Swedish flag.

ABC's Al Michaels had become famous around the country for his words in the final seconds of the Russian game: "Do you believe in miracles? Yes!" He was high up in the Field-house watching, but he wasn't covering the ceremony. It was probably a good thing. Years later he told me he had been wiping tears from his eyes the whole time. In the stands, Jeep looked at my football coach, and Deefa had tears rolling down his face. Then Jeep looked at my Uncle Tony, and he was crying, too. Finally, he looked at my mother, and she was wiping her eyes. At that point, Jeep couldn't hold back anymore, and he started crying, too.

When "The Star-Spangled Banner" came to an end, the crowd cheered, as loudly as in the Soviet game, as loudly as in the Finland game. I turned to where my family and friends were in the stands and punched a fist into the air to salute them. Then I turned back to my teammates. I was looking at them and they were looking at me, and nobody told us what to do. So I waved to them. "Come up on the stage! Come on!" I shouted. Bah and OC got there first, then Buzzy, Billy, Neal, Rammer, and the rest. Somehow all twenty of us squeezed onto the little platform, all of us with our medals, all together.

Al Michaels always says that was one of the most incredible sights of the Lake Placid Games. "That was one of the great, unexpected moments ever. How in the world did you get twenty pairs of feet on that little podium?" he told me once. "Maybe that was a miracle in itself. It just looked like the team had become so close that they could all fit together in this little space. I'll never forget that as long as I live, ever."

CHAPTER 14

POSSIBILITIES I NEVER IMAGINED

President Carter sent a plane to fly all 150 Olympians to Washington, and when I walked down the stairs from the plane to the tarmac, I couldn't believe it. A thousand people were screaming and cheering. They were lined up behind a small fence, waving American flags, signs, and posters. As soon as some of us appeared with our medals, the crowd started singing the national anthem. They called for autographs and reached out for handshakes. We had been way up in the Adirondacks. I hadn't known that people all across the country were watching. In 1980, hockey was played mainly in Minnesota, Michigan, and Massachusetts. But suddenly the whole country had become crazy for hockey and crazy for us.

All along the route to the White House it was the same—crowds lining up along the streets, cheering, waving flags, shouting "We're number one!" I saw one guy in the crowd holding a pole in the air, and hanging from it was a dummy wearing a hockey helmet and a red Soviet jersey—hanging a Russian hockey player in effigy. As we stepped off the bus at the White House, a Marine Corps band played "America the Beautiful" and "The Stars and Stripes Forever." Eric Heiden led us athletes up the White House stairs to the porch over-looking the South Lawn. When I got to the top, I shook Pres-ident Carter's hand and met Rosalynn Carter, the first lady. Then I looked out at the plush, green South Lawn. I couldn't help but think what it would be like to be out there with a pitching wedge and a bucket of golf balls.

The rest of the visit was a blur. They kept moving me from place to place to meet congressmen and senators and officials who wanted to have their pictures taken with the captain of the hockey team. It was a great honor to be in the White House. Whether you like the president or don't like the president, it's a thrill because of what the White House stands for. Then, be-fore I knew it, it was time for all of us to leave. OC, Silky, and I were flying to Boston. Jim Craig was headed to New York to be on TV the next day. Mark Johnson and Bobby Suter were headed back to Wisconsin. Mark was supposed to sign with the Pittsburgh Penguins. Kenny Morrow was going to make a quick stop at home in Michigan and then join the Islanders. The Minnesota guys were all taking a flight to Minneapolis.

I hugged the guys and shook hands and said good luck. Magic was getting married in the summer, so we knew we'd have a reunion in a couple of months. Then we were in the cab and on the plane. When Jack and Dave and I took our seats in first class, the other passengers clapped and cheered "USA! USA!" It seemed just a week since we had been in Norway skating Herbies in the dark. Only a week before, we had been celebrating beating the Czechs and pumped about maybe, pos-sibly winning a medal. And then we had beat the Soviets. And now here we were with gold medals. How had it all happened so fast?

I looked over at Silky, and his eyes were welling up. "Silky, what's wrong?" I asked.

He looked down for a second and then said quietly, "It's over." He turned to me and said it again. "It's over."

We had been together every day for six months. We had gone through so much, experienced so much as a team, and had achieved something incredible. None of us, no matter where we played or what we did, would ever play on a team like this again. And now it really was over. There would be no practice the next day, no more games. There would be no more joking around in the locker room. No more bitching about Herb. I loved these guys like brothers. Jim Craig had said it best when we were back at the White House. A reporter had asked about the team breaking up, and he had replied, "We were born in September, and we died last night."

That unbelievable day wasn't over, though. In first class, we could have anything we wanted. I ordered a Bloody Mary and the three of us made a toast: "To the team!" The other passengers cheered and joined in. When we landed at Logan Airport, hundreds and hundreds of people were waiting at the terminal. As soon as we came out of the jetway, they started screaming "USA! USA! USA!" A bunch of kids ran toward us. State troopers tried to hold them back. A couple women were holding babies in the air. A boy reached for my jacket and ran back into the crowd, shouting, "I touched him! I touched Mike!" Reporters and photographers crowded around. Flashbulbs were going off right and left. It was like we were the Beatles. We were rock stars.

Three limousines were waiting to take each of us home, escorted by police motorcades. Mine snaked through East Boston and turned right on Saratoga Street toward one of the two routes into Winthrop—the Belle Isle Bridge. I think half the town was waiting on the bridge, thousands of people. A gold Rolls-Royce was waiting for me. Inside the car were my parents. Jeep was talking to a reporter, still enjoying his moment of fame. There were flags everywhere, hundreds and hundreds of them. A big banner was stretched between light poles on Main Street. "Welcome Home Mighty Mike," it said. Winthrop policemen were lined up, holding hockey sticks in the air. The high school band, cheerleaders, and hockey players in their Winthrop jerseys were waiting to lead a parade to the Elks Club marina.

I got into the Rolls and stood up through the sunroof, and all of a sudden the crowd rushed the car. They banged on the windows with their hands, rocked the car, leaned across the fenders and doors. I'd never imagined I'd get this kind of reception over winning a couple hockey games. "I'm not a hero!" I shouted over the crowd. "I haven't changed!" Surrounded, we couldn't move, and the Rolls was getting trashed, people's zippers and buttons scratching the paint. I saw one lady shouting. At first I thought she was asking for an autograph, but then I heard her over the din. "The car's on my foot!" The police called for an ambulance for her and a cruiser to take me to the marina and to get people away from the Rolls.

I love Winthrop. I can't imagine a better place to grow up in. I was always proud to play for Winthrop High, to wear our navy-blue-and-gold jerseys. I've always felt the town has given me so much. And on that day, with that reception, I felt like Winthrop loved me, too.

As we moved through the streets, people were standing on roofs, leaning out of apartment windows, waving and shouting. More than five hundred people were so jammed inside the Elks Club that nobody could move. I was supposed to get up and say a few words, but the crowd just kept cheering "USA! USA!" Some of the cheerleaders pushed their way to the front and asked me to give them a kiss. One of the girls shouted, "Come on, just a little one!"

That kind of thing wasn't going on just in Winthrop. It was the same in Minnesota—for Pav in Eleveth, for Bah in Virginia, for Buzzy in Babbitt, Davey Christian in Warroad. In Michigan, Kenny Morrow was greeted by a cheering mob in Davidson, and it was the same for Mark Wells in St. Clair Shores. Magic and Bobby Suter were hailed in Wisconsin. Charlestown went nuts when OC arrived. Scituate had a big parade for Silky.

When I finally got to go home, the police had Bowdoin Street cordoned off to keep crowds and cars away from my house. Even so, a big group of people was clapping and shouting when I arrived, and they kept calling for me even after I went into the house. So I went out onto the second-floor porch. I felt like the pope, up high, talking to my flock below. I thanked all of them for their support and explained that I needed to take some time with my family and unwind for a while. It had been a long, exhausting day, and it still wasn't over. NBC wanted me on the *Today* show in the morning. At about 10:00 p.m., a couple policemen sneaked me out and took me back to Logan. On the plane, I got cheers again. The captain let me sit in the cockpit jump seat for takeoff and landing. When we got to LaGuardia, he handed me the flight data sheet. He had signed it. His name was Captain Robert

Frister. I would have given him my autograph, but he didn't ask for one.

The phone was ringing off the hook. People from all over—Philadelphia, West Virginia, Indiana—were calling even before I got home. "I know he isn't home, but please thank him for us," people said. There were stacks of letters. Five of them were marriage proposals. Companies were calling asking me to do speeches and appearances. Reporters called nonstop for interviews. IBM wanted me to go to Florida to speak at a meeting of its top salespeople. Bob Mathias, the winner of two gold medals in the decathlon, was the main speaker. I would have to speak for only eight minutes, and for that the company was going to pay me $3,000. In Toledo, I'd had to play eighty games and make sure no one took my head off to make that much money. Now I could make $3,000 just for saying a few words at a sales meeting? Sure, I'll do that.

IBM flew me to Florida first class and put me up in the Fontainebleau in Miami. This was a new life. I'd never stayed in a five-star hotel. The company asked if I wanted to do anything in Florida. IBM had taken some customers and VIPs out deep-sea fishing. I said that sounded like fun. The next thing I knew, it had chartered a whole boat—just for me. I called a high school football friend who was living in Florida, and we rounded up a group and had the boat all to ourselves. A whole day fishing for free. When it came time to do my speech, I walked out onto a stage in a banquet room, and everyone in the crowd stood up and started chanting "USA! USA!" just like in Lake Placid. There was a clock at the edge of the stage to tell me when my eight minutes was up. The audience kept cheering and cheering, and the clock kept counting down. Six minutes, five minutes. Just cheering and cheering. When they finally sat down, I had a minute left. "Ladies and gentlemen," I said, "a week ago, my teammates and I did something incredible, something no one thought we could accomplish. Thank you very much." And that was it. Easiest $3,000 I ever made. The funny thing is that IBM loved it and said it had four more meetings in Florida and five in San Francisco, and it wanted me to speak at those, too. For ten speeches, I was going to make $30,000—more money than my father had ever made in one year.

When I got back to Winthrop, a gleaming gold Mazda RX-7 was parked in front of my house, brand new. I went upstairs and found my mother sitting in the kitchen. "Ma, whose car is that?"

"You're not going to believe it," she said, "but it's yours." For a second, I thought maybe she'd been dipping into the homemade wine. I had never owned a new car in my life. "I'm telling you," she went on. "This guy from some dealership came by and said he wants you to have the car and dropped off the keys." She was right, and it had a special red, white, and blue license plate: "USA 21."

The next day, the governor of Massachusetts, Edward King, invited me, Jimmy, and Silky to the State House on Beacon Hill. OC couldn't make it; he was in Chicago negotiating with the Blackhawks. Our families were invited, too. My mother, Vinny, and my sisters were excited. My whole family was going to meet the governor. Except Jeep. He said he couldn't go; he said he couldn't take a day off work. My sister Nanci called the governor's office and got it all arranged: he'd get a paid day off at the sewage plant to go visit the State House. Then Jeep still said he couldn't go, and here was the real reason: there was a horse running at Suffolk Downs. Its name: Famous Father.

"I have to play that horse!" Jeep explained. "I'm the famous father!" Nanci and my mother dug their heels in and told him no way, you have to go.

At the State House, Jimmy, Silky, and I were supposed to stand at the end of a receiving line, like at a wedding. First the governor and other state politicians came through and shook our hands, followed by anyone, members of the public, who wanted to see the gold medalists. By then, Silky's voice was raspy from the nonstop talking and interviews he had done, and my right wrist was sore and swollen from shaking so many hands. Hundreds of people, mostly kids, showed up, and instead of waiting in line, they rushed at the three of us as soon as we appeared. I signed a picture for one girl, and she ran away shouting, "I can't stand it! I can't stand it! I can't stand it!" I never found out what it was she couldn't stand.

Because of the crowd, we had to duck into Governor King's suite and continue the reception there. That's when my father approached the governor and asked if there was a phone he could use.

"Certainly. There's one in my office," Governor King said.

After a while, my mother and Nanci and I started to wonder what was keeping Jeep. Nanci found him in the office, behind the governor's desk. Putting a hand over the receiver, he explained, "Famous Father, I'm playing Famous Father."

My family got invited to the State House, and my father used the governor's phone to call his bookie. That was Jeep.

Jim Craig was signed by the Atlanta Flames right away. Six days after winning the gold medal, he won his debut game in the NHL. That night the Flames' arena, the Omni, was sold out. Coca-Cola hired him for a TV commercial. Everyone wanted to see the golden goalie. Mark Johnson went to the Pittsburgh Penguins, and Steve Janaszak was picked up by the Minnesota North Stars. Mike Ramsey and Rob McClanahan signed with the Buffalo Sabres. Jack O'Callahan and Bill Baker signed contracts and went to the minors. The Winnipeg Jets got Dave Christian and moved him to forward, his natural position. In his first game, on his first shift, he scored. It took him just seven seconds to get his first NHL goal. The Hartford Whalers still owned my rights from back when they had been in the WHL and drafted me when I was at Boston University. Their general manager wanted to sign me to a minor-league contract, have me start with their AHL team, and then see if I could work my way up.

Every day, reporters called my house and asked what I was going to do. I believed I could play in the NHL. I wouldn't have been a big star, and I wouldn't have had a ten-year career. But I could have been a three- or four-year guy, a good third-line or fourth-line player, a good guy in the locker room, a good guy in the community. My father would have been absolutely over the moon to see me in the NHL. Some of the guys from the Olympic team were signing for good money—at that time, top rookies in the NHL were getting salaries of $85,000 a year, with signing bonuses of $50,000. I had other opportunities. I was going to make $30,000 just for doing some speeches for IBM. I was hired to do color commentary on Stanley Cup broadcasts. There were possibilities I'd never imagined.

One person who had mixed feelings about all of it was Donna. She was happy for me to have success and the new opportunities. But she had waited for me when I was going to BU. She had waited when I went to Toledo. She had waited while I played for the Olympic team. Now she knew she'd have to wait some more.

The Whalers eventually made a formal offer, and I talked with Bob Murray, my agent, and put a lot of thought into it. After beating the Russians, beating Finland, and winning a gold medal, I decided I wanted to be remembered as Mike Eruzione, captain of the 1980 gold medal–winning US Olympic hockey team. When it came down to it, I felt I didn't need an NHL career. Winning the gold medal had been the ultimate. Nothing could top that. Why not go out on top?

ABC, which had broadcast the Olympics, invited me onto *Wide World of Sports* on a Saturday to reveal what my plans were. My life would be just fine without an NHL career, I said. I'd been offered a college coaching job—with Jack Parker. I'd been a hard worker all my life. If I had to, I could get a job. "I can paint houses or bridges," I said. "I will always be able to go into a bar with that gold medal and tell stories."

Everything was happening so fast. I was getting twenty or thirty letters a day, and I got Donna to help me deal with them. Offers were coming in from all kinds of companies. A couple executives from Prince Spaghetti came to the house to talk to me about endorsing a new product they had called Superoni. Jeep listened to the conversation and decided to suggest a slogan: "Mike Eruzione, he eats-a Superoni." Jeep thought it was brilliant. My mother and everyone else in the house rolled their eyes.

"Dad," I kidded him, "if you don't watch out, you're going to make me famous."

Jeep had become famous himself, at least in East Boston. People would come into Santarpio's just to see the father of the guy who had scored the winning goal against the Russians. I was no longer Jeep's kid; Jeep had become known as "Mike's father." He had pictures of me printed and gave them to anyone who came into Santarpio's to meet Mike Eruzione's father. He signed them "Eugene Eruzione, Famous Father."

Within a few weeks, I had engagements booked all the way through Christmas. I would leave for five days, come back for two, go back out on the road for a week. Usually I'd take my gold medal with me, because everybody always wanted to see it. When I was home, I kept it in a safe place—in Jeannie's lingerie drawer.

Every time I walked through an airport, strangers stopped me, thanked me. It was a little scary because everybody knew who I was but I didn't know them. One person would stop me, and then two more would come over and more after that. I was hired to be a technical adviser for a TV movie called *Miracle on Ice*. I had to spend a lot of time in Los Angeles, so I got an apartment in Venice Beach. It wasn't exactly the greatest movie. None of the actors could even skate. It's pretty hard carrying yourself as a hockey player if you've never played hockey. For some on-ice scenes, I had to push the actor playing me into the shot. One time the actor playing Jim Craig tried to curl his hair to look more like Jimmy, but he overdid it and burned his hair. They put a ball cap on him to cover it up. I quickly realized that the producers didn't need me on the set very much, and I started enjoying being out and about in Los

Angeles. A producer suggested I try acting. I didn't follow up on that. One day I made a brief appearance on a game show, *Hollywood Squares*. For sitting there for a couple minutes, I was given $1,000 in gifts. One was a dishwasher. I gave that to my mother. It was the first dishwasher she'd ever had.

My whole life, I'd never had money to spend. Hadn't had a quarter for the toll to Boston. Now, suddenly, I had money. I wasn't going to become a millionaire, but for the first time in my life, in my father's life, in my mother's life, we could afford to live a little. I wanted to buy my father a car. "Just get me a set of tires and replace the fan belt," Jeep said. I wanted to buy my brother a car. My mother said absolutely not. I did get my parents a new living room set and sent my mother to Puerto Rico for a vacation. Jeep didn't go—his fear of flying.

My sister Nanci thought it would be a good idea to put some of the money I was earning into a house. It seemed like a good idea. I found a three-family house in Winthrop not far from my parents. Nanci joked about it, recalling the days when the neighbors had called the cops on us: "Oh, the neighbors will love it—the Eruziones are spreading out, taking over the neighborhood."

Once I bought the house, the trick was getting permission to live in it. In my family, you weren't allowed to move out until you got married. That was my mother's rule. So Nanci and Connie told my mother I would have to live in the house in order to be able to reap the tax benefits. Of course, it wasn't true, but my mother didn't know that. So I was allowed to move into my house.

The offers to do speaking engagements just kept coming, and I kept doing the ones I could fit in. But I knew, and Bob Murray knew, that there would be an end someday. At some point, it would all fade away. People would move on to other things. The gold medal would be forgotten. Whenever the money stopped, I'd get a job and go to work. In ten years, I figured, I'd be living a quiet life in Winthrop, coaching hockey probably. That's where I'll end up, I thought. Because nothing lasts forever.

CHAPTER 15

"THREE INCHES TO THE LEFT"

In the weeks and months after our triumph in Lake Placid, we all went our separate ways. Ken Morrow joined the New York Islanders, and three months after winning the gold medal, he won the Stanley Cup. Though a dozen guys were in the NHL, Bah Harrington and Buzz Schneider decided to play in Switzerland. Phil Verchota signed with a Finnish club. Herb spent a year coaching a Swiss club team in Davos. For a few years, weddings brought us together in the summer, but as the years went by, the time between our gatherings grew. We had been together for the most searing six months of our lives and accomplished something that would stay with each of us forever. But now we were on our own, pursuing separate paths in life.

For me, the Olympics had opened up opportunities I had never imagined. I was hired to do color commentary on Rangers games for Madison Square Garden Network. I lived in Winthrop, and on game days I took a shuttle to New York, called the game, and then caught the last flight back to Boston. It was fun and kept me in the game. The Rangers captain was Phil Esposito. I would tease him about what he had said to me at that training camp back in 1977. Phil always had a limo waiting to take him home after the game. If I was ever tight on time for catching the last flight back to Boston, he would let me take his car to the airport while he was showering. By the time he was done, the driver was back in Manhattan, waiting for him.

Herb Brooks became the Rangers' coach in 1981. He would call me into his office in Madison Square Garden to talk, and it was just like when we had been with the Olympic team. It was Herb talking about hockey, his schemes, players, concepts, while I nodded and listened. I'd leave his office and wonder, "What did we just talk about?"

I never really got to know Herb that well, even after the Olympics. He was a very intense person, but he didn't show you his emotions or his thoughts. One time he had a reunion for the players' parents at his place on a lake in Minnesota. A lot of the guys were still playing hockey and didn't make it, but I did. At one point, Herb and some of the wives and parents were out on the water on paddleboats. He was laughing and smiling, animated, joking around. I couldn't believe what I was seeing. I stood on the shore wondering, Who is that guy? Where did he come from? I had never seen Herb relaxed and having fun.

While we had been on the Olympic team, he had never celebrated with us when we won. He had never told us we played well. I'd always thought he considered me a good player, but I was never really sure. There has always been a question of whether the players actually voted me to be captain or Herb just picked me. It was always hard to understand how I had gotten enough votes, with all the Minnesota guys on the team. Years after the Olympics, Craig Patrick told me what he knew about it. Herb asked Craig at one point if he thought I'd make a good captain, and then sought his opinion on related question: Should Herb let the team vote for the captain, or should he just name someone? Eventually, Herb told Craig he would leave it to the team to choose, saying, "The team will vote, but I'm doing the counting." It wouldn't be right to go around asking all my teammates who they voted for. But I did ask Jack O'Callahan. He said he couldn't remember who he voted for, but it definitely wasn't me—because he didn't think I was going to make the team. So I know I became captain without Jack's vote. Did Herb just pick me to be captain? Maybe, maybe not. Craig never saw the vote and never asked Herb what the vote was. I did ask Craig if he thought the votes went in my favor, and he said they most likely did. It really doesn't matter. We won.

I am not a romantic guy.

Of course, I have feelings and emotions like everybody else, and I love Donna more than anything. She's always believed in me and always supported me. She means the world to me and is my best friend. I don't know what I'd do without her. She's a fabulous wife and a fabulous mother. I feel so lucky to have her.

But I am not a romantic guy.

It was three days before Christmas in 1981. By then we had been dating for nine years. I was twenty-seven. Donna was twenty-five.

"I haven't gotten you anything for Christmas," I said. "What do you want?"

She just looked at me and stared. She didn't have to put it into words.

"Okay," I said. "Pick it out."

Donna found one she liked, wrapped it herself, and put the box under the tree. On Christmas Day she opened it, and we were engaged. She slipped it onto her finger, and I got to see her engagement ring for the first time.

We were married the following August. All of the guys on the Olympic team, fifteen or twenty BU guys, some of my teammates from Toledo, plus all of my own family and cousins attended—more than 500 in all. We had a party at the Bowdoin Street house with two hundred lobsters chilled in a rowboat filled with ice in the backyard; that was the day before the wedding. At the reception, my father spotted Jack Parker and decided he'd finally confront my coach about something that still bothered him.

"Why did you break up my Michael and my Ricky?" he asked Jack. Jeep had never forgiven Jack for breaking up me and Ricky during our senior season.

Jack came up with a story on the spot. "Jeep, I've got to tell you something," he said. "Ricky said he didn't want to play with Mike anymore. It wasn't me. It was Ricky. Sorry, Jeep."

My father walked away with his mouth open. Jack came over to me and Ricky, and all three of us had a good laugh.

Donna gave birth to our daughter, LeighAnn, in 1983. Michael arrived a year later and Paul in 1988. To my mother's delight, we bought a new house that was two doors away from the house I'd grown up in. I could stand in my backyard and talk to her or my father on the back porch.

As the kids grew, I was away from my family a lot. Companies, charities, convention organizers, youth sports groups—they all wanted to hear about the "Miracle on Ice." A lot of the other guys on the team weren't as available to tell the story because they were still playing hockey. So a lot of speaking requests came to me, thirty or forty a year. I'd be gone for a week for a golf tournament, back for a few days, and then back on the road.

"When are you going to stay put?" my father would ask. "When are you going to get a real job?"

It was hard on Donna, having the three kids on her own so much. But I was trying to provide for my family. That's how it was in my house growing up. Fathers weren't home a lot. They worked. I had had a modest life growing up in Winthrop, and now I had access to a different world of VIPs and celebrities. I played golf with Dan Marino, Charles Barkley, Mario Lemieux, John Elway, Michael Jordan, singers, actors, comedians. I threw out the first pitch at Yankee Stadium, Fenway Park, and Wrigley Field. I introduced Ronald Reagan at a banquet. Frank Sinatra invited me and Donna to his house, and Tony Bennett was there. At another banquet, Donna and I were seated with Muhammad Ali. He saw me and pointed. "Eruzione! I want you! I want you!" The Greatest of All Time knew who I was. One time we were invited to stay at the Kennedy compound in Hyannis for a tennis tournament. Ted Kennedy took us sailing. I remember chasing LeighAnn around the lawn—the same lawn where JFK and his family used to play touch football.

Even *GQ* magazine did a story about me. *GQ?* I had never even read the magazine. It sent a photographer to Winthrop and brought a hairstylist, and every time the wind blew, the guy rushed over to fix my hair. They did some pictures of me in the house, sitting in a chair with my shirt off and my gold medal around my neck. It was bizarre, but that's what they wanted.

At one point I appeared in a promotional video for Boston University. The producer asked if the school could do anything for me in return.

"Yeah," I said, "give me my degree." Fifteen years after graduating, I finally got my degree.

All the shuttling to New York for Rangers games became a grind. Every time I flew back and landed in Boston, I heaved a sigh of relief. I'd cross into Winthrop over the Belle Isle Bridge, and it felt like a big iron gate was closing behind me. I was safe. I was home. I could be Mike. Not Mike Eruzione, gold medalist. Just Mike. I could put on a beat-up pair of jeans and meet friends for lunch or hang out at the golf club. I could ride my bike to the beach. I could go anywhere in town—and no one would stop me to talk about 1980. The only times I heard about the Olympics were when my Winthrop friends wanted to bust my chops. If I wore a jacket with Olympic rings, they'd say, "You're just wearing that so people will ask you about the gold medal." Anytime I mentioned some trip to Hawaii or playing golf with a celebrity, they'd give me grief about my goal against the Russians: "Mike, three inches to the left, and you'd be painting bridges."

Doing Rangers games enabled me to run into OC, Ken Morrow, Magic, Mark Pavelich, Dave Christian, and a few other guys when they were playing in New York. But when Madison Square Garden Network wanted me to move to New York, I said no, and it let me go. I started seeing the guys even less. I wasn't having an NHL career like some of my teammates, so I had to find ways to earn a living. ABC had me do Olympic broadcasts every four years. Public speaking became a second profession. Eventually I returned to Boston University to work for the school in development.

When I was on the road, I was stopped by people all the time—in hotels, restaurants, airports, golf courses. And the odd thing was, they usually didn't want to hear me talk about Lake Placid. Instead, they wanted to tell me *their* story—where they had been, who they had been with, and what they had been doing when they watched the game or heard the news. Every story starts the same way: "The night we beat the Russians . . ." Not *you* but *we*. Sometimes I kid people and say, "We? I didn't know you were on the team."

Some people had been driving and honked their horns like crazy. Other people had stopped and pulled over, found other people had done the same, and strangers started hugging each other. I've met people who were at Radio City Music Hall to see *Snow White and the Seven Dwarfs* when the announcement was made that we had beaten Finland for the gold medal. The audience erupted in cheers and sang "The Star-Spangled Banner." A lot of people tear up recalling watching the game with their father or grandfather. More than a few times, Vietnam War veterans have told me they had come home confused, hurt, disappointed. They had doubted our country. And they swear they began to feel proud of the United States again when we beat the Russians.

I wasn't trained as a public speaker, and nobody ever tells you how to handle yourself if suddenly people know who you are. Living in the Boston area, though, I'd seen one athlete who seemed to do it with ease. I'd watched Bobby Orr when I was growing up, and he was like a god to the people of Boston. The thing I noticed about him was that whenever he was in public, he was always so polite. He always signed autographs. He always shook people's hands. He always had a smile on his face. He always gave fans a few minutes of his time. Nobody anywhere ever had a bad word to say about Bobby Orr. I decided that if I was going to be out in public, he was the guy I wanted to be like. And why wouldn't I give anyone a moment to talk? They always smile. How can you not feel good if you give someone a few minutes to relive that joy?

The requests to speak just kept coming. Bob Murray, my agent, figured I should take most of the offers while I could because at some point it would all fade away. Surely, eventually, people would lose interest.

Since I was traveling so much, I missed a lot of my daughter's dance recitals and didn't get to see LeighAnn much when she was a cheerleader. One time she was running hurdles in a track meet and I was able to be there. During the race, the girl next to her hit a hurdle and fell hard. LeighAnn stopped to help her. People were yelling "Go! Go!" But LeighAnn saw that the girl was hurt.

"What were you doing, helping her?" I asked her after the race. "You're not supposed to help her! You're supposed to win the race!"

LeighAnn didn't see it that way. "But she fell and she was bleeding!" she yelled back. As it turned out, the girl had actually broken her arm. I took that as a sign that LeighAnn wasn't going to be a track star. I should probably have taken it as a sign of what a kindhearted, compassionate person she is.

As LeighAnn got older, having the Eruzione name brought a lot of attention that she didn't want. One time when she was seventeen, she smoked a cigarette with some friends. When she got home, Donna was already standing in the doorway with her arms folded and a look on her face. Someone had seen LeighAnn and called the house. LeighAnn would say she hated "the eyes"—people always watching her, noticing her because of her last name. She just wanted to be able to do normal adolescent things without always being under a microscope. "I am being held to a higher standard because of a man who's not even here!" she complained to her cousins. It was hard for her to understand where she stood, what her place was, with a famous last name. If a boy asked her out, she wondered if he really liked her or was just interested because her father was Mike Eruzione. She used to say she couldn't wait to turn eighteen so she could change her name.

"When I go to college, I'm leaving this stupid town and this big name behind me." Donna and I heard that a lot.

It was easier for me to relate to Michael and Paul. Both are good athletes, and I often took early flights home or arranged my schedule so I could get home to see them play. At hockey games, I usually stood away from the crowd, watching from a corner, usually with my brother, Vinny. I waited until we were in the car or at home to tell them how I thought they had played. I tried to be the opposite of my father.

Jeep went to all of their games. There was one time when Paul was pitching one evening in Little League. When my father sat down next to me in the stands, I saw he had a big clunky phone in his hand—the cordless phone from the house.

"Dad, what are you doing with that phone?" I asked.

"Every evening my buddy calls me at seven o'clock, and I don't want to miss him," he explained.

"Dad, that's not a cell phone. It only works in the house. It won't work all the way down here."

"Oh," he said, "I was wondering why I can't call nobody and nobody can call me!"

That was my father.

In high school, Michael played football and hockey, ran track, and had the potential to be a college athlete. But he separated a shoulder in football and broke his forearm in hockey. After graduating, he went to Phillips Academy in Andover, Massachusetts, for a postgraduate year, hoping to be noticed by college coaches. He was a tailback on the football team, and in the second-to-last game of the season, he got tackled from behind in an awkward way. When he got up, he limped off the field. His ankle was broken so badly that he needed surgery and pins and screws to put his leg back together. It took months for him to recover, and he was able to play only the last three hockey games of the year. Having missed so much of the year, he didn't have a lot of options for playing in college. Jack Parker gave him a shot to make the BU team, but his ankle wasn't the same. After one season with the Terriers, he gave up the idea of college athletics.

Paul was terrific at hockey and baseball and was the best athlete in the family. He once hit a ball clear out of the stadium at Winthrop High. The ball traveled about 450 feet, bounced in the street, and landed on someone's porch on the other side of the road. And it was a grand slam, too. I didn't get to see that, though. I was on the road.

When Paul did a year in prep school, he had a slight tear in his groin. He got treatment but didn't let on how much pain he was in. He had that competitor mentality: you gotta play hurt. That went on for a while until one day when he came out of the locker room before a game looking pale. "Dad, it feels like someone's kicking me in the balls," he said. The tear was worse than we'd thought. The adductor muscle was torn clear off the bone, and he needed surgery to repair it. That ended any hope he had of playing big-time college hockey. A year later, he went to Curry College, where my brother is the athletic director. Paul played one season of varsity hockey, but eventually saw it was no use. He still had some pain. The injury limited his flexibility and leg strength. Before one practice, it hit him. He packed up his gear and literally walked away from the game while his team was still on the ice.

I hardly ever had serious injuries. In four years at Boston University, I played 127 games in a row. Never missed a game. My sons weren't so lucky. If you're an athlete yourself, you can't help but want to see your children play and excel. When you see them get hurt and have their potential cut short, it's frustrating and sad. Paul went into a funk after he stopped playing. He had had so much desire to be a good athlete. That was his whole identity: being a star player, a competitor. After that injury, he had to let go of all of that. Finding a new direction was hard. He would come to me and ask, "Dad, what happened to the old Paul?" He struggled, and for a couple of years, Donna and I really worried about our son.

While the distance between me and my Olympic teammates seemed to grow, I reconnected with the place and coach who had given me a chance to play hockey.

In 1994, Jack Parker called and said he needed an assistant coach. He had once again turned the Terriers into a powerhouse. They had gone to the Frozen Four four times in five seasons and reached the championship game twice, losing both times, unfortunately. I joined the staff for the 1994–95 season, and we beat BC in the Beanpot, we won the Hockey East conference, and we reached the Frozen Four yet again. There we faced an old foe: the University of Minnesota. This time there was no brawl, and we beat them. In the championship game, we faced the University of Maine. We scored the first three goals, Maine got the next two. In the third period, we scored three more, and Jack had his second national title. It was great to see the players celebrating and hoisting the championship trophy. I felt proud, because I had played at BU, and anytime BU wins, I feel part of it. But it was still bittersweet. I still wish I had won one on the ice, not on the bench.

I coached one more season with Jack and cherish those two extra years I got to spend with him. If it hadn't been for Jack Parker, I wouldn't have the life I'm living today. He will always be my coach. Anytime I have a problem or a decision to make, Jack is the first person I call. We still get together from time to time, and when it's time to part, I tell him, "I love you, Coach."

He wasn't the only old coach I'd connect with. After I stopped doing Rangers broadcasts, I still heard from Herb every once in a while. The phone would ring, and Donna would say, "Michael, it's Herb."

I'd stop whatever I was doing and think, Uh-oh, what did I do wrong? I hope he's not going to yell at me. I was forty, forty-five years old. I had a wife and kids, a family of my own, and a mortgage, yet to me Herb was still the coach who had made us skate in the dark in Norway. But then I'd find out he was just calling to catch up. And it was the same as always—Herb would talk and I'd listen. The only thing Donna would hear was me saying, "Yeah . . . okay . . . uh-huh." I probably could have put down the phone, made a sandwich, and come back without his knowing.

Herb called one day in 1990. He said he was going to be inducted into the US Hockey Hall of Fame, and he asked me if I would do the introduction speech at the ceremony. I was floored. I had been captain of the Olympic team, but we hadn't seen each other that often since I had left broadcasting. There were guys who played for him at Minnesota. He socialized with them a lot more often than he saw me. I was honored that he asked me to do this for him. When I introduced him, I threw his own words right back at him.

"Herb," I said, "you were born to be a coach. You were meant to be here. This moment is yours."

CHAPTER 16

A BOND THAT CAN NEVER BE BROKEN

After almost two decades, events started bringing our team together more regularly.

In 1999, *Sports Illustrated* hosted a giant gala at Madison Square Garden to honor the greatest achievements in sports of the twentieth century: the top baseball player of the last 100 years, the top football player, the sportsman of the century. It was also going to name the greatest sports moment of the twentieth century. Three incredible moments were among the finalists: Bobby Thompson's home run, the "Shot Heard 'Round the World," that had won the 1951 National League pennant for the New York Giants; Mark McGwire hitting his sixty-second home run in 1998 to set a new single-season record; Muhammad Ali knocking out Sonny Liston to win the heavyweight boxing title in 1964.

The fourth was us. The 1980 US Olympic hockey team beating the Soviet Union in Lake Placid—the "Miracle on Ice."

That night was the closest we had come to a full reunion of the team. When the tenth anniversary had come in 1990, eight of us had gone to a celebration in Lake Placid. We'd had gatherings and gotten fifteen, sixteen, seventeen guys. The night of the *Sports Illustrated* gala in New York, Mike Ramsey was an assistant coach for the Buffalo Sabres and had a game the same night. A few guys called Mark Pavelich to get him to come. Mark was always the quietest guy on the team, he likes staying at his home up in the woods in Minnesota, and he doesn't like to fly. "It's too glitzy for me, Rizzo," he said when I called him. There were eighteen of us there for the event.

It was like the Oscars for sports. We walked down a red carpet lined with reporters, fans, and photographers to enter Madison Square Garden, with flashbulbs popping like fireworks. Inside were the greatest athletes of the day: Bill Russell, Billie Jean King, Jack Nicklaus, Jim Brown, Muhammad Ali, Wayne Gretzky, and many more. We were all dressed in tuxedos, to be celebrated for what we'd achieved. It felt odd being back in Madison Square Garden, though. The last time all of us had been there was when the Soviet team had killed us 10–3.

When it came time to name the greatest sports moment, the highlights of all four events were played on the scoreboard. Then Al Michaels came out onstage, took the microphone, and asked, "Do you believe in miracles?" It gave me chills. Herb, on the other hand, was flabbergasted. He knew it had been an incredible upset. He knew what it had meant to hockey. "Do you believe this?" he kept asking me. "Do you believe this, Mike?" Even twenty years later, he didn't really understand how that game had touched people outside of hockey and all across the country.

"C'mon, Herb," I said. "I told you this was big."

The following summer, 2000, Jack O'Callahan organized a reunion at Secession Golf Club in South Carolina. All expenses were covered by royalty money that comes from the use of photos of us. By then our group was expanding. Ralph Cox and other guys who had been in the original twenty-six players picked by Herb joined us. I had always considered them part of the team, and the other guys who played in Lake Placid did, too. That's another example of how unique 1980 was. Today, Olympic hockey rosters have twenty-four or twenty-five players. If it had been that way in 1980, Ralph and the five others would have been with us in Lake Placid. Al Michaels comes to a lot of gatherings, too. I didn't have much contact with Al in Lake Placid, but we've played golf many times and have become good friends. Al helped make us famous. He's as much a part of the story as I am.

Reunions with my teammates always go the same way. It's never a formal handshake. It's "Boy, are you getting fat" and "Man, are you bald." Lake Placid hardly ever comes up in conversations. Instead, it's catching up with each other's lives: How's the family, how are the kids, who's divorced, who's remarried? Before long, it goes right back to the wisecracks, like we never left locker room 5 in the Olympic Fieldhouse.

"Rizzo, how did you ever get to be captain? How did you even make the team?"

I get grief for giving speeches for a living. Herb used to say, "Mike Eruzione believes in free speech, but he never gave one." Billy Baker busts my chops by insisting that he tipped my shot into the Soviet goal and he should be the guy giving speeches and playing in golf tournaments.

A few months before the 2002 Winter Games in Salt Lake City, I got a call from Mitt Romney. He was serving as the head of the Salt Lake City organizing committee. Years later, in 2012, when he ran for president, he would ask me to speak at the Republican National Convention. But in 2002, he had a tough job. The Olympics had been beset by a bribery and corruption scandal, and Mitt was there to clean it up. That wasn't the only challenge he had. The 9/11 attacks had just taken place, and the Salt Lake City organizers wanted to put together an opening ceremony that would lift the country's spirits. The committee thought the 1980 hockey team could help do that. Herb couldn't; he was making an encore, coaching the US team at those games. We tried to get all twenty guys to participate. It took some convincing, but Pav joined us. Rammer was then a coach with the Minnesota Wild. He had a game and couldn't make it.

The night before the opening ceremony, the hundreds of people participating in the spectacle had a rehearsal at the Olympic stadium. The details were kept secret to make it a surprise for the worldwide TV audience. We knew our team had a role but didn't know exactly what it was. As the rehearsal went on, one famous American athlete after another passed the Olympic torch around a sheet of ice in the stadium. Then Picabo Street, the great downhill skier, and Cammi Granato, a gold-medal winner with the US women's hockey team, together carried the torch up a long flight of stairs, 117 feet high, to a stage where a steel tower rose higher into the sky, with the cauldron at the top. And that was where the hockey team came in.

They had chosen us, as a group, to light the cauldron to open the 2002 Winter Games.

I got back to my hotel room at about 2:00 a.m. Donna was still awake.

"We're lighting the cauldron. The whole team," I said.

She cocked her head to one side and gave me a look. "What bar have you been drinking in?"

"No, it's true," I told her. Besides, we were in Utah, a dry state. There were no bars that stayed open until 2:00 a.m.

The ceremony the next night was a spectacle meant to evoke the Wild West. There were covered wagons, bears, wild horses, skaters, dancers. A color guard of first responders presented a tattered American flag pulled from the rubble of the Twin Towers. Then the torch entered, and Picabo and Cammi arrived at the top of the stairs. I was about to step out into the spotlight to take the torch from them when Mark Johnson tapped me on the shoulder.

"Mike, four billion people are watching on TV. Don't drop it," he said with a laugh.

I took the torch, and as I had been instructed, I held it high for a moment. Then I called the other players to join me on the stage—just as I had called them up to the stage at the medal ceremony in Lake Placid twenty-two years before. We gathered together, just as we had in 1980, and as a group we touched the torch to the bottom of the steel tower. The flame climbed upward until the cauldron burst into a giant flame.

When I think of all the great athletes who've won gold medals for the United States over the decades, I feel so proud that our team is now among the elite group to have opened an Olympics on US soil, a group that includes Muhammad Ali, who opened the 1996 Olympics in Atlanta, and Rafer Johnson, who lit the torch in Los Angeles in 1984.

On the morning of August 11, 2003, I was in New York, set to catch a flight to Boston that afternoon. Herb Brooks had a flight to catch that day, too. He was in Eveleth, Minnesota, playing in a celebrity golf tournament for the US Hockey Hall of Fame. He played in the morning and left around noon in his minivan, heading to Minneapolis, where he was scheduled to board a flight to Chicago.

We landed in Boston on time, and I turned on my phone. Waiting for me were about thirty voice mail messages.

"I just heard the news."

"What a terrible thing."

"I'm very sorry about your coach."

At home there were more messages from radio stations, TV stations, newspapers, all asking for comments. Sometime around 1:00 p.m., Herb's minivan had swerved across a highway in Minnesota and rolled over, killing him. He was sixty-six.

Herb had a brilliant hockey mind. He was stubborn and headstrong and always thought he had better ideas than anyone else. And he did. The way hockey is played now is the way he taught us to play—four decades ago. I wish I had been able to know him better than I did. During the Olympics, he wasn't friendly with any of us. That was part of his method; he made us a close-knit team by making himself everybody's enemy. But even when I was fed up with him, I always respected him. All the players did. Our team was like a family, and Herb was the father. You love your father, but sometimes you hate him when he's tough on you, when he's demanding. Herb took on that role, and I think it made the Olympic year very lonely for him. He didn't join the celebrations on the ice when we beat the Soviets and the Finns. He left the bench and went off by himself. That was part of his coaching scheme, but I firmly believe he would have loved to be there on the ice, in the middle of it, with all of us.

One thing that set Herb apart from other coaches was how he was able to get into the heads of his players. He knew what buttons to push. He knew he could yell at me and I'd get mad and work harder. He knew he didn't have to yell at Mark Johnson and Ken Morrow. With Herb, everything was planned and had a purpose. He yelled at Jack O'Callahan a lot, and after the Olympics, I found out why. Herb had had an understanding with Jack. When Herb yelled and called him Jack, it meant that Herb really was yelling at Jack. But when Herb yelled and called him OC, that meant he was really yelling at the team. When he threatened to cut me, he knew he was lighting a fire under everybody else. If he was going to cut the captain, nobody's spot on the team was safe. When he went after Rob McClanahan between periods in the Sweden game, everybody's adrenaline started running—exactly what he wanted. When OC intervened and dragged Herb out of the locker room, he got a glimpse of Herb's face and saw a smirk. Years later, Craig Patrick told me Herb admitted afterward he'd only done it to stir up the team. Craig was Herb's roommate for seven months, so he was privy to a lot more of what Herb was thinking than we were. "He definitely did it for a purpose," Craig said. Craig added that Herb felt he could pick on Robby because he'd coached him at Minnesota and felt more comfortable targeting him than anyone else. Herb scheduled the Madison Square Garden game against the Soviets months in advance, knowing they would surely dominate us. I'm sure he figured that if we played the Soviets a second time in Lake Placid, we wouldn't be in awe of them and would be better prepared. And maybe, just maybe, the Soviets would be complacent and overconfident. He was right about that, too.

When Herb said, "There's a method to my madness," he wasn't joking.

And that brawl between BU and Minnesota back in 1976?

I always suspected Herb must have orchestrated that in some way, and years later I found out how he had pulled it off because Steve Janaszak and Bill Baker were on that Minnesota team. In the days leading up to the game, Herb kept telling his team that those eastern players and Canadian imports think they're better than you, they think they're smarter than you, but they don't like to be hit. They're soft. Go ahead. Hit them, and you'll see. That's the mind-set Minnesota had when they played us in Denver in 1976. It wasn't that different from what he did in Lake Placid, when he made fun of the Soviets and got us to believe we could beat them.

His funeral was held at the Cathedral of St. Paul, and 2,500 people came out to say goodbye: players, coaches, trainers, managers, from college, high school, the NHL, the Olympics, international hockey. Thirty-three honorary pallbearers raised blue hockey sticks in a salute. A bagpiper played "Amazing Grace." Four air force jets flew over the cathedral in the missing man formation. When I was called to give my talk, I read remarks from other guys on the team. I thought all of us should eulogize Herb, not just me.

Then I imagined Herb up in Heaven: "Right now, he's saying to God, 'I don't like the style of your team. We should change it.'"

"Miracle on Ice" is a catchy phrase, and I understand why people say it and like it, and it's fine if they do. People always refer to us as "college guys," and it's true that we all played college hockey and we weren't professionals at the time. But I see the events of 1980 a little differently.

Neal Broten was only nineteen years old in Lake Placid,

but he would eventually play seventeen seasons in the NHL, more than 1,000 games, and would win a Stanley Cup. He was the first American-born player to score 100 or more points in a season. Ken Morrow won four Stanley Cups in ten seasons with the Islanders. Mike Ramsey had an eighteen-season career with the Sabres. Mark Johnson played eleven seasons in the NHL, Dave Christian played fifteen, Jack O'Callahan and Dave Silk seven, Mark Pavelich six, Rob McClanahan and Steve Christoff five, Bill Baker three. Yes, we were college players, and we were young. But we were a lot better than anyone realized.

You also have to look beyond what those guys did on the ice. After retiring, Bill Baker became an oral surgeon. Steve Janaszak is a successful bond trader. Mark Johnson began coaching the women's team at the University of Wisconsin and has won five national titles. He was the best player on the 1980 team and has gone on to become one of the best women's hockey coaches in the world. As for Jack O'Callahan, after retiring he went into commodities trading in Chicago and built up his own company. Always a Terrier at heart, he called it Beanpot Financial Services. Phil Verchota and Bah Harrington both played in the 1984 Olympics, and then Phil became a banker in Minnesota. Bah has been a college coach for two decades. Craig Patrick won two Stanley Cups as general manager of the Pittsburgh Penguins. Buzzy Schneider played in Switzerland and then went into real estate back home.

The guys on our team brought more to the table than their hockey skills. They brought their values—hard work, pride, commitment, respect, the intangibles that made our hockey team so special. Herb always said he recruited people, not athletes. The players he picked were all strivers and achievers. He picked players who were willing to work and sacrifice, to put the team ahead of themselves. He picked winners.

People always remember my goal against the Soviets, but the truth is, Billy Baker's goal was the most important goal of the Olympics. If Billy hadn't scored in the last minute against Sweden, we probably wouldn't have had the confidence to beat the Czechs. We probably wouldn't have gotten to the medal round. There would have been no game with the Soviets. The second most important goal was the one Mark Johnson scored with one second left in the first period against the Soviets. Mark's goal gave us energy and emotion. It knocked Vladislav Tretiak out of the game. It changed the direction of the game and opened the door for us.

Everybody on the team did something at some point that helped us win. The Conehead line was spectacular against the Czechs. Mark Wells, Phil Verchota, and Eric Strobel gave us tough, gritty, important minutes. We would never have beaten the Russians playing just three lines. Jack O'Callahan came back from his injury when no one else thought he could play. Dave Christian switched to defense and played so well.

The game against the Soviets is usually portrayed as our being dominated the whole game and hanging on by our fingernails to win. The Soviets did outplay us in the first and second periods. But in the third period, we were the better team, and it was our defense that made the difference. The Soviets had more talent, but we made plays. When a shot needed to be blocked, Ken Morrow or Mike Ramsey took one for the team. When we needed a big save, Jim Craig was there. Before the game, I was confident that we would score some goals. The question was: Can we keep the Soviets from scoring goals? They had averaged ten goals a game until we faced them, but we held them to just three. And when the game was on the line, we outplayed them. After my goal, the Soviets got only three more shots on Jimmy—all from outside our blue line. In the last five minutes, they didn't get a single shot. Not one.

It's fine to call it a miracle if you want. In my mind, it wasn't a miracle and it wasn't a fluke.

About six months after Herb died, the movie *Miracle* brought the team together again. There were a few prerelease screenings for us, and each one became a reunion for the team. For the premiere in Hollywood, we walked the red carpet together like movie stars.

It's a great movie. Kurt Russell was brilliant playing Herb. Kurt had played minor-league baseball, so he carried himself like an athlete. When I saw the movie, I got goose bumps. He was dead-on as Herb. Disney also used college and minor-league hockey players to play us guys on the team. Instead of trying to get actors to act like hockey players, they got hockey players and taught them to act, and it gave the film a realistic feel.

One scene people remember most is when we skated Herbies in Norway. Kurt Russell, playing Herb, orders the players to skate up and back, up and back. Then he shouts, "Who do you play for?" And the actor playing me, gasping for air, shouts back, "I play for the United States of America!"

People ask me about it all the time, and many are very disappointed when I tell them it didn't happen. I didn't say that. Herb didn't ask who we played for. It's a dramatic scene that was written into the script to show the players coming together as a team—the US team. A lot of times people are really upset to hear that it was fiction. Sometimes people tell me that they don't care, they're going to believe it was real anyway.

Before the movie came out, the people who stopped us on the street were almost always people who had actually watched us on TV when we beat the Soviets and won the gold against Finland. But after its release, it was more and more kids stopping me in airports and hotels, sending me letters, asking for autographs. They usually say, "I wasn't born in 1980, but I've seen the movie *Miracle*." The movie brought the story of our team to a new generation. Youth coaches call and ask if I can speak to their teams before big games. And not just hockey teams; women's teams, men's teams, soccer, lacrosse, football, swimming teams. Almost every year, I hear about a college hockey team that watched *Miracle* the night before playing in the Frozen Four. Even pro teams call on us for inspiration. In 2004, when the Red Sox were trailing the Yankees three games to one in the playoffs, the Red Sox asked if I'd attend game five and walk the game ball to the mound for the first pitch. The public address announcer introduced me, and as I stepped across the green grass of Fenway, the scoreboard showed highlights of the Soviet game and my goal. The crowd was going crazy. I reached the mound and pumped my fist, and the cheers got louder. The highlights ended, and a message appeared on the scoreboard: "Ladies and gentlemen, it has happened before . . ."

The Red Sox won game six in New York, and before game seven, the Red Sox players watched *Miracle* in the clubhouse. The Sox won, becoming the first major-league team ever to come back from three games to none. Then they beat the Cardinals to win the World Series for the first time in eighty-six years.

In 2016, the US Ryder Cup team invited me to speak at a team dinner at Gillette Stadium, where the Patriots play. I was pretty nervous. Those were some of the top golfers in the world. What did they care about Mike Eruzione? To win, that Ryder Cup group felt they needed to play more as a team than as a collection of great individual golfers, and they wanted to hear how the hockey team had done it in Lake Placid.

After the dinner, they invited me to join them in Minnesota, where that year's Ryder Cup was being played. On the last day, I followed Phil Mickelson during his round. He was playing against Sergio Garcia, and they both made birdie after birdie. It was incredible golf. After Phil won one hole, he gave me a high five and said, "This is awesome, isn't it?" He was so calm, you would have thought he was going bowling, not playing one of the world's most intense golf championships. I didn't make a single putt, so I didn't have anything to do with it. But the Americans won that Ryder Cup, too.

If you ask guys on our team who was their favorite teammate, a lot of them would say Bobby Suter. In college, players hated playing against Bob. He wasn't that big, but he hit hard. He'd whack you on the back of the legs and skate off. He was intense and tough. If there was a scuffle, he was right there backing up his teammates. He was the guy you hated playing against, but you loved it when he was on your team. After the Olympics, Bob opened a sporting goods store in Wisconsin, Gold Medal Sports. He donated to and volunteered for youth hockey. He coached his own son Ryan, who made it to the NHL. In 2014, we lost Bobby when he died of a heart attack.

That made me and most of the other guys think. How

many more chances will we have to get everyone together? About six months after Bob died, NBC covered a weekend-long celebration of the thirty-fifth anniversary in Lake Placid. All nineteen guys participated. Soon afterward, we started an annual fantasy camp in Lake Placid at the Olympic Field-house, which has been renamed Herb Brooks Arena. Every March, about sixty amateur players show up. We put them through drills and evaluations and then split them into teams coached by players from the 1980 team. The campers play a tournament, and the winners are awarded medals. The camp has become a reunion for us. We don't get all of us there each year. Ten or twelve guys usually make it. But it's on everyone's calendar. It ensures that some of us—or most of us—get together at least once a year.

Many of the great stories in sports involve teammates or rivals who are forever linked with each other. You can't talk about Larry Bird without talking about Magic Johnson. It's the same with Tom Brady and Bill Belichick, Bo Schembechler and Woody Hayes, Muhammad Ali and Joe Frazier. They share a bond that can never be broken, and so do all of the guys from the 1980 US Olympic hockey team.

We are twenty different people with different personalities. We don't have the same interests and views on life. But we endured hardship together. We triumphed together. We achieved something people thought was impossible, and it remains a central part of the lives of every member of that team. I think about those guys and 1980 every day of my life. We will always be linked together, no matter where we go, no matter what we do, no matter how often we see one another.

* * *

One morning in 2019, I got an email from Captain Robert Frister. He was the pilot who had flown me to New York that delirious night after we had won the gold, after I had arrived home in Winthrop. He was the one who had let me sit in the cockpit. He emailed because he was writing down his fondest memories for his grandchildren, and one of them, he said, was our brief encounter thirty-nine years before. That, to me, shows what a grasp the team has on the American imagination. Captain Frister is a highly accomplished pilot, and he's been all over the world. But as he looks back on all he's experienced over the many decades of his life, he still cherishes a one-hour flight with a hockey player in his jump seat.

I didn't answer his email. Instead, I signed a few pictures and put them into an envelope with a short note. It was about time Captain Frister got that autograph.

My agent, Bob Murray, and I have always asked each other, "How long is this going to last? How long are people going to be interested in this story?"

Four decades later, my phone is still ringing.

CHAPTER 17

HOW CLOSE TO HOME

My mother worked every day of her life. By the time she was in her seventies, she had been diagnosed with a kidney disease. She was put on dialysis for a time, then had a stroke and broke her hip, and her health slowly declined. She knew her grandchildren but never got to see them grow up and flourish. In 1997, she passed away at the age of seventy-six. Her funeral was the first time Donna saw me cry.

I wasn't sure how my father would get on after losing the woman he'd known his entire life. He stayed in the second-floor apartment by himself. He insisted on it. The kitchen stayed exactly the same as when my mother was alive. The same plastic tablecloth. The *Boston Globe* story comparing me to Pete Rose on skates was still tacked to the wall. He continued working at Santarpio's and hanging out with his buddies there, signing pictures of me for anyone who asked: "Famous Father." People would come into the restaurant, and he would let them know right away, "I'm Mike Eruzione's father."

He lived on his own for more than a decade. Donna and I and the kids were right around the corner. So many times, I was sitting out on my deck and he'd come out on his back balcony and yell, "Mikey! Are you home?" I don't know why he'd ask that. He could see me plain as day on the deck. I'd tell him to come over for a beer—a cold one. For him it always had to be ice-cold. It was probably no more than a hundred steps from the front door of his house to my house, but my street has a slight incline. My father didn't like walking down and then back up. So he would get into his car and drive around the block. After he had a beer or two, he'd get back into the car and drive back home.

One time, he came home from a night out with the boys and sat down on the glass coffee table to take off his shoes. The glass gave way, and he fell backward, shards poking into the heavy winter coat he had on, pinning him down. My cousin Tony was walking up the stairs and heard a faint voice: "Help! Help!" Tony rushed in and found my father stuck in the broken coffee table, like a turtle lying on its shell. Tony couldn't help but laugh, and he paused a second to think, "Should I get a camera?" My father was fine, just a few minor cuts.

Eventually, after working and hanging around at Santarpio's for more than fifty years, Jeep said goodbye to the place for good. But not because of his age. The restaurant hired waitresses. "I can't work with women," my father said. "I have to work with guys."

"Dad," I told him, "things change."

"Not at Santarpio's."

By the time he reached ninety, all of us were keeping a close eye on him. We had food delivered. We dropped in every day to check on him. We got him a medical alert alarm he could wear around his neck and press if he ever fell or needed help. Sometimes he would hit the alarm, and the automatic signal would go out to the local ambulance company. They would call the house to ask if he was okay, and Jeep would say, "Yeah, I'm fine, but I can't get the cable TV to work." It happened so many times that eventually we took the alarm away. That was Jeep.

Eventually he decided he wanted to move into the Soldiers' Home, a home for aging veterans, in Chelsea. It was a ten-minute drive away, and my sisters, my brother and I, and other people in the family dropped in on him all the time. He loved it. The residents all wore their military caps showing their branch of the service. He was on a floor with about fifteen other vets, and right away he was like the mayor, entertaining the other guys with jokes and stories, just the way he used to entertain us when we were kids.

In June 2011, my son Michael was getting married. I visited my father the day before. Jeep was too frail to attend. The next day, as the wedding ended and we were filing out of the church, I saw my sister Nanci walk off with a cell phone to her ear. She came back with concern on her face but said nothing. We all enjoyed the reception, and the next day, Nanci told us: he had passed away on the wedding day, right after the ceremony was over. Typical Jeep. He waited until after the wedding to pass, so as not to disturb the ceremony. He lived to be ninety-four years old. His funeral was the second time Donna saw me cry.

When you lose your parents, it gives you pause to consider your own life, your own mortality, what you will leave behind, and what you still want to accomplish in the time you have on earth. Two years after my father died, I thought maybe it was time to sell my Olympic gear and memorabilia: the white number 21 jersey I had worn against the Soviets, the stick I had used to score the goal, the blue jersey from the gold-medal game, my hockey pants, my shoulder pads, my gloves, my white cowboy hat, the blue warm-up suit I had worn for the medal ceremony, my opening ceremony outfit. They were all just sitting in the attic, in the original hockey bag from 1980. I never looked at them, never took them out. What was I going to do with two jerseys and three kids? I could have framed the white jersey and put it on the wall, but I thought it would be better to sell it. I didn't need the money myself, but someday my children and grandchildren would. I also thought I could do a lot of good for other people with what the jersey and the other things would sell for. I'd be able to do something meaningful with the money, and I could do it while I was still alive.

I was concerned about how it would look: Mike Eruzione cashing in, selling his jersey to the highest bidder, raking in money. LeighAnn was reluctant, but Michael and Paul thought it made sense. Jack O'Callahan and Robby McClanahan said go ahead, do it. I texted several guys on the team. No one objected. Finally, I asked Jack Parker, and he said, "Good for you." That was the clincher for me. If Jack had said I was making a mistake, I would have held off. But knowing that Jack was behind me, I felt okay. I hoped the public would be okay with it, too.

My gold medal is in a safe-deposit box. It's chipped and scratched in places from the times I've dropped it. I take it out if someone asks me to visit kids in the hospital. LeighAnn, Michael, and Paul all got to take it into school for show-and-tell, and now my grandchildren want to do that, too. But I don't see it that often. If I want to relive the moment, I can always watch a video of the game. If I want to recall the feelings I had when we won, I can just close my eyes and take myself back to Lake Placid. I don't need to see the medal or put it on display anywhere. But the medal is different from the jerseys and the stick and the gloves. The gold medal means I was an Olympic champion. It's what all twenty guys on that team played for. It's why we worked so hard. It's why Herb pushed us so hard. That gold medal will never be sold, at least not in my lifetime.

My memorabilia were sold in an auction in 2013, and the white number 21 jersey went for $657,250. With the rest of the stuff, the auction brought in more than a million dollars. I gave some of the money to LeighAnn, Michael, and Paul, to give them a start in their future lives. I put some money into a foundation I had started years before, Winthrop Charities, which helps needy families in town and supports a variety of programs in Winthrop. I used the rest of it to endow a scholarship at Boston University. Now, every year, a hockey player is awarded the Helen and Eugene Eruzione Scholarship.

When we won in 1980, the players and coaches were given championship rings. That's another thing I didn't sell and will never sell. My father had mine for years. Today it is in a box with my other rings: my BU rings, the Goaldiggers ring I got for winning the Turner Cup. One ring in that box has nothing to do with sports. It's a gold tiger's-eye pinky ring that someone gave me a long, long time ago. She told me to keep it, and I did. Always.

Every speech I give starts the same way. I show a short clip of highlights from Lake Placid: Mark Johnson's incredible goals, Jim Craig keeping the game close, my goal. When it ends, the audience always cheers. Sometimes they chant "USA! USA!" Sometimes they stand up and chant. Sometimes they won't sit down. When the applause finally ends, I say, "There you have it. The story of my life in four minutes." Gets a laugh every time.

Winning the gold medal and being part of the 1980 team was an incredible event for me. It's the reason Donna and I live comfortably. It's the reason we have been able to give each of our children an education and a helping hand as they reach the milestones of adult life: getting married, buying a home, having children. It's the reason we are able to provide a future for our grandchildren.

But winning the gold medal hasn't defined my life. The most important thing that ever happened to me was being born to the parents I had, being surrounded by the family I have, and growing up in the town I've never left. Everyone encounters opportunities in life. It's what you do with them that makes the difference. I was lucky to have great opportunities come my way: Jack Parker giving me a chance, Herb Brooks offering me a tryout, big-name companies inviting me to speak about the incredible, extraordinary thing our team accomplished in Lake Placid. The times I was able to make something out of those opportunities, it was because of all the things that had come before, what my parents had taught me, the values they lived by, the values I hope I've passed on to my children.

Years ago, LeighAnn and I found we shared a love of musicals and theater. It was a thing we did together for a while. We would go in to Boston to see shows often and run down to New York a few times a year to see splashy Broadway productions. Not surprisingly, my daughter has made compassion her career. She's a social worker and runs a substance abuse prevention program. She never left Winthrop as she threatened to do back in high school. LeighAnn and her husband bought a house that's not even a five-minute walk away. They named their first son Michael. LeighAnn had asked her brother about giving her son that name. She said she wanted to name the first grandchild Michael as a gift to me, and my son Michael agreed. LeighAnn also has two other sons, Leo and T.J. Donna and I see our grandsons practically every day. Sometimes I take them skating at the rink here in town. It's now called the Mike Eruzione Center. My grandsons don't know who Mike Eruzione is. To them, I'm Papa.

My son Michael and his wife also have a son. His name is Michael A. Eruzione III. Michael asked LeighAnn about that. He told her he thought that since he has my name, wouldn't it be nice to continue it for another generation? And she said by all means, do it. So I have two grandsons named Michael, with different last names. To keep them straight, we call Michael III "Trey." In 2019 Michael and his wife had a second child, and this time we were blessed with a granddaughter—Rayley Marie. My son Michael lived here in Winthrop for a time, but his wife longed to be closer to her mother and her big, close-knit family. Donna and I can understand that. They now live in Connecticut. A couple times a year, Michael suits up and plays in alumni games with other former Terriers. Paul plays beer-league hockey in winter and softball in summer. And he's pursued his passion: he's a Winthrop fireman. Paul lives just around the corner from LeighAnn. Vinny, my brother, took his eleven varsity letters from Holy Cross and made a career out of athletics. He lives ten minutes from me in Winthrop and is the athletic director at Curry College. My sister Nanci moved out of Winthrop to be near her daughter, but Connie and Jeannie are still in town. Sadly, my sister Nettie passed away unexpectedly in 2018. That was the third time Donna saw me cry.

My cousin Tony lives in the house he built on the lot that used to be Three Cousins Stadium. My cousins Bubba, Linda, Richie, Laurie, and several others all live nearby. In Winthrop you can find at least twenty homes of people who can trace their lives to the three-family house at 274 Bowdoin Street. If you count Donna's side, there are at least ten more. Thirty homes—that's about a hundred people. As impossible as it once seemed, that fairy tale of my mother's has come true. We didn't hit the lottery, and we didn't buy a big piece of land, but just as my mother hoped, we all live together—not in one house but right here in Winthrop.

Every time I sit on my deck and glance to the south, and I see the back of the triple-decker, it reminds me of my mother hanging the laundry on the clothesline. I think of those windy days, when the clothes would fly off into the tree and I'd have to climb up to retrieve them. Then more memories come flooding in: Sunday dinner, meatballs and pasta and sausage, my sisters in their housecoats. In my mother's house, girls weren't allowed to sit at the table without their housecoats on. I remember playing hockey in the backyard, my mother and aunts on the back porches, watching from above. I think of the fun we had in that house, one big, extended family. I remember how happy my mother was when I told her Donna and I were moving in two doors away.

The house on Bowdoin Street is very different now from when I was growing up. Cousin Richard had the house renovated. The striped wallpaper was torn out. The old appliances were replaced. The floors and porches are now refinished and shiny. The night before the house was gutted, about fifty of us got together for one last visit, to say good-bye to the house as we knew it. I hadn't been inside in some time and had forgotten how small the kitchen was, how small the bathroom was. The corridor to the bedrooms seemed huge when I was a kid. Tony and I played basketball in a little area in the hallway. Now the two of us can barely fit into that space. Yet we made up games and played there hour upon hour. How did my sisters ever share a single bedroom? How did we fit so many people into the house when we had parties with everyone laughing and singing and Jeep playing his guitar? Before closing the door a final time, we poured shots of Fireball and drank toasts to the old place.

Every Fourth of July, I sip a glass of cabernet sauvignon and marvel at the scene in my backyard: my brother and sisters and their families, dozens of cousins, nieces, nephews, in-laws, splashing in the pool, laughing, eating, drinking. It's at least a hundred people. Ricky Meagher visits that day. After BU, he played more than seven hundred games in the NHL over twelve seasons. He has come to my house for the Fourth of July for more than forty years now. He stays in the finished part of my basement. Donna and I call it "Ricky's room." I notice the other guests. Coach DeFelice. He still looks like a Marine. He arrives with a couple guys I played football with, and it usually doesn't take them long to start kidding me about "Three inches to the left."

I take in that Fourth of July scene, and it comes back to me like an echo. Five decades ago, it was my father drinking beer and playing horseshoes and all my cousins and siblings running into and out of the house. Three floors, no doors. This has been my life for more than fifty years, almost exactly in the same spot, with almost exactly the same people. I'm still here.

I consider how far life has taken me, yet how close to home I've remained. Then a new thought comes to my mind. I smile and whisper to myself, "Man, I'm glad that shot went in."

ACKNOWLEDGMENTS

Mike's acknowledgements

So many people have helped and supported me over the years. I'm humbled by the thousands of people who offer such kind words, share their own memories of 1980, and treasure the story of that US Olympic hockey team as much as I do. Their enthusiasm for what our team accomplished brings so much to my life.

The town of Winthrop embraced me long before I had a gold medal around my neck, and has never stopped. I'm thankful to be part of such a great place. My thanks, too, to so many hometown friends—especially Frankie, Wayne, Higgie, Fenway, K.D., Boyhood, Tom and the Thursday night dinner guys, and Jack Anderson and the Sunday afternoon lunch crew. Also a shout-out to Dale Dunbar and Mike Norris, who've allowed me to remain a part of Winthrop hockey, and to all my friends at Tedesco and in Jupiter.

I had fabulous teammates in all the sports I played, at all levels. I feel a great sense of gratitude for all the guys I played with at BU. In Toledo, thank you to Jim McCabe, Randy Mohns, Paul Tantardini, Tony Peroski, Lindsey Middlebrook, and all the people there who gave me a second home. As for one particular teammate: I cannot express what it means to have played with Ricky Meagher, to have accomplished so much, and to remain as much like brothers today as we were at BU.

I had great so many great coaches—Paul O'Brien, Jim Evans, Bob DeFelice, Pop Whalen, Ted Garvin, and the BU assistants Bob Murray, Toot Cahoon, and Andy Fila. For more than forty years, Bob and his wife, Lin, have been friends and trusted advisers, and have provided so much wisdom and guidance.

BU is close to my heart and I will always be thankful for the opportunities the school has given me. To President Robert Brown, Athletics Director Drew Marrochello, and all the other outstanding colleagues I've worked with in the athletics, alumni, and development offices, a sincere thank-you.

I appreciate all the athletes and celebrities who've invited me to play golf and raise money for so many worthy charities, as well as my own golf groups.

Not a single day goes by that I don't think about Jack Parker and the role he's played in my life, his belief in me, his kindness, his character. Grateful doesn't begin to describe what I feel. My admiration for him is boundless. It is no exaggeration to say that none of this would have happened without Jack Parker.

Certainly there would have been no gold medal without a special group of talented, hard-working hockey players who are also absolutely some of the best people and friends you could ever meet anywhere. What great fortune it was to have pulled on the USA sweater with Steve Janszak, Les Auge, Ken Morrow, Gary Ross, Mike Ramsey, Bill Baker, Rob McClanahan, Dave Silk, Neal Broten, Mark Johnson, Steve Christoff, Jack Hughes, Ralph Cox, Mark Wells, Mark Pavelich, Jack O'Callahan, Eric Strobel, Bob Suter, Dave Christian, Dave Delich, Buzz Schneider, Phil Verchota, John Harrington, Jim Craig, and Bruce Horsch.

Craig Patrick is an unsung hero and was so important to our success. Thanks as well to team staff members Buddy Kessel, Gary Smith, Warren Strelow, Ralph Jasinski, and Doc Nagobads, and to Katie Million, Jeff Potter, and all the people in Lake Placid who have worked to keep the story of the "Miracle on Ice" alive. I cannot forget Al Michaels, a great friend whose TV call helped turn the game into a miracle.

All of us on the Olympic team were supremely fortunate to be led by one of the greatest coaching minds in any sport. Herb Brooks didn't make it easy on anyone, but he brought out more in me as a hockey player and as a person than I knew I had. Our victory in 1980 and so much of what Herb accomplished after Lake Placid has helped make American hockey what it is today. I feel forever indebted to him, and I know all of my teammates and millions of hockey fans across the country do, too.

Family is the heart of this story, and I was truly blessed to be born to parents like my mother and father, and to have grown up in our home on Bowdoin Street. I am deeply grateful to my sisters, Connie, Nanci, Jeannie, and Nettie; my brother, Vinny; my cousin Tony, and all my many, many other cousins, uncles, aunts, nieces, and nephews, for all the love and support they've given me. Further thanks to Victor and Barbara Alioto and all of their children, who welcomed me into another big Italian family.

My three children, LeighAnn, Michael, and Paul, and their own growing families, have given me so much happiness and so many reasons to feel proud. My grandchildren, Mikey, Leo, TJ, Trey, and Rayley Marie, are a new source of joy in my life. They were the inspiration for this book. More than anything else, I wrote it for them, so they would know my life was more than just Lake Placid, and how far family, hard work, and respect can take a person in life.

And, finally, I am so grateful Donna Alioto walked home with me that evening in 1973. Donna is my wife and my best friend. She has given me a life and a family beyond my wildest dreams, and has stood by me always, with love and patience and beauty.

Neal's acknowledgements

I am deeply grateful to Mike and Donna Eruzione for the trust and faith they placed in me, and to the extended Eruzione clan for welcoming me into their homes and sharing their stories.

I'd also like to acknowledge four great teachers, Robert H. Mitchell, Robert Wozniak, Gerald R. Powers and David Wessel. My thanks to our agent, Richard Abate of 3Arts, for his unwavering belief in this project. Our editor, Matthew Harper, lent a deft hand that brought vibrancy to this story.

There was no greater break than connecting with Mitchell Zuckoff of Boston University's College of Communications. I was aided greatly by assistance from Bernard M. Corbett, Rick Sacks, David Quinn, and Albie O'Connell. BU alums Glenn Rifkin, Ed Sharrow, Kevin Quirk, and Allison Moore were generous with their advice. John U. Bacon, a great writer and an even better friend, provided invaluable guidance and encouragement, as did my *New York Times* colleague Bill Vlasic, another fellow Terrier.

Jack Falla and Jeffrey Zaslow passed away too soon to see this book, but they have been sources of inspiration for years, and remain so to this day.

I could not have reached the finish line without Robin, Alice, Joe, Olivia, and Clara, whose love and support carried me through the long nights and solitary days at the keyboard.

Most of all, I want thank my father, John, who taught me to play hockey, and my mother, Mary, who passed on her love of words and stories to me.

APPENDIX

Mike Eruzione's Statistics

YEAR	TEAM	LEAGUE	GAMES	GOALS	ASSISTS	POINTS	PENALTIES IN MINUTES
1973–74	Boston University	NCAA	31	21	19	40	14
1974–75	Boston University	NCAA	32	27	29	56	20
1975–76	Boston University	NCAA	30	21	27	48	18
1976–77	Boston University	NCAA	34	23	41	64	18
1977–78	Toledo Goaldiggers	IHL	76	30	56	86	43
1978–79	Toledo Goaldiggers	IHL	74	27	45	72	28
1979–80	US Olympic Team	1980 Games	50	21	25	46	22

ABOUT THE AUTHORS

MIKE ERUZIONE is the director of special outreach at his alma mater, Boston University. He has been a television commentator, a motivational speaker, and a hockey coach. He lives in Winthrop, Massachusetts.

NEAL BOUDETTE, also a graduate of Boston University, is a reporter for the New York Times. He lives in Ann Arbor, Michigan.